CRUSADE AGAINST SLAVERY

CRUSADE AGAINST SLAVERY

Edward Coles, Pioneer of Freedom

KURT E. LEICHTLE AND BRUCE G. CARVETH

Southern Illinois University Press

Carbondale and Edwardsville

14 13 12 11   4 3 2 1

Library of Congress Cataloging-in-Publication Data
Leichtle, Kurt E., 1949–
Crusade against slavery : Edward Coles, pioneer of
freedom / Kurt E. Leichtle and Bruce G. Carveth.
    p. cm.
Includes bibliographical references and index.
    ISBN-13: 978-0-8093-3042-3 (cloth : alk. paper)
    ISBN-10: 0-8093-3042-3 (cloth : alk. paper)
    ISBN-13: 978-0-8093-8944-5 (ebook)
    ISBN-10: 0-8093-8944-4 (ebook)
1. Coles, Edward, 1786–1868. 2. Governors—Illinois—biography. 3. Slavery—Illinois—History. 4. Slaves—Emancipation—Illinois—History. 5. Freedmen—Illinois—Biography. 6. African
Americans—Illinois—Biography. 7. Illinois—Race
relations—History—19th century. 8. Illinois—Politics and government—To 1865. I. Carveth, Bruce G.,
1951– II. Title.
F545.C695L44 2011
977.3'03092—dc22 [B]   2010039079

Printed on recycled paper. ♻
The paper used in this publication meets the minimum requirements of American National Standard
for Information Sciences—Permanence of Paper for
Printed Library Materials, ANSI Z39.48-1992. ∞

To Barrie and Karen, whose patience and loving support were the leaven for this work

Contents

List of Illustrations   ix

Acknowledgments   xi

"Dust in the Balance": An Introduction   1

PART ONE

1. River and Opportunity   7
2. Man of Property   17
3. Release   42

PART TWO

4. Beginning   69
5. A Rough Land of Great Promise   80
6. Contest and Convention   92
7. A Prairie Firestorm   100
8. The Chasm   109
9. The Complaint   131
10. The Emancipator   150
11. The Devastating Truth of Madison's Will   157
12. The Aging Historian   167
13. The Preacher   183
14. Prodigal Virginian   191
15. The Woodlands   200

Epilogue   207

Notes   213
Bibliography   247
Index   263

Illustrations

Portrait from *Sketch of Edward Coles* 3

Coles's house at Rockfish Plantation 18

Landscape at Rockfish Plantation 19

Mural depicting Edward Coles freeing his slaves 65

Prairieland Farm and the properties purchased by
Edward Coles on behalf of his former slaves 85

Summons of Edward Coles 122

Portrait of Edward Coles 168

Portrait of Sally Logan Roberts Coles (1809–83) 168

Photograph of Edward Coles taken shortly before his death 204

Acknowledgments

We acknowledge with sincere appreciation: David L. Holmes, whose reading of materials related to the Reverend James Madison provided important insights; Jim Travisano, whose early reading of opening chapters gave much-needed support and encouragement; and Charlotte Johnson, whose special knowledge of Robert Crawford opened a wealth of new information to us. We also sincerely thank the Virginia Foundation for the Humanities, which provided a grant in support of research and a traveling public exhibit of the Edward Coles story at an early phase of work. We thank Ian Muehlenhaus, Geography Department, University of Wisconsin–River Falls, for the map of Edward Coles's property in Illinois. Thanks also to Beth Taylor and to James Madison's Montpelier, Orange County, Virginia, for their generosity in providing detailed information about the slaves of James Madison.

"Dust in the Balance": An Introduction

Edward Coles was fifty-eight years of age when he recalled the day he emancipated his slaves: "The morning after we left Pittsburg, a mild, calm and lovely April day, the sun shining bright, and the heavens without a cloud, our boats floating gently down the beautiful Ohio, the verdant foliage of Spring just budding out on its picturesque banks, all around presenting a scene both conducive to and in harmony with the finest feelings of our nature, was selected as one well suited to make known to my negroes the glad tidings of their freedom."[1]

Coles had wrestled for more than ten years with the complex moral and practical difficulties of emancipating his chattel slaves. Giving freedom was, he had discovered, far more than putting pen to paper to make a deed of gift. It had taken a decade to assemble the resources to emancipate and to shake not only his own doubts and hesitations but also the resistance and criticisms of his family and friends. The moment of freedom had arrived and now, recalling it twenty-five years later, his emotions spilled across the page as he penned the words.

Coles viewed the emancipation of his slaves as an experiment. For "his" slaves, he wished the pleasures of self-determination, and he firmly believed in liberty as their natural birthright. He intended this experiment as a demonstration that slaves could be freed to good effect and that they were capable of living free in the republic. He was curious to see for himself what the moment of emancipation would produce. What would be their reaction to it?

A breathless quality fills this scene: the quiet waters of the Ohio seem to acknowledge the majesty of the unfolding moments just before the arrival of freedom. Coles is almost giddy with expectation. The reader knows, in general, what is coming and the emotion of a simple, dramatic and heartfelt gesture is on the rise. The scene's unfolding may be reckoned a panorama, the expectation of lives forever changed, now captured in a river setting. Some lives will blossom; others will cease. Illness and loss, marriage and preaching and love—these are the things that flowed from the freedom given by Coles to his slaves. His "experiment" will unwind over the decades. The emancipation will affect his own future and the futures of those he freed in ways he could never have imagined.

This biography concerns the life and times of Edward Coles, but it also follows the lives of those he freed. Three elements argue for including their stories with his. First, the close interest that Coles preserved in those he freed and the ongoing support he provided to them necessarily weaves his story with theirs. Second, anyone interested in the remarkable course of Coles's commitments to end slavery in America might well ask: What were the effects of his own "experiment" in freedom upon his freedmen? Third, the history of slavery in America is not only the story of Africans and later African Americans in servitude, and it is not only the story of the white master-race. This biography attempts to join a black history with a white history and help to build an American history as a story of black and white people together. The intent is to acknowledge that American history, in part, is a racial dialog.

Coles's life spanned a time of transition. The deaths of Thomas Jefferson and John Adams in 1826 (when Coles was forty years old) and of James Madison ten years later signified the passing of what has been called the founding era. In its place emerged a powerful new motif variously called the era of the common man, the age of Jackson, the market revolution. Coles was wed to the earlier era. He denied many of the racial compromises made by the founding fathers, but he was tethered to other founding-era views on race, economy, and republican governance. Coles was eclipsed as the nation moved away from the republican ideal, inventing itself anew during a contentious era of change leading to the clash of North and South. This transitive time in American history is lit up in new ways, we believe, by knowing something of the life of Edward Coles.

Frank O. Lowden (Illinois governor from 1917 to 1921) introduced the reissue of the first published biography of Coles with a personal assessment of the significance of his life. Had Coles not stopped a nefarious effort to put slavery into Illinois' constitution, Lowden believed

Portrait from *Sketch of Edward Coles, Second Governor of Illinois and of the Slavery Struggle of 1823–4*, by E. B. Washburne (Jansen, McClurg, 1882).

Illinois would have become a slave state. The great debates between Abraham Lincoln and Stephen A. Douglas would not have occurred; Lincoln would not have become president. "Indeed, with Illinois a slave state," Lowden went on, "it is altogether possible that the Confederacy might have won."[2] This is hyperbole. And while this tribute by Governor Lowden is some testament to Coles's historical relevance in Illinois, we find no good reason to admit Coles to any pantheon of heroes writ large.

The crux of Coles's life is revealed in the singular and private moment on the Ohio River. History's meanings are made more whole by moments such as this instant of emancipation on the Ohio River that morning in April 1819. The threads of this moment touch the lives of Jefferson and Madison and their struggles with slavery. The threads are wound about the constitutional battles of the State of Illinois. They entwine with the 1831 debates in Virginia's statehouse over the future of slavery in that commonwealth. That moment on the Ohio River reached far beyond its place in time because Coles made it so. Still, Edward Coles was not a great man of history. He was a common man who made uncommon history.

* * *

Edward Coles was a young man of twenty-one years in 1807 when he announced to his family his opposition to slavery and his intention to free any slave who belonged to him. His father was newly buried, Edward's inheritance in slaves and land newly received.

Edward's family begged him not to act hastily, rather, to weigh carefully the cost of such a gesture. They pressed him with the standard arguments of the time. They pointed to the many benefits enjoyed by the slaves of a humane master. Edward was a planter with no other profession. The slaves were a third of his inheritance. He might not survive financially without them. His family was tenacious in resisting Edward's proposal. Arguments came from all quarters and took many forms.

Reflecting later on this painful time in the life of his family, Coles describes the moral equation that propelled him, "But all this [opposition to freeing my slaves] is dust in the balance, when weighing the consolation & happiness of doing what you believe right, with the corroding of feelings, & the upbraiding of conscience, at doing what you believe wrong—a great wrong too, by which you deprive your fellow man of the greatest of all earthly blessings, the enjoyment of his liberty, that liberty which we are taught to believe is the gift of God, & the inherent & unalienable right of man."[3]

PART ONE

1

River and Opportunity

In the early 1730s, when John Coles arrived, Richmond was a rough smudge of a Virginia frontier camp.[1] It was a river town of sorts; people called it "the Falls." But the Falls was more bottom than river. The James River at Richmond was an impassable, frothy confusion of water and boulders rising gradually for seven miles west. The river then found its depth again, filling out for seventy or eighty navigable miles inland.

From his father, William Byrd II inherited the Falls and twenty-six thousand acres surrounding the rocky-watery barrier to the expanding upland enterprise that was central Virginia. He took his father's beginning in land and location and built it into a commercial empire. John Coles arrived, rode the boom, and shared in the building.

John Coles knew something about commerce. His father, Walter Coles, had been the local customs officer—or *portreeve*—in the Irish town of Enniscorthy, Wexford County.[2] No doubt, John became well acquainted with the trade of goods along the River Slaney and the money to be made in their transshipment to the Irish countryside. The first decade of his life in Richmond made John Coles. He became a wealthy merchant, shipping wheat and other commodities to England and importing goods for sale in Virginia. Like most Virginians, he put his money into land to protect his investments and ensure his legacy. By 1741, he had purchased fifteen parcels of Richmond property, three thousand acres of land on Albemarle County's Green Mountain from the heirs of pioneer settler Francis Eppes (sometime between 1740 and 1747), some lands in Louisa County north of there, and additional plantation lands farther south on the Staunton River.[3]

Coles became an active and visible colonist and a faithful man of business whose skills and personal qualities appear to have been the leaven for some of Richmond's growth. His election as a member of the vestry of the old Curles Church solidified his position and status in the community. On 10 June 1741, the Council of Virginia appointed John Coles and two others as commissioners of the peace for the County of Henrico. The following year, Coles presented a petition to the legislature requesting recognition of Richmond as a new town.[4] Within a decade, Coles had built a business and established himself as a leader in the civil and sacred spheres of life in Richmond. He had become a gentleman of note—no small achievement. At some point, Coles married Mary Ann Winston, youngest daughter of Isaac Winston, a prominent Quaker.[5] They had five children; one was John Coles II (born 29 April 1745), father of Edward Coles.[6]

Nineteen years after his father's death, John Coles II, now twenty-one years, claimed his inheritance, Enniscorthy (named in homage to the family home in Ireland).[7] Enniscorthy sits on the Green Mountain, part of a modest ridge called the Southwest Mountains. Generous folk might call it a foothill range of the Blue Ridge. It runs for forty miles, following the line of the Blue Ridge but sets apart about ten miles east. John Coles's land was at the southern end of the range.

On the same hill but a day's easy ride northeast is James Monroe's Ashe Lawn plantation. Carter's Mountain is beyond that, next to Thomas Jefferson's Monticello. A break in the ridge provides a pass to Charlottesville. Continuing farther along the ridge is Montpelier, home of the James Madison family. A nearly straight line joins these four great plantations of Central Virginia. Each was well located for delivery of tobacco and other produce to market: Enniscorthy was closest to Richmond and was situated by the Hardware River, a tributary of the James. Monticello was on the Rivanna, another James River tributary. Montpelier was close to the headwaters of the Rapidan that, flowing north and east through Fredericksburg, provided a second route for trade and development of the Virginia interior that the Madison family had followed for three generations. The Southwest Mountains, of which Green Mountain was a part, was the perch for some of central Virginia's loftiest families.

John Coles II began to develop Enniscorthy almost immediately from hunting camp to profitable farm. His account book shows an entry during that first year, 1766, in payment to his neighbor Colonel John Fry "for a month's work of your sawyers."[8] So began a habit of building that would ultimately place the Coles family in the top ranks of Albemarle builders during the next century. Three years after moving permanently to Albemarle County (on 9 February 1769), John Coles II married Rebecca Elizabeth Tucker, half-sister of Henry Tucker of Norfolk, who had married John's sister, Mary. Before the year was out, Rebecca gave birth to a son, John (affectionately Jack). Walter arrived next, in 1772. A total of thirteen children were born to Rebecca. Ten grew to adulthood; five boys and five girls.[9]

John Coles II developed a successful plantation at Enniscorthy; a diversified operation that produced goods and services for both local and international markets. The cash business was based on tobacco, but hemp contributed also to Coles's ledger, as did lumber, brandy, flour, and horses. The ledger of John Coles captures only the narrow story of his financial activities, recording the business of Enniscorthy through the decades. The sons of John Coles II made entries to its pages as they grew. Scattered references to clothes bought, tuition paid, and trips made play through its pages, showing a family's expenses. The death of John Coles II in 1808 brought the passing of the business to his offspring and the final pages of the ledger document the activities of the new generation.[10]

The journal shows that John Coles II loaned money to his neighbors at a small profit. He sold brandy to the neighbors, sometimes in small quantities but rather often. His journal entry for 1797 recognizes 385 gallons produced that year.[11] His cherry trees were harvested for their wood: eighty-eight feet in 1804 for Jefferson (resulting in the cherry wood making a rich visual counterpoint in the parquet flooring of Monticello's music room).[12] The diversification of income streams demonstrated John Coles's wisdom and hence his success. The Coles plantation was one of very few in central Virginia that was successful over the long term in using an unholy trinity (slaves, tobacco, and land) to accumulate durable wealth.

Coles's success in business led to the expansion of his holdings. By the time of his death, his various plantation businesses had prospered such that his Enniscorthy property had more than tripled in size (to 9,299 acres). His total holdings amounted to 14,475.5 acres, including properties at Meadows of Dan (a high-meadow area south and east of Roanoke,

Virginia) and a smaller plantation in the Rockfish Valley just a score of miles from the home place. John Coles II started out with nine slaves from his father's will. By 1784, the Albemarle County tax rolls show that he owned seventy-one slaves. Only the Carter family and Thomas Jefferson held more Albemarle County wealth in slaves at the time.

Birth of a Republican Prince

Edward Coles was born at Enniscorthy on 15 December 1786. His eldest surviving brother, Walter, was born fourteen years before. Then came John (that is, John Coles III hereafter), Mary, Isaac, Tucker, and Rebecca. Edward was next. (Then, four more children were born to John and Rebecca Coles of Enniscorthy; Sarah, Elizabeth, and Emily would survive into adulthood.)[13] Edward was solidly a member of Albemarle's aristocracy—the landed gentry of both Virginia and the new nation. The scion of a wealthy plantation family with excellent connections when the Virginia aristocracy was at the height of its influence and power, his life held much promise even at his birth.[14]

Edward Coles was tutored rather than being sent to a one-room field school. Some tutors may have lived at Enniscorthy. A tutor would have had a full class of students. Edward received part of his training at the neighboring plantation of Wilson Cary Nicholas, a large landowner whose plantation served as a community focus. Some of Edward's fellow students boarded at the Nicholas plantation, but Enniscorthy adjoined the Nicholas property, so Edward probably lived at home.[15] From his tutors, Edward presumably learned the basics of reading, writing, and arithmetic, some French, Latin, and perhaps a brief introduction to Greek.[16] Since all of his brothers went to college, Edward would have taken such college-oriented courses as might be available. Edward finished his college preparation at Dr. William B. White's Academy, located in the White home near Dyer's Store, at the crossroads on the way to Scott's Landing on the James River.[17] Once again, Edward appears to have commuted from home rather than lived at the school.

In 1805, Edward joined his cousin Tucker at Hampden-Sydney College in western Virginia. Edward was a tall lad, fully six feet, with a thin and high forehead. He considered his face too sharp to be pleasant, but his features were intelligent and fine, and his chestnut hair curled casually.[18] The term began in the summer of 1805. On the fifth of September, he wrote his father about various problems and conflicts at the college. In addition to his participation in a riot over the quality of food in the dining hall, he complained about the college's academic quality. He and other students had lodged complaints about the school's curriculum and the conduct of the masters. The curriculum lacked practical courses such as mathematics and surveying. The library, he felt, was poor in quality and quantity.[19] Hampden-Sydney did not, in Coles's view, provide the sort of rational, practical education in the sciences that he had hoped to find. He proudly boasted to his father that rebelling students had won something of a victory: "The very men that threatened to expel us for the most rebellious and unpardonable behavior, now say that we have done ourselves a great deal of honor, and showed a great degree of public spirit." In the same letter, he noted that the disturbances had caused the enrollment to decline from seventy students to fifty-five.[20] At the end of the term, he joined the exodus. Coles left Hampden-Sydney for the College of William and Mary in Williamsburg, the alma mater of his four brothers.

Reason: The Handmaid of True Religion

When Coles arrived at Williamsburg, he found a struggling college in a nearly deserted, decaying town. Williamsburg, Virginia's capital beginning in 1698, commenced its slide when the state capital shifted to Richmond in 1780. The legislators had moved, so the newspapers, taverns, and theaters followed. During the next year, the venerable College of William and Mary was forced by the war raging around it to close its doors for some months. The college had been an "English" institution, tied closely to the Church of England. Its professors of divinity prepared young men for the Anglican priesthood. Its endowment had been heavy with British investments. When the war was done, William and Mary's assets, stature, and teaching staff were, comparatively, a trifle. The school, almost a century old when the new nation was born, had to start from scratch. William and Mary was a venerable institution brought to disastrously bad times by revolution—revolution in politics and revolution in knowledge. College president (and bishop) the Reverend James Madison—second cousin to the future U.S. president—set about saving it by embracing the revolutions about him. This remarkable catechist, First Bishop of the protestant Episcopal Church of Virginia, scientist, and champion of the Revolution, would ignite an ember somewhere deep inside Edward Coles.

* * *

On Thursday, 19 February 1795, (ten years before the arrival of student Coles), a congregation assembled to hear a sermon by the president of the College of William and Mary.[21] Bishop Madison, tall and thin, his graying hair combed back off his forehead, took his place in the pulpit. Madison addressed the assembly from Samuel 12:27, "Only fear the Lord, and serve him; for consider how great things he hath done for you." He noted, "There are few situations more interesting to the human race, than that which the people of America this day presents. The temples of the living God are everywhere, crowded, I trust, with worshipers, whose hearts, impressed with a just and lively sense of the great things, which He hath done for them, pour forth, in unison, the grateful tribute of praise and thanksgiving."[22]

Tied closely to the writings of John Locke but steeped in English and Scottish radical thought for a generation, Madison's vision—the republican ideal—grew out of a concern with the origins of authority and power, and their use or misuse by governments.[23] The key to this ideal rested on the belief that authority is tied to the rights of the individual by natural law. When the rights of the individual are in proper accord with public authority, the result is harmony. The natural laws that direct this relationship are like other natural laws. They are knowable. And they may be used to further a common good.

The republican logic, as it developed during the eighteenth century, conceived the world as subject to rational natural laws laid down by a superior being. Government allowed for the smooth administration of those natural laws to achieve the common good or happiness of all the nation's citizens. Threatening the ability of the government to achieve the common good were the temptations of power. Power could corrupt even the best leader unless outside checks were devised. The Dissenters and Whigs believed the history of the English government proved that without checks, leaders inevitably succumbed to the temptation to use their power selfishly to further their own rather than the common good. For the early republicans, a structure with carefully delineated checks and balances became an end in itself. The correct structure would, by definition, perpetuate virtue.[24]

The ideology developed and matured between the American Revolution and 1790. By the 1790s and the first decade of the 1800s, republicanism had become an identifiable ideology refined through public discussion and crystallized in the national constitution and in various state constitutions.[25] The division of church and state and the role of checks and balances were elaborations on the powerful and revolutionary view that government based on the rights of the individual satisfies natural laws of the universe and results in public happiness. A virtuous electorate produces a just government. Bishop Madison was a true-believer. He was an early exponent and an active promoter of republican views through regular correspondence with Jefferson and various colleagues, students, and friendly contacts.[26]

Madison's core commitment to republicanism was present in his sermon on that day of thanksgiving. He had warmed fully to his subject—reason was the handmaid of true religion. Madison believed that America was the new Jerusalem, slated to demonstrate God's will that moral and political adherence to the laws of nature would transform the world. The Revolution, to Madison, was a holy political crusade.[27] And in this is seen the germ of American exceptionalism, a theme that would prove enduring. The image of America as exemplar of the proper balance of rights and obligations and of the American republic as God's design for the world is, after all, but a short distance from the idea of human rights as natural law (if one adds just a dash of self-congratulation).

Although natural law was a framework within which Madison believed virtuous actions were judged, Madison was not a Deist. Unlike the Deists, Madison believed that God was more than the initiator of the universe: God was manifest in the world every day. Madison remained firmly placed within the Christian Church and believed God was the final judge of all actions. Madison interpreted his republicanism, in part, through the church.[28] It worked the other way, too. His Christian faith was republican. He was reputed to admonish any reference to the kingdom of heaven. Surely heaven is a republic![29]

* * *

Edward Coles arrived in Williamsburg for classes in fall 1805. He probably had no other choice. His first choice had been Hampden-Sydney, and he had come to regret it. Now he was sent to follow his brothers (no serious complaining allowed). Still, writing home in December, he lamented that the college was not a big improvement over Hampden-Sydney. He stewed about the poor library. In closing, he got to the point: please send money.[30]

On New Year's Day 1806, he had the misfortune of breaking his leg while wrestling with school chum Beverly Tucker. By the end of the month, he was back at Enniscorthy in recovery. He would not return to school until October. In November 1806, he wrote home again, annoyed this time at having to pay the masters for the time he had been away from school. To recoup some of his loss, he arranged to take applied mathematics from Mr. Blackburn in addition to his other courses.[31] His letter noted that his leg was much better by that time. He was even tempted to dance.

During the nine-month period from October 1806 to June 1807, Coles had a series of discussions with Bishop Madison on the incompatibility of slavery with republican ideals. With Bishop Madison and the Coles family moving in the same circles and Edward being the fifth of his generation at the school, the relationship was more than teacher-student examining texts and translations. Madison played roles of fatherly adviser, mentor, and quasi-friend as well as teacher. The meetings became explorations about life and its meanings. Coles's life changed, and it changed forever. Later in his life, Coles reflected on these conversations with Madison. Coles's determined and pointed questions forced Madison to admit that slavery "could not be justified on principle and could only be tolerated in our country by finding its existence, and the difficulty of getting rid of it." What Madison considered an insoluble moral dilemma, Coles came to consider a call for action. A citizen may omit to take advantage of a lawful privilege (such as the owning of slaves), but, Coles reflected later in life, he is bound to obey what he considers the will of God where it concerns a right of man.[32]

Edward Coles had become convinced that a higher law controlled the universe. This higher law forced him to renounce slavery as immoral: "I felt the just censure, as I conceived, of heaven and earth."[33] The rights and duties of man under this natural law meant that black people could never be property and that at no time had they been legitimate property. Holding slaves constituted a dangerous breach of virtue—dangerous to the republic and dangerous to the individual. The flow of Coles's argument against slavery and his call for action marked him as a republican of radical stripe. He rooted his conviction in a natural law ordained by God—that all men were created equal. Slavery was a corruption of that natural law and as such was not virtuous. If the citizens of the United States continued to practice slavery, the result could only be a decline into tyranny. Coles concluded that remedial action was necessary to save the republic.

Coles wrote that he greatly preferred collective action over individual action, but that if the people of the state neglected their duty in violation of fundamental values, then he must act alone and could not hold men as slaves. Coles was concerned about the violation of fundamental (that is to say, republican) doctrines. On this point, Coles remained in agreement with Bishop Madison and with Jefferson. Coles argued that as man had created slavery, then man could end it: "As to the difficulty of getting rid of slaves, we could get rid of them with less difficulty than we did the King of our forefathers. Such inconsistency on our part, and such injustice to our fellow man, should not be tolerated because it would be inconvenient or difficult to terminate it."[34] The problem seemed so obvious to him. As long as slavery existed, a virtuous republic based on a unified people could not survive. Slavery would corrupt the republic because it deprived a part of the people of liberty. So slavery had to be ended. That self-evident conclusion proved hard to implement. Coles struggled for the next several years to move from theory to practice. And he seemed at times to search for ways even of avoiding the entire messy, disruptive, and compelling question. Ultimately, Madison continued as a slaveholder while Coles persisted in a search for a way out, finally finding a way after years of searching.

As I Do Expect You Will Be a Farmer

In the spring of 1807, John Coles's letters to his son were filled with complaints about the hard times, poor prices, and bad crops.[35] Then, on June 10, John Coles wrote to his son that both he and Edward's brother Tucker had taken ill.[36] The crops were ripening. Tobacco, wheat, and fruits all needed to make their way to market, but first Edward must oversee the harvest. His father bluntly wrote, "For as I do expect you will be a farmer, it will be necessary to attend something to the business."[37] Edward would not be returning to William and Mary. Dutifully, he returned home on June 25, not graduated.[38]

Coles returned to Green Mountain a republican. From Bishop Madison, he had learned that the world was orderly, following divinely ordained natural laws. These laws were best exemplified in a republican form of government. Yet, he also learned that the republic required a virtuous citizenry. By encouraging one class of people to deprive another class of people of liberty for economic gain, slavery led to tyranny and ultimately to the destruction of the republic. Yet, he had returned to a world that had grown powerful with the institution of slavery. He had decided not to tell his father or his family about his views and his tentative decision not to hold slaves. Were his views known, his father might alter his will, replacing the slave properties he objected to with other properties more to his liking. The effect of this, Coles wrote later, "would be the same in perpetuating their bondage, as if I had sold the portion of them which I should otherwise have inherited."[39]

Edward Coles at the age of twenty knew that slavery must be ended, but he had no plan. He had no plan for his future and no plan for his slaves. He had no intention of keeping them and no notion as to how to free them. In this Edward Coles was adrift.

2

Man of Property

John Coles died in the winter of 1808. He was laid in the family cemetery behind his own Enniscorthy, close by the three children who had preceded him in death (Jack, who died of burns at the age of four in 1773; Isaac, who died in 1778 at five weeks of age; and William, who died at one year in 1794).

The family took up the last will and testament, signed by the master of Enniscorthy on 6 December 1795. It was an account of his success and a demonstration of his love. Properties human and otherwise were passed down among the children: Enniscorthy (to the eldest John) and then the Upper Quarter, the Beaver Dam Tract, Meadows of Dan (high country south of Roanoke), and properties south of Scott's Ferry. Slaves Harry, Lewis, Lucy, Lucy's child, Mariah, Edy, and Martin are mentioned in the will. Beloved wife, Rebecca, was remembered with three fellows (male slaves), three wenches (female slaves), four house servants, and her choice of a carpenter and all the offspring from these people. It was the wish of John Coles that the remaining slaves (those not mentioned specifically) be divided equally among his seven youngest children.[1]

The share for youngest son Edward was carefully specified. The father's testament was the initial act in a story of slavery and freedom that would play out for more than twenty-five years: "Item I give unto my Son Edward Coles the tract of land Containing seven hundred & eighty two acres I bought of Frances Mereweather on Rockfish River in Amherst County to him & his heirs for ever."[2] The Rockfish Plantation house still sits among hills just west of Pilot Mountain, about twenty miles west and south of Enniscorthy. The property is halved by the north fork of the Rockfish River. These days, the Rockfish is hardly a creek—not much more than a trickle, really. Two hundred years ago, it was navigable for small boats and gave irrigation to the plantation and water access for tobacco markets downriver via the James to Richmond. In February 1784, John Coles had purchased 782 acres in the Rockfish Valley from Frances Meriwether. Payments in cash were made 1 February 1784 and again exactly one year later, and the deal was finished off with the transfer of ten bushels of corn and a bull. The property came with a log house that had been Frances Meriwether's home. In all likelihood, it had been built by Frances's father, Thomas M. Meriwether, and may have been the area's claim house referred to as early as 1735.[3] Due to some small miracle, the house still stands (in 2011) perched on the tip of a rounded ridge, a knoll looking down on rich bottom land of the Rockfish Valley, house and knoll together point east down the valley toward sunup.[4] Various parts and pieces were added to the original house during the early 1800s, probably by John Coles II or one of his sons. A new living area and bedrooms were added on the west, kitchen, dining, and other bedrooms on the east.[5]

Coles's house at Rockfish Plantation. Photo by the authors, 2001. Used with permission of Michael McConkey.

Landscape at Rockfish Plantation. Photo by the authors, 2001. Used with permission of Michael McConkey.

During the twentieth century, electricity, updated plumbing, and white vinyl siding have brought the building in line with its neighbors. For all that, the building has not changed much in almost ten score years. Where the new bits fit imperfectly, one can still see hints of Meriwether's cabin. Today, a visitor can head down the stairs to the basement and look to one side to see logs and chinking where brickwork and lathing have fallen away. The basement room under the oldest part of the house has a small, stone fireplace at one end. The floor was, until very recently, of dirt hard-packed. The fireplace in this tiny basement room gave precious warmth and a means to cook.

Fertile river bottomland makes up more than half of the plantation given to Edward Coles by his father; hills suitable for grazing make up much of the rest. It was an operating farm in the Coles family for more than twenty years before Edward took possession of it. John Coles II worked the hills and rich bottom land to make the plantation pay. He stabled between eight and fourteen horses at various times, and he produced tobacco (as many as eleven hogsheads one year but more commonly six or eight). Tucker, Edward's brother (older by four years), worked Rockfish at one point as a diversified farm (corn, rye, timothy, apples, wheat).[6]

For all the industry that occurred there, however, Edward was saddled with a $500 debt owing on the farm when he became its master at his father's death. Satisfying the debt under the economic uncertainties of the day would be a very tall order. The Rockfish Plantation had been productive but not profitable. An old enterprise, the operation added volume to the overall Coles family business, but taken alone, it struggled along with its neighbors in a world turned upside-down by the turmoil of the 1790s, and its market opportunities were limited by the trade embargoes that followed later. A planter of the period could not count on a reliable foreign market, safe shipping, or a stable currency system. Virginia agriculture provided no easy living for Edward Coles or most of his neighbors. During 1808 (the year of John Coles's death), the family paid £14 17s 6d to an overseer for tending the slaves at Rockfish. In all likelihood, this was John Melton, the son of a former neighbor who had fallen on hard times and sold his land to John Coles II.[7] The property and its slaves were also rented out, giving a record of the slaves known to be there when John Coles died.[8]

Any 1808—Credits
By hire Tom £15, Ralph £15, Ned £12, Bob £6, Cate £3, Sukay £1.10
    from first March 1808 toward your 52.10
By rent of Rockfish for 1808   105
Hire of Polly for 1808   4

Edward Coles came into the human property that his sense of honor called him to make free. He had kept his thoughts on slavery from his father, a calculation to ensure that he would receive slaves in his inheritance. He had carefully schemed to own slaves so that he could free them.[9] Finalizing his ownership of these slaves would take months; the deed settling the distribution among his siblings was finalized on Christmas Eve 1808 and recorded at the Amherst County courthouse in 1812. These slaves were his (as described in the deed): Tom, Ralph, Ned, Bob, Kate, Molley, Franky's Susan, Polly, Kate's Betsy, Kate's Tom, Rachel's Nancy, and Grace.[10] A dozen slaves, now beholden to master Edward. What mix of sentiments brewed inside Edward when his share of slaves was placed in his own name? Surely, there was some turmoil in this moment, perhaps some dread, maybe some embarrassment.

Soon after the death of his father, Edward shared the shocking news of his beliefs and intentions with his family. He rejected the morality of slave ownership and would free those in his possession. The result was a protracted family crisis. No doubt, the discussions that followed were wrenching for Edward, painful and frustrating for those he loved. His family was unified in their opposition to his attitude and to this plan to cast a large portion of his inheritance to the winds. Edward's attitude could be taken as an affront to his parents and the work they had invested in building a family enterprise. His parents, after all, had worked hard to provide the wealth that Edward was proposing to squander in a senseless and destructive fit of foolish, unproductive, and potentially dangerous generosity. The effect of this act might lead to problems on the family's other farms. Word could circulate throughout the family's slave holdings and produce anger, maybe even insurrection, as the remaining slaves could demand similar treatment.[11]

Edward described discussions with his family in two autobiographical pamphlets written later in his life. The family advanced the common arguments favoring slavery and the benefits it offered to black people. They pointed to the clothing, food, housing, and lifetime of security bestowed on slaves by benevolent owners. They faulted him for his failure to declare his objections to slavery to his father, who would have replaced the unwanted legacy with other property. Edward patiently explained to them that this would have been a betrayal of his views. He likened such an action to selling his portion of the slaves by substitution. But Edward, they said, had no other profession besides farming. He would need the slaves to provide for himself and would otherwise be destitute.[12] Edward recognized the cost of freeing the slaves willed to him. They constituted a third of his worldly wealth. But the most serious privation, he believed, would be the separation from family and friends that might result from his actions. He believed that he could become a cast-out, ostracized from the community of Virginia planters by his seditious course.

The Grip of Slavery and the Grasp of Freedom

The circumstance that held Edward Coles was thorny. It may be that the objections to emancipation were "dust in the balance," as he asserted later in life, but this measure of dust must have weighed heavily on him at the time. In placing such store in the unalienable rights of man, he was embarking on a challenge that he could only partially have understood at the time. He faced a dense thicket of problems in this challenge: the strong but loving resistance he met from family and friends, the need for a large infusion of cash in order to financially survive his experiment in emancipation, the profound hold that slavery had on Virginia society and its entwined notions of white virtue and honor, the legal barriers to emancipation, and the manifold difficulties faced by free Virginia black people. Coles struggled for more than a decade to put his plan into effect in part because slavery held Albemarle County and the rest of Virginia so firmly in its grip.

Coles was proposing to free slaves in a county for which slave property was the single-largest tangible asset. Slavery was widespread, and its management was everybody's business. Moreover, slavery so marked Virginia economy, daily life, and civil views of honor and duty that a challenge to its integrity transformed the disposition of private property into a controversy of public moment. The hold that slavery had in Albemarle County shaped the options that Edward Coles could consider.

* * *

Albemarle County was fully "slaved" from the start. Slavery arrived with the very first settlement in Albemarle, recorded in 1735: Thomas Meriwether had eleven slaves on his Totier Creek property, one of the earliest establishments in the county. And slavery grew right along with the population. Nine hundred and forty-one Albemarle households paid taxes in 1782 (four years before Edward Coles was born); 4,409 slaves were counted as property among them (an average of 4.7 slaves per household).[13] The distribution was: 54 percent of tax-paying households owned at least one slave, and of those, the largest number, ninety, owned only one. Forty-two percent of slave-owning families had three or fewer slaves. In short, the majority of white families owned a slave or maybe a few. A very few households (fewer than 1 percent) owned fifty slaves or more.[14]

The going price for a good field hand in the 1780s was between £100 and £150. John Coles paid a total of £200 for the construction of his first family house at Enniscorthy. It was a good house but not a big one. Nobody would have called it grand or fancy. So, the cost of a prime slave approached the price of a small house. To buy and keep a slave, then, were business acts of some moment for most people. The loss of a slave, whether by death or escape, was somewhere between serious financial embarrassment and ruination. The emancipation of slaves, carrying with it a message of hope for those remaining enslaved, was a real and understandable concern for those who had invested in slave property.

By the close of the eighteenth century, two stanchions held the institution of slavery steady in Virginia: laws of property and beliefs about race. The central fact defining the lives and fortunes of enslaved African Americans throughout Virginia was their clear legal status as property. Slavery in Virginia began as an informal means of dealing with a persistent labor shortage. The responsibilities of slave ownership (of benevolent treatment of an inferior race) were often viewed as emblematic of white honor. Slaves as property grew into a hallmark of white honor and of white liberty. Edward Coles was implicitly challenging this hallmark. He was calling into question what white Virginians assumed as a right of birth: an extensive system of laws that protected their property, their means of livelihood, and, more broadly, their way of life.

Laws governing slavery reflected the views of the legislating class and focused largely on their rights to own and control property. The right to property had been a key right in Locke's political theory, so for those lower on the economic ladder, it became a key indicator of success. Threats to the stability of any property were viewed as a fundamental danger. Between 1782 and 1806, Virginians were permitted to exercise their rights to dispose of property. Manumission, that is to say, was allowed. But it was restricted in 1806 when a new law required freed slaves to leave the state within twelve months. The effect was to preserve the right to dispose of property while removing the threat that freed African Americans would undermine the institution of slavery through the example of hope. Add to this the strong impetus to empty the state of free black people lest white people be forced to live among them.[15]

Law, convention, and white honor notwithstanding, the logic of the Revolution led in some measure to the waning of slavery. Northern states moved more firmly and clearly to emancipation; southern states softened to manumission. Virginia Quaker Daniel Mifflin freed a hundred slaves in 1775. Robert Pleasants freed eighty in 1777. Robert Carter III (and his heirs and executors) freed 450 slaves between 1792 and 1852.[16] Charles Stockly of Accomack County freed 33 in 1787. That same year, William Parramore, John Treackle, and George Corbin of Accomack freed eighty-seven slaves among them.[17] Eva Sheppard Wolf estimates that ten thousand slaves were freed during this twenty-four-year period, representing almost a third of the free black population in 1810 (or about 2 percent of the total black population of Virginia).[18] Wolf's study, based on a review of 350 deeds and wills from eight Virginia counties, found that antislavery sentiments were common. But she shows that emancipations dawned under many and diverse ethics. Many emancipating Virginians were fearful of the wrath of God. Others were inspired by the moral implications of the American Revolution. Some were prompted by both. Others were propelled by more practical questions. Freedom would be a reward for past service in some instances; in others, a promise to be fulfilled in the future, pending good behavior. This was a surprisingly common feature of emancipation deeds, this promise of future emancipation as a means of motivation for earnest and reliable future work.

More than half of the deeds examined by Wolf give a reason for emancipation. Of those, nearly two-thirds professed slavery a wrong. Wolf demonstrates that these instances often show a mix of religious views with enlightenment ideals. Emancipations to fulfill religious and moral ideals were sometimes done "in community." That is, groups of like-minded neighbors (or church congregants) might emancipate groups of slaves together. (Accomack County shows the strongest example of this, but waves of emancipation overtaking communities can be pointed out in other parts of the state as well.)

An earlier study by Theodore Babcock finds a weak economic pattern among Virginia wills and deeds, suggesting that slaves tended to be manumitted when the cost of it was relatively low and when the pressures to pass on assets to heirs was least.[19] While the emancipation window was open in Virginia (1782 through 1806), freedom was given for many reasons. Freedom was often granted as a benefit to the slave, a gift in support of emerging American ideals of human rights and the fulfillment of the golden rule. And freedom was often granted as benefit to the slaveholder in support of the American ideal of individual control of property. But it must be said that emancipation, while explicitly an expression of the right to dispose of property, was also a subversion of the institution of slavery and was considered by many to dishonor the white community and the burden of leadership it saw as its God-given destiny.

* * *

The Coles family was a pillar of Virginia slavery and a paragon of the virtues many believed were the mark of white society. The Coles family like many Virginia families had already wrestled with the issue of slavery. The family was quite aware of emancipation and had direct experience with its effects. In 1761, John Payne married Mary Coles, the sister of John Coles II. They bore a daughter Dolley, who would later charm the nation with her warmth and hospitality in the White House. The family originally settled in a Quaker area in North Carolina. After a brief stay (1765 to 1769), they moved back to Virginia and settled on a plantation near Mary's father's country seat, Coles Hill.[20] As a strict Quaker, John soon began to doubt the legitimacy of slavery. In 1782, with the passage of the law legalizing manumission, John Payne freed the many slaves that had made his farm a success. In 1783, he moved north to Philadelphia, becoming one of the first Quakers in Virginia to free his slaves and sell his plantation.[21] John Payne tried to make a living as a starch maker but was skilled only in farming. He went bankrupt in 1789, was rejected by the Quaker community for failure to pay his debts, and died in 1792, broke and broken.

Experience of the Coles family with manumission also included Elizabeth Russell, sister of Patrick Henry (who was a nephew of John Coles I). She manumitted her husband's slaves upon his death, recognizing it to be "both sinful and unjust, as they are by nature equally free as myself, to continue them in slavery."[22]

Virginia was slaved. Not all white Virginians liked it slaved. Some Virginians freed their slaves (pleading variously for the will of God and the rights of man). But emancipation remained relatively rare, and Edward Coles's inclination to emancipate was decidedly out of step with the social order and with prevailing views of race and honor.

* * *

For the Coles family wrestling with well-intentioned but wrong-headed Edward, the test of family bonds was extreme. In time, his family came to accept Edward's conviction as unshakable, even while his plan was not defined. His immediate inclination was to free his newly acquired slaves outright.[23] But this option was complicated by a new law. Two years before his father's death, the Virginia legislature had passed the law requiring that freed slaves leave the state within twelve months of gaining their freedom. Freed slaves were required to give up family and home. Failure to leave brought the prospect of being sold back into slavery.[24] And as the numbers of free black people grew in Virginia, so did the perceived threat to stability.

Coles was well aware that free African Americans were saddled with a long string of restrictions and they could count on being subject to white suspicion and derision (and the accompanying threat of violence). There was a registration system for free, black Virginians. There were restrictions on travel. There were restrictions on employment and restrictions on assembly. Free, black Virginians were not free in the same way that white Virginians were free.[25] To sidestep these problems, Coles proposed not to register his freed slaves with the court. He would hire them at his Rockfish Plantation. Papers of emancipation would be registered by will upon his death. He discussed this option with his family and with neighbors but came to see that the slaves' legal status would fall into a dangerous state of limbo, and his action would set a precedent that could enflame the desires of other slaves in central Virginia, thus inviting the wrath of other slave owners.[26] And he came to understand that he might not be able to perfectly control the settlement of his will. The freedom of the slaves, furthermore, would be publicly recognized only in the distant future. What form of justice would this be, delayed and kept under wraps as if it were shameful? Some of his slaves were much older than he was; he would very likely outlive them. This would be justice denied.

Worried about the hostile public reaction toward manumission and worried about his family's position in society and politics, Edward, with his family's enthusiastic support, rejected the immediate manumission option. He also rejected his family's offer to buy the slaves from him[27] And he rejected their pleas to remain with the family in Virginia.[28] Edward Coles came to accept a duty to free his slaves as a necessary act of personal honor and republican justice. To do so, he would have to leave Virginia. In fact, rejecting Virginia became, over time, a defining element in his personal statement rejecting slavery. He would reject slavery and not live in a state that would support it. With the rudiments of a plan now in hand and his father's property newly divided, Coles undertook a trip by horseback to explore the area northwest of the Ohio River.[29]

In 1809, late in the year, he placed his Rockfish property on the market, hoping to realize enough from the sale to permit a move out of

Virginia and the emancipation of his slaves. But times were lean. For the next decade, Coles tried to sell his property for a good price. And his family searched for an alternative career, the fascination of which might distract Edward from this morbid interest in emancipation. In due course, they found one. In the city of Washington, D.C., young Mr. Coles would find as much distraction as his situation could fairly stand.

The Departure of Isaac Coles

Isaac A. Coles (older than his brother Edward by six years) is described as one of the most handsome eligible young men in Washington. With a bachelor of arts degree from the College of William and Mary in hand, he worked (at the age of twenty-four) as a courier for President Thomas Jefferson in Europe during 1804 and became Jefferson's private secretary in 1805, filling in for William A. Burwell as necessary.[30]

Soon after the inauguration in March 1809, just as the James Madison administration was forming, Jefferson, presumably with Madison's blessing, once again dispatched Isaac to France as a courier delivering critical diplomatic packets at a time when clouds of war were beginning to form.[31] On 4 September 1809, Isaac accepted an invitation from President Madison to join the official family in the same capacity as he had served Jefferson: personal secretary to the president. He lived in the White House, enjoying the use of a sitting room on the East Wing's ground floor and continuing to labor at copying letters and delivering messages to Congress.

On November 29, Isaac delivered the president's annual message to Congress. What transpired in the lobby of the senate chamber is not entirely clear. All agreed that Isaac Coles struck Maryland Representative Roger Nelson. Coles later stated that this was in response to a verbal insult from Nelson. One witness reported that Nelson had extended his hand to Coles, who came back with a smack to the representative's face. Another said that Coles had grabbed Nelson roughly by the collar and whacked him on the temple or forehead. Later, Nelson denied saying anything injurious to Coles. The story made the rounds. As it did, details appear to have been added. British envoy Francis James Jackson reported in a 10 January 1810 letter to his brother in Philadelphia that Coles had "horsewhipped" a member of Congress.[32] No direct evidence exists that the incident involved riding gear.

Isaac suffered for his new notoriety. He recognized the damage done to his reputation in Washington and proposed to leave the White House as soon as Madison could find a replacement.[33] He submitted his resignation to Madison on December 29 and set plans in motion to leave the city.[34] He took with him Madison's letter to his brother Edward, offering him the position of secretary to the president. Isaac retreated, tail between his legs, into the army on January 12.[35]

The offer to Edward seemed perfect to everyone. Isaac wanted a quick and discreet escape from Washington. The family saw the job as an opportunity to interest Edward in something other than the self-ruinous notion of freeing slaves—anything to take his mind off slavery. To Edward, the position was a call to public service; a situation that would tide him over honorably until he could sell his plantation and do something about his slaves. The position also offered him great potential in terms of future advancement and experience. Coles did see himself first as a farmer, but public service called out to his sense of republican duty, and Washington was, after all, a jolly alternative for a Virginia farmer.

Edward was interested in the position, but when he wrote Madison, it was to decline the offer, citing his lack of preparation.[36] Coles held his honor close and high. He saw the position as an opportunity for service and as part of his duty as a citizen. Yet, he worried that the job offer might be seen as patronage: a sop from his family and derived via family ties to the new president. How could he accept it and not lose standing in his own mind, if not others'? Added to that issue was his youthful lack of confidence in his direction and skills. In this decision, he seemed a typical twenty-two-year-old. On the one hand, his idealism and sense of adventure said "go" while his insecurity about his skills and his position held him back. The exasperated tone of his family's letters suggest the amount of discussion that went on.

On his way to the post office with the letter, chance brought Albemarle County resident (and future president) James Monroe to cross his path. Learning of Coles's decision, Monroe urged him to reconsider and accept the position. Monroe cited the potential contacts and experiences that would be valuable later, especially if Coles decided to leave Virginia. Already under pressure from his family, particularly from Isaac, and with his inclination to accept in spite of his slavery problem, Coles capitulated. He wrote a second letter, this time accepting the position.

Coles clearly wanted to search out new horizons, and Monroe's argument had given him a new perspective on the offer.[37] Four days later, Coles left for Washington.

His slaves were still in bondage. He was sure of only one thing: his intention to free them. He was unsure of all the rest. How should he free them? And when? And where?

At the Republican Court

Washington was a rancorous and divided capital when Edward Coles arrived. Jefferson's policy of embargo and neutrality toward England and France was proving neither effective nor popular.[38] Congress contained groups from the south and west who advocated war with Britain. Others from New England wanted to rescind the embargo and get on with trade. Opposition had been growing during Jefferson's term. Now, under Madison, action was demanded by both sides.

James Madison tried to thread a policy needle: keep the nation from either precipitous war or craven surrender. As a result, his presidency was marked by conflict in Congress, conflict in his cabinet but finally conflict with England.[39] The heaving tides of impending war were amplified by various new factions that were adding to an already-stormy political sea.[40] The three branches of government were evolving, becoming differentiated in location and function.[41] The committee system in Congress had emerged and had produced some efficiencies, but the committees also introduced new bases of power. Finally, Monroe's opposition to Madison in the presidential contest signaled the beginnings of a movement that would break up the old party system and lead to a new one a decade later. It was Madison's good fortune that the White House was beginning to provide a diplomatic haven under the focused but cordial inspiration of Edward's cousin Dolley Payne Madison.

Coles arrived in Washington and took up residence after Dolley Madison's breathtaking transformation of the White House: marble mantle pieces, forty new pieces of furniture including two sofas, and silverware from Philadelphia. Mrs. Madison's parlor had been transformed into a cheery oasis of sunflower yellow. The sofas and chairs were covered in yellow satin. Yellow festoons billowed at the windows. Yellow-fringed drapery made a sunny cornice around the ceiling. In the oval drawing room (then called the "Elliptical Saloon"), the walls were papered in cream, and the woodwork finished white. Blue and gray highlights suggested masonry. Dolley insisted on silk-velvet curtains of sun-bright crimson. Surrounded by this energizing decor, Dolley Madison had begun to dazzle Washington society with the warmth of her personal attentions. Washington discovered that the White House under her gaze was a colorful and inspired oasis of social intelligence. The White House was a salon for Dolley and a crucible for Madison's political agendas. Edward Coles became a prominent feature in the capital's social tableau.[42]

In May of 1809, Dolley opened the White House for the first of many Wednesday "sitting rooms" as formal receptions. By the time Edward arrived in Washington (January of the following year), these weekly affairs had become a powerful social hub around which the Washington galaxy revolved. As many as two hundred people would attend these Wednesday salons, most arriving by foot, many by carriage alighting at the north entrance.[43] Madison (pale and small, dressed in demure black) and Dolley (grand, buxom, glowing, plumed, and satined, effusive, rosy, and glamorous) would receive their guests at the door to the drawing room. Madison was socially diligent, and no one doubted his intellectual power or range. When one-on-one at gatherings such as these, he was charming and "artful in convincing others of his guilessness."[44] Chairs were set into small groups as semi-circles; couples moved arm-in-arm about the house. The table in the dining room held cakes, meats, syrups, and ice cream in hot pastry (a Madison specialty). Waiters passed coffee and wine. Whiskey punch was served. The delicacies were in such abundance that a current rhyme circulated to tease about the largesse: "Tom Tingey, Tom Turner, Tom Ewell, Tom Digges, / All go to the palace to eat up the figs."[45]

Edward Coles, a cool and remote Virginia gentleman of position, became fascinated by the cheery abundance and happily took in the scene, puff pastries and all. At formal dinners, he normally sat at the head of the table, opposite his cousin Dolley. This arrangement freed the president, who sat in the middle, from any need to get up during the meal to attend to the needs of his guests. Edward saw to these details instead.[46]

Through Dolley, Coles's social horizons broadened immeasurably. No longer were his acquaintances limited to the Virginia aristocracy. The Madisons helped to open to Coles the high societies of Philadelphia,

New York, and Boston. President Madison became a major influence on the young Coles, who described Madison as uncommanding in appearance but secure in his poise and personality. And of Madison, Coles asserted, "Few men possessed so rich a flow of the language, or so great a fund of amusing anecdotes, which were made the more interesting from their being well-timed and well-told."[47] Throughout their relationship, Coles displayed the greatest respect for Madison, treating him almost as a surrogate father. And Coles returned Madison's faith in him with deep and durable personal loyalty.

As Madison's secretary, Coles's duties were varied but often routine in nature. Most of his time was spent copying letters and papers and carrying messages to Congress. In the course of his work Coles oversaw patronage, gathered political intelligence, and tried to manage public relations. During the administrations of Jefferson, Madison, and Monroe, every document that left Washington crossed the desk of the president, who had only one aide, his secretary.

Coles became an important cog in the patronage machine. From 1800 to 1824, friendship and section of the country were more significant criteria for appointment than was party.[48] Men seeking favors from the administration often contacted Coles about appointments. William Pinckney, for instance, wrote Coles urging the appointment of Howard Goldborough for an office in Maryland.[49] A college friend asked Coles to help him obtain a commission as a major.[50] During April 1813, while in Philadelphia recovering from an illness, Coles interceded for a Dr. Barton who wished an appointment as treasurer of the U.S. Mint in Philadelphia. Later, in November, Nicholas Biddle, a close personal friend in Philadelphia, most often remembered as president of the Bank of the United States from 1823 to 1839, asked Coles to have Madison appoint his father as commander of the Pennsylvania militia.[51] Coles sent out many of the appointment letters over his own signature.[52] As far as Coles was concerned, however, the granting of offices was a rancid necessity. And patronage was the spleen of government (notwithstanding the fact that Coles's own position was, awkwardly, a product of the same).

Coles acted as a buffer between Madison and the crowds of office seekers threatening to consume Madison's time and energy. Coles tried also to protect Madison's political interests. Several months before Biddle's request, for example, Coles had warned Madison that there were problems with the Pennsylvania militia. The troops had nearly rioted, he reported, because too many appointments were going to the Leib faction. Michael Leib, senator from Philadelphia, had openly opposed Madison's policy toward Britain. The appointments, Coles wrote, made Madison appear the fool.[53] In 1814, then, when Postmaster General Gideon Granger appointed Leib postmaster for Philadelphia, Madison immediately countered, removing Leib.[54]

Coles served Madison in the field, both collecting and distributing information. He collected political intelligence for the president and dispensed political advice from his growing store of knowledge of the president and his cabinet. He was tied, for instance, to a weekly Sunday dinner with Julien Poydras, congressman from the Territory of Orleans, who insisted on keeping Coles close at hand, relentlessly pushing his territory's interest in entering the Union.[55] Inventor Robert Fulton, too, harangued Coles throughout his somewhat-mad scramble to attract government investment in his torpedo and submarine schemes.[56]

* * *

Government operations slowed considerably in the summers. Congress met seasonally; it vacated Washington in the sweltering months. Even the president retreated to the cooler and drier breezes of Montpelier. In the summer of 1811, Coles joined the exodus from Washington with his brother John. They toured the north (Philadelphia, New York, and Boston) to get a change of scenery and, no doubt, relax in cooler weather during Congress's summer recess. He had written to John in March that the duration and route were somewhat unsure, and they were free to follow their inclinations toward improvement and pleasure.[57]

Coles left Washington weighed down with letters of recommendation and introduction.[58] Using one such letter from family friend James Monroe, Coles met Biddle in Philadelphia. Coles's friendship with Biddle strengthened in coming years. He would write his mother that Biddle was so fine a friend that a place was always set, as it were, at the table for Coles, even at Biddle's in-laws.[59] Biddle had much in common with the Virginian. Though he was from a different section of the country, he was, like Coles, idealistic and fully republican in his politics. Biddle had a lively sense of humor and enjoyed an evening's fun. The two men corresponded freely and often for fifteen years, trading light amusement and dry political commentary in a steady stream.

Biddle's situation in Philadelphia suggested an opportunity: Coles could move to the city and become a businessman. Philadelphia's attractions tempted Coles constantly. Pennsylvania was free soil. Perhaps his slaves could be resettled there. In 1815, even as he was deciding on a strategy to move west, the Philadelphia option seemed very tempting, and Biddle's presence there played no small part.

Coles made other contacts during his 1811 tour of the north, many predicated on Madison's need for candid and reliable information about his opposition. In Baltimore, Coles stayed with the family of Samuel Smith, whose civil treatment of their guests did not hide the aching offense they took against Madison—offense they parlayed into a small industry of public resentment and villainy. Madison had dismissed Secretary of State Robert Smith for cause; the Smith family was deeply emotional over the slight, and Coles reported the contact in some detail to Dolley.[60]

When Coles arrived in Boston, he stopped to deliver another of Monroe's letters of introduction to Governor Elbridge Gerry and added to his insights the extent and sources of northern opposition to Madison's policies. The same was true in Philadelphia during Coles's visits with Drs. Benjamin Rush and Caspar Wistar.[61] New England was a key source of resistance and animosity toward Madison. Coles's trip provided a valuable opportunity to explore the political terrain and gauge the depth of feeling.

The Coles brothers spent the greater part of two days with the irascible John Adams and, of course, the fiery-but-wise Abigail, engaging the former president in free and extensive talk about the early years of the republic and, more specifically, about his experiences while president and incidents related to the election of 1800. Many years later, Coles described the meeting with Adams in some detail in a letter to Henry S. Randall.[62] The gist of it: Adams vented several grievances over Jefferson's treatment of him during the 1800 campaign. Coles could not reconcile this with feelings he knew Jefferson had for Adams, notwithstanding the well-known estrangement of the two former brothers in revolution. Coles repeated specific statements he had heard Jefferson make, noting Jefferson's appreciation for the grace that Adams had shown during numerous dinners shared by the two men during Adams's administration. Coles told Adams that Jefferson had agonized about the timing he should use in approaching him after the election of 1800. Too soon and Adams might believe Jefferson was exulting; too late and Adams might take it as a slight. When he judged the time right, Coles said, Jefferson went to Adams and found the president to be alone. Adams advanced to Jefferson in a hurried and agitated step and with a tremulous voice said, "You have turned me out, you have turned me out!" Jefferson's meek reply: the election was a public review of parties and policies, not a personal contest. The meeting progressed. Tensions softened. The two former friends, Coles went on, acknowledged various differences of view. Adams was impressed with the details of the meeting that Coles had mastered (not having been there in person, of course), confirming that it had gone exactly as Coles had described. Adams had not known that Jefferson had taken his feelings into such account, agonizing over the timing of their first meeting after Jefferson's victory over Adams at the polls. As the conversations went on, Adams's memory of Jefferson warmed, and he complimented his service to the country, especially during the Revolution. Adams went further, expressing how much he loved Jefferson—still did love him!

On his return to the south, Coles met with Jefferson at Monticello, telling him in some detail about his conversations with Adams. Soon after, the famed reconciliation took place, and the celebrated interchange of letters began. Coles's function in bringing the two men back together is certified in a 5 December 1811 letter of Jefferson to Rush.[63] The letter speaks to the reconciliation. It describes two men who traveled the north country recently (these two were, assuredly, John Coles and Edward Coles), who met with Adams and, as described in Coles's letter to Randall, came to know Adams's deep affection for Jefferson. Jefferson acknowledges the effect of this mediation on his desire to renew his interrupted friendship with Adams. It was Rush who had actively pursued reconciliation between Jefferson and Adams over a period of years. Yet, there can be little doubt that Coles was the wick bringing two flames of the Revolution back together again as friends after a decade of coolness and estrangement.

* * *

Whether Coles was meaningfully involved in making administration policy is not clear, but he was certainly aware of and consistently supported Madison's positions. As war approached, Madison was peppered with criticism from all sides. Some historians argue that Madison approached the declaration of war in 1812 hesitantly, stymied by gales of criticism, and that he was driven into war by Congress.[64] Biographer Ralph Ketcham sees Madison as more assertive.[65] Edward Coles makes a case for the resolute Madison, who, he claimed in a letter to his brother, had decided the matter as early as July of 1811. He knew that the country needed to prepare before war could be declared. He delayed until more-cautious members of Congress could be convinced that war was inevitable and until steps could be taken to bolster the military. By May of 1812, republican Coles, still firmly in support of the president's agenda, joined those calling for war.[66]

In August of 1814, British warships pushed up the Potomac River, cleared defenses at Fort Washington, then deposited troops who seemingly waltzed into the nation's capital and put the torch to the White House, the Capitol, and various other official buildings and private residences. Coles was not present in Washington at the time. An illness had driven him to Philadelphia to seek relief and left him in pain for more than a year. By August of 1814, he was mostly recovered but opted for a short holiday in the comfortable and sparkling atmospherics of the White Sulphur Springs resort, nestled in the foothills of the Allegheny Mountains just west of Virginia's Shenandoah Valley. Coles lamented the burning of Washington and especially the rough treatment of the president handed out by the press.[67] He commented to his cousin (Madison's stepson, Payne Todd) on the conduct of the battle as it was presented in a Congressional report, complaining that the rambling depositions revealed little but inconsistencies. Laid bare, he said, were accusations that were frivolous. Congressional investigation and reporting on the failures of the battle in the nation's capital settled nothing. Coles recognized that the battle and its aftermath left the public depressed, especially in the cities, where talk was of surrender.

Later, Coles reported that successes at Lake Champlain and in Baltimore had restored the public's spirit. The war did not strain Coles's faith in the virtue of his fellow citizens, but he did worry about the virtue of its leaders. To Payne Todd, he groused that Congress was in an unspeakable mess—it was not worth the paper to discuss the matter.[68] He ranted to Biddle, suggesting that the states arm themselves since Congress was obstructing the national government's constitutional duty to provide for the nation's defense.[69] As the war ended in the winter of 1815, Coles believed that republican government had virtually ceased to exist in the welter of bickering and fighting in Congress. To Coles, good government was courteous government. Rancor was vulgar; rancorous government lacked virtue. Pettiness and selfishness imperiled the Republic. He looked down with disgust from the same kind of republican perch he shared with Madison and Jefferson.

The New Englanders were at fault, Edward said. Stooping to call them "Yankees," he traced much of the discord to the Federalist Hartford Convention and raged to Payne Todd that the Federalists were English sympathizers: "Every bone and sentiment brethed [*sic*] in their public speeches, in their prints, and in all their proceedings clearly show their desire of blowing up in a tempest of discord and Civil War."[70]

Biddle commiserated with Coles about the Federalists but warned him that Congress as a whole was the problem, not just the New Englanders. Congress, he said, had to act to strengthen the war effort or risk losing support.[71] Coles believed that the problem lay with a few individuals in Congress. Sweep away those lacking virtue and the republic would be fulfilled. Biddle saw the problem as one of a weak central power that needed to be strengthened. He presaged the new Whigs while Coles reflected the old republican faith in good governance as a law of nature mediated by human virtue.

Edward Coles at twenty-six years was deeply loyal to Madison, lonely, widely sought after but distant and detached. Coles was a man whose passions were guarded and cerebral. He was devoted to republican ideals that were increasingly dated and fast growing irrelevant in the political sphere he was treading. He was an idealist, unsympathetic to the gathering clouds that were beginning to drive some elements of the republican ideal into the background of American political life. At first, Coles seemed to thrive on the social whirl in Washington. He concluded, as early as 1812, that the important work of the Congress was done less on the floor of the Capitol than on the floor of the ballroom. And he played an important, if indirect, role on several occasions in readying the stage for policy successes.

In late November 1812, the thirty-six-gun frigate USS *Constellation* lay in Washington's Eastern Branch (the Anacostia River), ready for sea but awaiting its complement of hands. The ship provided the setting for a reception that would have some impact on the appropriation of funds for the nation's meager navy. Coles managed this grand fete as a member of a committee of ten gentlemen. Whatever his enthusiasm for the political importance of this ball, Coles nurtured a personal interest. To his brother John, he admitted enthusiasm that the party may draw coquettes from the country, ladies who are at once "consumate, artful, hypercritical and perfidious."[72] Edward Coles was an idealist, true. He was also a young man interested in what young men are interested in: girls.

The party was a hit. All heads of departments attended with their wives, as did many members of Congress and the French minister.[73] The *National Intelligencer* reported on November 28, "The day was spent in the utmost concord and hilarity, no accident intervening to damp the gaiety of the scene." The next day, still bubbly with excitement over the "hilarious" party, Congress made the navy larger by twelve ships.[74] Coles played his role so well that two weeks later, the navy asked him to manage another ball. It was known as the Macedonian Ball and was held in Tomlinson's Hotel. The president did not attend; he was waiting for confirmation that Captain Stephen Decatur's USS *United States* had in fact defeated the HMS *Macedonian*.[75]

Coles's reaction to Washington and its social life matured over time. His first letters complained of mundane things, such as the cold weather and his lack of money. Six months later, he nearly chirped that he was so occupied that dining home in the family manner had not occurred more than three times in the previous fortnight.[76] And two months later, the social life had worn thin: "I am sick, yes heartily sick with the number of our parties. I have not been out of company one evening for more than two weeks." Spending every evening in idleness gives to the mornings additional labor. Coles complained that by the balls, levees, private dancing, and dinner parties, he was continually hurried and continually behind.[77]

Although Edward Coles had ample opportunity to graze in a rich field of social clover, he was unable to find a companionable sprig to his taste. In theory, he held that marriage is a happy and natural state; marrying and settling down were essential to a full life.[78] Yet, he was hesitant and easily distracted. He came to Washington a twenty-four-year-old bachelor and left it a thirty-year-old bachelor. To his brother, he sent all encouragement that marriage was, in his view, the most natural and therefore the most happy state.[79] And to John Hawkins, he sent a cheerful note celebrating his friend's impending marriage, dooming him to a blissful state and insulating him from any unhappiness or distress.[80] To his college classmate Tench Ringgold, Coles recommended a country girl rather than a city girl: they are more practical, he advised.[81] Between 1810 and 1815, his thoughts on women and his prospects for marriage fluctuated. He celebrated first the sophisticated, urbane woman suitable to townhouse or plantation and with the gift for light conversation; then he wanted the tough, practical woman with whom he could venture into the wild frontier.

Coles had at least one chance (possibly two) to marry and settle his family aspirations while he was in Washington. They show both the urgency Coles felt about finding a wife and his genteel, cerebral, and mostly practical take on the feminine mystique. In 1812, he wrote to his brother John that his wedding plans had "changed" but that he was still on friendly terms with the girl in question (probably a certain Miss Swann), who, in sum, was a perfect riddle and incomprehensible.[82] Three months later, he appeared to have found a replacement for Miss Swann, the perfect riddle. He told John he was waiting on a letter from "Miss A." of Richmond, and things seemed as well set as he could hope.[83] But again, the marriage was not to be. In the case of Miss Swann, the marriage fell through because the couple decided they did not have enough money to live at an appropriate level.[84] The fate of Miss A. and her reasons are unknown. William Preston described Coles as a "thorough gentleman, one of the best-natured and most kindly-affected men it has ever been my fortune to know."[85] Preston's portrait suggests a southern gentleman.[86] Coles left Washington unmarried, and he continued to worry about his bachelor state until he finally did marry in 1832 at the age of forty-six.[87]

Plantation Owner

Edward Coles was a messenger and agent for Madison. He was a manager of Washington parties and a gentleman with connections in Philadelphia . . . throughout also a slave owner and planter. He tried to be a model planter and slave master, though he did not consider himself an economic success.[88] Coles charged John Melton, manager of his Rockfish Valley plantation, with strict limits on harsh treatment of the slaves under his care. In retirement, he reflected (with some pride, it appears) that he had treated his slaves with all the kindness and attention in his power and forbid whipping in every case but one.[89] His plantation followed a diversified cropping pattern including tobacco, hemp, and wheat.[90] Diversified agriculture had worked for his father and for other planters; it had seen his family through good times and bad. And Coles was determined that as long as he owned the farm, he would make a success of it. He would try at least to clear the debt that ran with his inheritance.

During the time he lived in Washington, he peppered his brother John with letters demanding information or giving advice about selling crops and other farming matters.[91] He rejoiced when things went right, as in 1810 when Melton got the crops to market at the right time.[92] But, in 1812, Coles fell into despair when he received his accounts from John. After four years, two-and-one-half with a salary from Madison, he remained unable to pay off the $500 debt he had inherited with the estate.[93] The debt weighed heavily at this time (he planned to marry), and so he brooded half-seriously, "[I]f I can do no better on Rockfish, I must move elsewhere."[94] Coles rehearsed this conversation frequently in the coming years as he grappled with the nexus of his ideals and the practical needs of life.

In 1815, Coles was still trying to make money by farming, going so far as to hire additional farmhands (slaves) from his sister.[95] He was now also diversifying his holdings by buying bank stock.[96] He had been trying to sell the plantation since 1810, when it was appraised at $17,000. He was willing to accept $15,000 with $5,000 down. But the war and the embargo made Rockfish unmarketable within even those more generous terms.[97] He did not sell the plantation for several more years and then only to his brother Walter in 1819.[98] Edward summed up his position by telling John that he wanted to sell the plantation, but "I am not so much bent on it as to make a sacrifice."[99] Keeping the plantation from going further into debt marked his determination and steadfast attention to his business (surely recognizable as a family trait). But the years of war were generally a depressed time for Virginia agriculture in the piedmont.

Edward Coles harbored a sense of failure stemming from the fact that he had not freed himself from the slave system. He was unable to sell the plantation and unable to gather enough capital to emigrate. Stretching before him appeared to be a lengthy road of struggle to erase his debt, sell his farm, and keep his self-respect in the face of his awkward state as a slave owner. Youthful confusion over the course that his life should take and the high cost of his dream to emancipate played to his natural indecisiveness. Coles was pulled both toward the lively life of the city and to the virtuous and manly challenges of the frontier farm. His moral compass was strong, but the general direction of his life was susceptible to the magnetic currents swirling about him. Coles was faced with choices but lacked a clear way to sort them out. The mental turmoil may even have affected his health.

* * *

Coles was ill during a third of his tenure in Washington. He traveled in search of health. In a September 1812 letter to Madison, Coles, from his family's plantation, said that he would be indisposed at least three or four weeks and suggested that Madison replace him.[100] Then, as later, Madison either did without a secretary or had Payne Todd or Dolley fill in while Coles was ill. Exactly what troubled Coles is difficult to determine with authority. One historian refers vaguely to tumors.[101] Coles listed various complaints. In November 1812, he lamented to his brother John that despite the efforts of Drs. Everett and Ebsey, the ulcer on his chest would not respond to treatment.[102] Still sick in the spring of 1813, he went to Philadelphia on Dolley Madison's recommendation to consult Dr. Physick (Philip Syng).[103] Physick removed two "sacks" from Coles's rectum (the symptoms point to pilonidal cysts). This treatment seemed to have solved the problem, but recovery was slow.[104]

In May 1813, Coles was still under treatment; his complaint was that his illness cramped his ability to socialize. Still, that spring, he indulged his taste for Philadelphia glitz and attended his first major Philadelphia party. Going with James Gallatin and James Bayard to George Dallas's house, he was, however, "much disappointed in the beauty and elegance of the circles of belles."[105] His health continued to improve, and later that month, he forwarded letters to the president from Gallatin and handled various business matters, including patronage. On May 22, he thanked Dolley for allowing him to remain in the employ of the president and promised that he would be recovered in two weeks.[106] The expected recovery was interrupted. A relapse in the summer led to another rectal operation. In September, he still felt miserable and exhausted.[107] As late as August 1814, still following Dr. Physick's instructions, Coles took a vacation.[108] This two-year period marked the only major illness he suffered until 1834. This was also the period when he devoted much time to thinking more deeply about his plight—about slavery and that he still felt sullied by slaveholding.

Shortly after his ultimate recovery, he began to plan seriously for his move westward.[109] His illness provided time to think, time for his thinking to settle, time to draw the residue of his beliefs and experiences into a focus. It gave him time to settle on a future for himself as an emigrant to America's western frontier.

3

Release

African Americans were conspicuous in Washington, D.C., during Coles's time. Slave and free, they made up almost a quarter of the population in 1800, forming a deep pool of black culture in the urban life of the nation's capital. Slaves were domestic servants; they delivered produce by wagon from the wharves in Georgetown; they operated tables at the farmer's market; they were used extensively (and profitably) as laborers during the capital's construction boom. Slaves accompanied their congressional masters on daily rounds, waiting outside on Washington street curbs as business was transacted indoors. Slaves were everywhere, and they were taken for granted, including by northerners.[1]

The Washington area grew quickly into one of many slavery centers in America. The area's growth attracted slave owners who could make good money hiring out their slave property for labor in the new capital to throw up cheap quarters and fancy residences. One of the largest of the slave traders was located in Alexandria just across from the city and the Capitol dome.[2] Slaves were auctioned for hundreds of dollars in Washington. They were then sold in Georgia and other deep-south states for thousands where the cotton gin multiplied the value of and demand for slave labor.[3]

Auction houses and "Georgia pens" (holding cells for slaves going to the block) dotted the town of Washington. The area known now as Potomac Park held an auction; Roby's Tavern at the corner of Seventh Street and Maryland Avenue had another. One was on B Street in southwest Washington. Another on F Street near Thirteenth. One of the largest auction operations was located at Lafayette Square, in sight of the White House.[4]

Edward Coles was a slave owner during his Washington years. He was also an occasional manager of slavery business for family and friends. At times, he made arrangements for slave hiring and their transport to and from Virginia.[5] Coles appears to have drawn a perimeter around his involvement with slavery in Washington. He neither bought nor sold slaves, limiting his activities to arranging for transport and matters of contracting. Was he, perhaps, playing at the same game as did James Madison and numerous other southerners, tending to associate the worst sins of slavery with the buying and selling side of things? Auctions broke up families and broadcast misery. Ownership, however, was a matter of stewardship, a benevolent means of protecting slaves from mistreatment by less-scrupulous people. Slave ownership was, in the view of many, a white man's burden that produced honor when carried with compassion and a sense of responsibility. There is certainly some of this in his reminiscence of earlier days when he recalled nostalgically that he had fed, clothed, and treated his slaves with all the kindness and attention in his power.[6]

Coles did not subscribe wholeheartedly to the game. He was probably reluctant in undertaking these business favors. They betrayed beliefs he held closely. He was a Virginia gentleman for whom family loyalty was a prime virtue that certified and expressed his honor. Allegiance to his family and friends was cardinal, a motivating force for Coles throughout his life (notwithstanding the exception they took over his views on slavery). In other ways he asserted his contrary view of slavery: He could have brought a servant to Washington to wait on his needs, but this he did not do. And he found ways to express himself candidly on the topic of slavery. James Madison and Edward Coles, walking together along a street in Washington, passed a slave coffle on its way to the slave market. Coles turned to Madison, congratulating him that he was not then accompanied by a foreign minister and thus saved the mortification of witnessing "such a revolting sight in the presence of the representative of a nation less boastful perhaps of its regard for the rights of man, but more observant of them."[7]

The War of 1812 had driven home to Edward the fragile nature of the republic. The contrast between "low" political realities and "high" republican ideals was painfully obvious to him. Those high republican ideals were now his ideals. He was frustrated with the disorder in Congress and the failures of the war—they pointed to a (congressional) leadership wanting in the virtues that would keep the country morally strong. Memories of Bishop James Madison's lectures on the importance of a virtuous citizenry combined with the problems Coles saw in Congress during the War of 1812 may have heightened his concern about the ever-eroding effects of slavery on that virtue.

Seven months before the war ended, Coles began a correspondence with Thomas Jefferson on slavery and the future of the republic. Coles was growing hungry for the bread of freedom; Thomas Jefferson's cool response would leaven that bread.

* * *

In the summer of 1814, five years into his retirement, Jefferson was living the exalted life of letters. His correspondence played upon wide-ranging topics: classification in natural history, Lord Napier's Theorem, the constitution of Spain, foundations of the morality of man.[8] Pamphlets, books, and treatises arrived in surplus. This was the draft of life that Jefferson had thirsted after while president and from which he drank as deeply as he could in retirement. He reveled in a private life of family, farm, friends, and ideas. He would not be budged from it.

Jefferson dreamed of building an "academical" village in Central Virginia; he'd dreamt of it for decades. Peter Carr gave that dream an outlet in 1814. Carr was proposing to set up the Albemarle Academy, a private secondary school in Charlottesville. Jefferson was placed on the board during that year and began at once to reshape the project in the much-grander vision that ultimately would produce the University of Virginia, a viable new model for a republican university.[9] Jefferson, man of letters, man of study, threw himself into fulfilling a distant vision. He would not, during the same season of his life, invest so much as a jot in a cause—the end of slavery—for which he had often professed support. Edward Coles turned to wise family friend and public hero Thomas Jefferson for action.

Washington, July 31, 1814

Dear Sir:

I never took up my pen with more hesitation, or felt more embarrassment than I do in addressing you on the subject of this letter. . . . I will not enter on the right which man has to enslave his brother man, nor upon the moral and political effects of slavery on individuals or on society; because these things are better understood by you than by me. My object is to entreat and beseech you to exert your knowledge and influence in devising and getting into operation some plan for the general emancipation of slavery. . . . And it is a duty, as I conceive, that devolves particularly on you, from your known philosophical and enlarged view of subjects, and from the principles you have professed and practiced through a long and useful life, pre-eminently distinguished as well [by] being foremost in establishing on the broadest basis the rights of man, and the liberty and independence of your country.[10]

On three pages in his well-formed hand, Coles implored the sage of Monticello to take up the cause that he fully believed Jefferson cared about as deeply as did he. Coles armed his letter with a battalion of compelling arguments, soldiering to a just cause. If the writer of the Declaration of Independence made an appeal against slavery, the nation would surely listen. Even if the effort should fail, grateful posterity would forever remember him by his efforts to secure the rights of man. Coles reminded Jefferson of his unequivocal statements in the Declaration and asserted slavery as unfinished business from the Revolution. Jefferson should feel not only interested in this noble battle but also obligated to fulfill the Revolution's promise to those still oppressed. Coles closed with a personal note.

I will only add as an excuse for the liberty I take in addressing you on this subject which is so particularly interesting to me, that from the time I was capable of reflecting on the nature of political society, and of the rights appertaining to man, I have not only been principled against slavery, but have had feelings so repugnant to it as to decide me not to hold them; which decision has forced me to leave my native State, and with it all my relations and friends. This I hope will be deemed by you some excuse for the liberty of this intrusion, of which I gladly avail myself to assure you of the very great respect and esteem with which I am, my dear Sir, your very sincere and devoted friend,

Edward Coles[11]

In *Notes on Virginia* and elsewhere, Jefferson had placed hope for the future of the republic on the shoulders of the second generation: Coles's generation.[12] Perhaps Coles hoped that once reminded, Jefferson would provide the necessary impetus to mobilize that generation. Jefferson replied on 25 August with a janus letter. This letter has become a basic document in the painful study that tries to comprehend how the author of the Declaration of Independence could have feet of Virginia clay for the eradication of slavery (at his plantation or anywhere else, for that matter).[13] Jefferson wrote back to Coles.

Monticello, Aug 25, 1814

Dear Sir:

Your favor of July 31 was duly received, and was read with particular pleasure; the sentiments breathed through the whole do honor to both the head and heart of the writer. Mine on the subject of the slavery of negros have long since been in the possession of the public, and time has only served to give them greater root. . . .

. . . Your solitary but welcome voice is the first that has brought this sound to my ear, and I have considered the general silence which prevails on this subject as indicating an antipathy unfavorable to every hope, yet the hour of emancipation is advancing in the march of time. . . .

I am sensible of the particularities with which you have looked towards me as the person who should undertake this salutary but arduous work; but this, my dear Sir, is like bidding old Priam to buckle the armor of Hector "trementibus aevo humeris et infutile ferrum cingi." No, I have overlived the generation with which mutual labors and perils begat mutual confidence and influence. This enterprise is for the young, for those who can follow it up and bear it through to its consummation. It shall have all my prayers, and these are the only weapons of an old man. . . .

Th. Jefferson[14]

Emancipation could be accomplished, Jefferson explained on his page 2, only if accompanied by an exodus of the newly freed black people out of the country. Jefferson admitted his own plan (published in his *Notes on Virginia*) needed a long time to succeed. Coles, he argued, could best serve the cause by remaining in Virginia, setting an example as a kind master, and continuing to be active in politics. As Coles rose in political circles, Jefferson hoped, he could eventually help to achieve the emancipation that flowered in his hopes.

He would go no further.[15] Here is Jefferson. Here is the sphinx as captured by Joseph Ellis in his insightful biography.[16] More theoretical than operational was Jefferson; politic to preserve his future influence. Bold in thought, more cautious in action.[17] Here is the man to whom is attributed some responsibility for the 1778 law closing Virginia to the international slave market, the substance of the 1782 law permitting manumission in the state (taken largely from his 1769 bill submitted by Richard Bland), and a 1783 draft of a constitution (to replace that of 1776) setting emancipation within its terms. Still, as early as 1784, at the age of thirty years, Jefferson had given the same message to friends that he later gave to Edward Coles: he would not participate directly in efforts to abolish slavery in Virginia.[18] In a letter of 31 March 1801, Jefferson had written tellingly to Dr. Walter Jones: "We see the wisdom of Solon's remark, that no more good must be attempted than the nation can bear."[19] This became Jefferson's creed of action on slavery in Virginia. John Quincy Adams was correct: "Mr. Jefferson had not the spirit of martyrdom."[20] Jefferson offered Coles no concrete help beyond his prayers—a strange pledge for a deist. In essence, Jefferson recommended that Coles follow Jefferson's own course of action (the very definition, in some regard, of inaction). Coles had received similar unsatisfying advice from his family.

Scarcely more than two weeks later, Jefferson wrote an astonishing letter to Dr. Thomas Cooper, including an elaborate comparison of social relations in England and in the United States. Jefferson asserted that slaves in America were better cared for and more prosperous than were day laborers in England and no more coerced than were seamen impressed in His Majesty's navy. On the other hand, he said, "I am not justifying the wrongs we have committed on a foreign people, by the example of another nation committing equal wrongs on their own subjects. On the contrary, there is nothing I would not sacrifice to a practicable plan of abolishing every vestige of this moral and political depravity."[21] "Nothing I would not sacrifice"? Only weeks ago he could offer up nothing but his prayers.

Coles, of course, was not in receipt of this astonishing letter. Certainly, the reply that Coles did receive was not what he had expected from one of the Revolutionary fathers. Jefferson took a cautious view that did not solve the crisis Coles believed was destroying the virtue of the citizenry. The very cornerstone upon which the republic rested was crumbling. The problem called for boldness, but Jefferson met Coles's proposal with diminution, retirement, withdrawal, (tactical) retreat, abdication. Coles had hoped that Jefferson would live up to the Jeffersonian ideals that Jefferson had put into his Declaration of Independence. It was hope misplaced.

Coles's response to Jefferson's letter of 25 August followed some weeks later, because Jefferson's letter arrived while Coles was on vacation.

Washington, September 26, 1814

I must be permitted again to trouble you, my dear Sir, to return my grateful thanks for the respectful and friendly attention shown to my letter in your answer of the 25th ult. . . .

Your prayers I trust will not only be heard with indulgence in Heaven, but with influence on Earth. But I cannot agree with you that they are the only weapons of one at your age; nor that the difficult work of cleansing the escutcheon of Virginia of the foul stain of slavery can best be done by the young. To expect so great and difficult an object, great and extensive powers, both of mind and influence, are required, which can never be possessed in so great a degree by the young as by the old. . . . It was under these impressions that I looked to you, my dear Sir, as the first of our aged worthies to awaken our fellow citizens from their infatuation to a proper sense of justice, and to the true interest of their country; and by proposing a system for the gradual emancipation of our slaves, at once to form a rallying point for its friends, who enlightened by your wisdom and experience, and supported and encouraged by your sanction and patronage, might look forward to a propitious and happy result.

Your time of life I had not considered as an obstacle to the undertaking. Doctor Franklin, to whom, by the way, Pennsylvania owes her early riddance of the evils of slavery, was as actively and as usefully employed on as arduous duties after he had past your age as he had ever been at any period of his life.

With apologizing for having given you so much trouble on this subject, and again repeating my thanks for the respectful and flattering attention you have been pleased to pay to it, I renew the assurances of the great respect and regard which makes me most sincerely yours.

Edward Coles[22]

This series of letters, presented by most writers without Coles's response of 26 September, remains a useful aid to understanding Jefferson.[23] It is, however, an indispensable aid to understanding Coles at this point in his life. The correspondence grapples with the paradox discussed by James Oakes.[24] What definition of freedom would not reject slavery as incompatible? In the logic of white, liberal, republican society, freedom defined the individual; a slave could not be an individual. Coles had first confronted this twisted notion at William and Mary and revisited it in his correspondence with Jefferson. Coles turned the logic right side out: If the individual is defined by his freedom, there can be no slave. From that vantage, the way to Illinois became clearer.

As the War of 1812 concluded, he had begun to sort his options. He did so slowly, hesitantly, unwilling at times to accept the conclusion of migration to the west. Edward Coles never wavered in his intent. His general plan to leave the state and free his slaves outside Virginia appeared not long after his father's death but shifted among the various priorities that competed for his intentions. His family requested that he not announce his plans to his slaves in advance—the knowledge might incite other family slaves to hope for similar treatment or to run. Coles respected their request. The agreement was probably in place as early as 1810. But the how and where of this plan emerged slowly. Coles was unsure, careful, methodical, and sometimes distracted. His intent was not irresolute.

The letters to and from Jefferson pushed Coles beyond the precipice. He had determined to act on his views and would not stay in Virginia. His response to Jefferson points to newfound certainty in his mind. Coles would henceforth put his shoulder to the daunting challenge of freeing himself from the slavery that still owned him, however vague and elusive the specific plan might remain for some years.

It had been seven years since he had left the protected halls of The College of William and Mary, seven years since his moral sensibilities had been awakened by Bishop Madison. Coles's own slaves, in fulfillment of the promise to his family, knew nothing of his. But he had made his intentions known to Presidents Madison and Jefferson. His family had struggled with the question that nagged at the wayward son. It will take him almost five years more before the yeast of his determination would rise to confidant action.

* * *

The Treaty of Ghent was signed on 24 December 1814, exactly four months after the British had made a mockery of American defenses in Washington. The president and his family moved into one of Washington's most interesting residences, the Octagon House, at the invitation of the French minister.[25] The upstairs circular room was made into a study for Madison; he signed the Treaty of Ghent there on 15 February 1815. Wednesday drawing-room parties continued, but they never achieved the brilliance and flash that were so celebrated in the White House. They did provide a rallying social venue and continued to make a back stage on which Madison could set his political ideas in motion.

Edward Coles returned from Philadelphia. He was in White Sulphur Springs sometime between 31 July and 26 September 1814 while Washington was picking up the pieces. Shortly after Madison's signing of the Treaty of Ghent the following February, Coles submitted his resignation to the president.

I Hope I May Yet Find a Country

For all the winter and spring of 1815, Coles agonized more. In a letter to Payne Todd, the struggle and his own future loomed as a sacrificial (yet still obscure) burden.[26] He even suggested to Nicholas Biddle that the west with its Spartan frontier environment might harm his physical well-being. Coles was being dramatic in his descriptions of the sacrifices he would make. He seemed to be convincing himself that the move west would be as heroic as remaining in Virginia to fight against slavery. Various friends, among them his school pal Tench Ringgold, urged him to stay in the east and not to sacrifice himself in the wilderness.[27] By the end of March 1815, the decision became firm again. The remaining questions were where and when and how. Coles wrote again to Biddle, reporting that he had left the president with no intention of returning and was busily preparing to visit the frontier northwest of the Ohio River with every hope of ultimately escaping from the scene of slavery and its oppression.[28] In June, he left Enniscorthy, traveling west to explore the potential that the frontier held as his personal Eden. He needed to deal with the practical problems to find a pleasant, affordable place to live that might approximate the social life of the east. He traveled by horse and buggy, taking with him a second saddle horse and his slave Ralph Crawford. Ralph was a short fellow, about forty years of age, trained as a coachman, and held in some regard by the Coles family. Together, the two men traveled first to Ohio. In July 1815, Coles wrote James Madison from Cincinnati, complaining that Ohio was too wet for comfort or health and that the acreage was too expensive. So he and Ralph pushed on farther west.[29]

In September, he paused in Kentucky to visit a college friend. Travel was slow and roundabout. The two men forded the Ohio River twice, and each crossing inflamed Coles's frustration. The lands he viewed were not to his liking, yet to return to a life in Virginia was to accept defeat.[30] Coles felt unmoored. The frontier towns were small, cluttered, and crude. Land prices were high. He found no bargain; acreage was as dear, in his judgment, as in Virginia. Still, he continued to search. To his brother John he wrote in September, "I hope I may yet find a country with which I may be so pleased as to determine to live in it and set about settling myself immediately."[31]

In Kentucky, he fancied that Indiana (which was about as far west as he could contemplate) might offer a home.[32] But once in Indiana, he found terrible roads and swamps that seemed to bloat the land and to draw vermin and insects. The National Road, the best the territory had to offer, consisted of little more than blaze marks on the trees and stumps. Settlers' cabins were widely scattered, and travelers were tempting targets for robbers and other scoundrels of the frontier. This was definitely not the sort of territory Coles had in mind as a future home. Like many travelers of the time, he concluded that Indiana was at least as bad as Ohio.[33]

He might have turned back, of course. But Virginia was a dead end. In Virginia, he could not justly free his slaves. So he looked farther west. He had concluded that if his Eden was anywhere at all, it must be beyond Indiana. It must be beyond the vanishing point of his own plans. In Illinois, perhaps. His letters began to register resignation to a life of isolation.[34]

After crossing Illinois, Coles discovered the American Bottom, a crescent of fertility hugging the southwestern Illinois shore of the Mississippi River. The land was fat, watered, and $1.25 an acre. St. Louis, just across the Mississippi, held hope of a chance for a more cosmopolitan life as well. In partnership with two of his brothers, Coles purchased 6,000 acres in Lincoln County, Missouri (now part of the St. Louis metropolitan area); 2,880 acres of Illinois farmland in the Military Bounty district just north of the Illinois Bottom; and several lots in the little French town of St. Louis.[35] Even in 1815, St. Louis, with a history already and a

European flavor of sorts, offered hints of civility that Ohio and Indiana failed to give the prospective pioneer.

The quantity of land Coles was able to purchase was a result of two factors. First, he had moved far enough west that land was cheap. Population was sparse and speculation not yet frantic. Second, he operated in conjunction with his brothers. Their combined assets allowed for purchase of large tracts under good terms. It happened that Isaac was considering a move to Missouri, so some family might be closer than Virginia. The land in Illinois and St. Louis appears to be owned by Edward while he partnered with Isaac on land in Missouri.

Coles wrote Biddle about his purchases. He was not entirely reconciled to his chosen life on the unsettled frontier. Biddle agreed that settling in Ohio would not have been wise, and he urged Coles to become a landlord instead of a "woodsman."[36] Biddle would have his own problems with Ohio land, trying to make money from a salt works. Coles, for his part, was disappointed with what he had discovered but was resigning himself to a chosen life on the frontier.[37] His words were hesitant, qualified, reflecting a mind as yet unsettled on his final course. The crux of Coles's predicament was society—specifically, marriage and friends.[38] Coles had met a west filled with roughnecks and yokels. He feared being bored to senility, despaired at the lack of society, and so concluded his letter wavering and equivocal.[39]

Coles was under pressure from friends (especially Biddle and Payne Todd) to remain in the east. Todd urged him to move anywhere *but* the west and suggested that Madison could arrange a post in Washington or Europe.[40] Ultimately, Coles (now nearing thirty) was worried about finding a suitable wife. He worried that the right type of woman would not be available on the frontier.[41]

In October, still in Illinois, Coles reached Shawneetown (in the southeast corner of the state) and then went west to Kaskaskia (an ancient town with but a single brick house). He sent Crawford back to Rockfish with one of the horses. Coles set out by keelboat down the Mississippi just before the setting in of winter. From New Orleans, he headed for home, traveling first by sea to Savannah, Georgia, then pushing on to Charleston, South Carolina, and making a short side trip to visit his sister Emily in South Carolina (now married to John Rutherfoord, a successful planter). Home, then, to Enniscorthy.[42]

Prometheus

During 1816, the Russian consul in Philadelphia, Nicholas Koskoff, was tried and convicted of the rape of a maid in his household. The Russian minister to the United States, Andre de Daschkoff, convinced Czar Alexander I that Koskoff's diplomatic prerogatives had been violated. In retribution, the czar barred the American chargé d'affaires from the Imperial Palace.[43] Levett Harris, the chargé d'affaires, had recently resigned, but a successor had not yet been named. President Madison was presented with a diplomatic puzzle. To use Harris for the negotiations without additional support would have appeared weak. Yet without access to the palace, the chargé could conduct no business at all. So Madison chose to send a personal envoy. This would appeal to the czar's sense of injury. By smoothing over the problem with a personal messenger, Madison hoped to apply a friendly, diplomatic salve, relieve the inflammation, and clear the way for a new chargé d'affaires to come into a more relaxed situation.[44]

In July of 1816, Madison approached Edward Coles, asking him to act as his envoy to Russia.[45] Coles would be seen as a personal representative, a member of the Madison household.[46] But Coles's plans for emigrating to the west were hardening. It took repeated requests from Madison before Coles finally relented. The U.S. State Department wanted to resolve the incident quickly; the U.S. Navy hoped to avoid having a ship ice-locked in St. Petersburg, Russia. Through an interchange of letters, naval-department officials selected the brig USS *Prometheus*, commanded by A. J. Wadsworth, to make the trip.[47] She sailed with a full wartime complement of officers but was undermanned before the mast, which emphasized the diplomatic nature of her mission. The crew was partially drawn from the frigate USS *Macedonian*.

Coles left Boston in the late summer for St. Petersburg, arriving on 30 September. His instructions ordered him to deliver his dispatches to Harris, who remained in charge pending the arrival of his replacement, and then wait for a reply. Coles would not be negotiating the resolution. He would simply bear the prestige of the president and add gravitas to the effort as Harris untangled the knot.

On 30 September 1816, the *Prometheus* docked at Kronstadt, a naval fortress and port of entry on an island in the Gulf of Finland, thirty-five miles from St. Petersburg.[48] The Russians detained Coles with a series of excuses—a diplomatic *opera buffa* was in full dress. First, an officer of the Russian guardship demanded a bill of health from the *Prometheus*. Clearing this up took a day. Next, the officer required that Coles send a letter to St. Petersburg seeking entry on diplomatic business. Finally, when the health assurances and various permissions were in place (these requiring some days), the officer required that the dispatches be smoked. The officer assured Coles that smoking diplomatic documents was normal and customary (of course). Smoking was completed. Finally, the officer required that the dispatches be jabbed with a fork. The officer assured Coles that stabbing diplomatic documents was normal and customary. Coles's dispatch to Secretary of State James Monroe angrily recounted the entire ridiculous scene. Was this absurd smoking of documents a Russian effort to fumigate out the spirit of American liberty? In the end, after threats, letters, smokings, and grand stabbings with dinner forks, Coles (much ruffled) was allowed to proceed to St. Petersburg.[49]

Harris convinced Coles that a formal protest against his detention at Kronstadt would accomplish little, so Coles merely noted the incidents in his report. This Russian comic opera appears to have been meant for a Russian audience as a domestic political affair. Coles and the *Prometheus* appear to have sparked an entirely local military tussle.[50]

Once Coles's papers were in Harris's hands, Harris contacted the Russian Foreign Office and discussed the Koskoff case with Count Karl Nesselrode. The count agreed to allow Harris to send an explanatory dispatch to the vacationing czar. The czar, duly impressed that Madison had sent a special envoy, accepted the explanation, and relations returned to normal.[51] Coles informed Secretary of State Monroe that the negotiations were successful and that he felt the czar would recall not only Koskoff but also Daschkoff. Coles remained in St. Petersburg for three months until the diplomatic mission could be completed. His return home commenced by land.

From Hamburg, Coles sent his report to Monroe, along with comments about his personal travel plans. The work finished, he wrote, he proposed to spend several weeks in Brussels after some time in the capital of the Netherlands. Then he would mount a tour of France in early spring, followed by some time in England.[52]

Coles arrived in Brussels on 4 January 1817, spending several enjoyable weeks with the American minister, William Eustis.[53] From Brussels, Coles proceeded to Paris and supped with the Duke of Wellington. He also went to the opera several times. During the three months he spent in France, he was seen often with the Marquis de Lafayette.[54] (He would again see Lafayette on America's frontier when the marquis would make his triumphal tour of the United States from 1824 to 1825.)

In Britain, several new friends organized Coles's stay. His papers contain a note from George Murn recommending a grand tour of Britain including Scotland and the industrial lowlands. Less grandiose were A. H. Rowan's plans in London. Rowan proposed to "do the town," beginning with the theater and ending with a sermon from a dissenting minister—hell followed by heaven in one evening.[55] American Minister John Quincy Adams introduced Coles into English society; indeed, he was presented at the Court of St. James.[56]

During a weekend tour of the Midlands, Coles began an important friendship. He met Morris Birkbeck, a social reformer and farmer, who wanted to escape taxes and high land prices in England by emigrating to the United States. Birkbeck hoped to develop an English-style landed estate with tenants working the land on the American frontier. He saw himself as a simple yeoman unable to advance in the class-ridden economic climate of England.[57] Coles spent five days with Birkbeck, discussing an immigrant's options in the American west. Clearly, Coles was somewhat of an expert on the subject. Birkbeck complained to Coles about the same problems with which Coles had been dealing—high land prices and bad climate. Coles saw in Birkbeck the type of person he had described to Biddle in his letter of 1815, the type of companion who could make the frontier livable. He spent the time ardently working to bring Birkbeck to Illinois.[58] Coles had turned Illinois promoter. Further . . . he had decided. He was ready to move. And his enthusiasm for home was radiant. His European tour solidified his faith in the American system, in its republican foundation, and in its power to promote the enjoyment of happiness.[59]

* * *

Coles arrived back in America in the fall of 1817. The most concrete result of the trip was a paper Coles wrote comparing Russian serfdom with American slavery. Slavery was harsher and immoral and thus threatening to the virtue of the United States. While the serf's life was restricted, Coles did not see the serf so constrained as to prevent enlightenment.

Whether Madison or Payne Todd had suggested the research, Coles's writing suggests that the project had been proposed as a means of dissuading him from his plan of emancipation. It was supposed to convince him that serfdom and slavery were similar and thus slavery tolerable because under the guise of serfdom, it was tolerated in another civilized nation.[60] The plan, if there was one, failed.

In the fall of 1817, Walter Coles, eldest of the Edward's brothers, purchased the Rockfish property. Edward had placed it for sale in 1810, but Virginia's economy had been slow in recovery from the Revolution, and it had declined further during the War of 1812. He was absent from Virginia while the property sat. The market was slow, and Edward was in no position to advance the sale. Walter's offer to purchase Edward's legacy must be viewed as a remarkable brotherly gesture—a testament to the bonds of family. Walter understood that he was empowering Edward to fulfill his pledge to free his slaves, a pledge that Walter disapproved of.

While Coles was in Europe, Monroe replaced Madison as president, the fourth and final dynamo in the Virginia dynasty. Coles's proven loyalty to Madison and the long-standing friendship and family connections with the new president, together with Coles's recent efforts in Russia, brought successive offers from Monroe for positions in the government.[61] Monroe asked Coles to remain in Washington to become his personal secretary. Coles rejected this offer, and a second offer invited Coles to name his own position. In private, Coles confided that Monroe, a more formal man than Madison, would have made any office a "perfect drudgery."[62] Instead, Coles returned to Illinois to make his final preparations. His Prometheus was behind him, and the sale of his farm provided him at long last with the resources he needed to realize his own future. His resolve was now matched with clarity, financing, and a plan.

From Kaskaskia to Rockfish

Edward Coles departed for Illinois (alone this time) in March of 1818. Well armed with letters of recommendation from the president, he sought out the leading citizens. His letters introduced him to Ninian Edwards, the territorial governor and the dominant political figure in the Territory of Illinois. Coles also renewed his acquaintance with Birkbeck, who had, by this time, relocated in Illinois. Birkbeck, along with Richard Flower, founded the "English Settlement" of Albion in southeastern Illinois, not far from the Wabash River.[63]

While in Illinois in 1818, Coles attended the state's first constitutional convention, convened in Kaskaskia. He remained several weeks. Slavery and the status of black residents were two of the major questions before the convention. Coles remarked later that he worked diligently to prevent the success of the proslavery faction, but Coles's role in this early antislavery fight remains speculative and (as yet) hidden.[64] Most Illinois historians have concluded that Coles's actions included writing an antislavery letter that appeared in June 1818 over the pen name "Agis." The letter was credited with swinging the convention against allowing slavery and a restrictive Black Code and has been a strong part of Coles's antislavery reputation. But attributing the letter to Coles is based on deduction, not on direct evidence. The style and general flow of the letter are typical of Coles's writings on slavery, but Coles does not mention the letter in any of his own writings. The evidence points to another. A series of "Agis" letters addressed various questions facing the convention. In May, George Churchill (a leading figure in Madison County who was destined to serve in Illinois' first House of Representatives) noted in his diary that he had written a letter that he had signed "Agis" and dropped it off at the newspaper's office. This particular letter dealt with the issue of the secret ballot. Because Churchill was a delegate at the convention and was also antislavery, a better case can be made for his authorship of all the "Agis" letters.[65]

Coles spent the summer and autumn exploring the territory of Illinois. Much of the time he spent traveling to small settlements. He took two excursions beyond the settled areas: one trip of three weeks, another of one. With a guide, provisions, and blankets for sleeping under the Illinois stars, Edward Coles came to be more cheerfully reconciled to his chosen future.[66] On his return to Virginia during the winter of that year, Coles collected the remaining payment from his brother Walter, completing the sale of his Rockfish property.[67] Coles also made one final decision: he needed a firm source of income that was not related to farming.

Applying to James Monroe for a position was awkward for Coles and, notwithstanding Monroe's efforts to enlist him two years earlier, Coles hated to lower himself in the seeking of it. He found his voice, however, and contacted Monroe for an appointment as Register of Lands in the

Illinois town of Edwardsville.[68] On 15 March 1819, Monroe quickly and enthusiastically granted Coles the position as register that he desired, which gave Coles the financial security that sealed his decision to move. Finally, twelve years after the idealistic college student had made his tentative decision, the actual emigration to Illinois began.

* * *

Perhaps, as the spring of 1819 burst upon Nelson County, the slaves on Coles's Rockfish plantation had become a little complacent about the sale of the farm, believing that the breakup of their families was a receding possibility. Rockfish had been for sale since 1810, after all. When the actual sale did occur, the plantation had gone to a family member eighteen months ago. The slave families were still together. None had been sold at Charlottesville's auction yet. Perhaps life would go on as before?

When Ralph Crawford, the oldest man of the group, had traveled with Coles four years ago (in 1815), he was probably aware of Coles's views on slavery.[69] Even so, a realistic view of the matter might sober any hopeful slave. Were Coles like other slave owners (yet wishing to free himself from the holding of slaves), he would send them all away for sale in New Orleans. He would free himself from slavery but not sacrifice the largest portion of his wealth. He'd make a profit, in fact. And Ralph's family would be scattered.

At some time in the early spring of the year, Edward Coles assembled his slaves at the plantation.[70] Perhaps they gathered around the tobacco shed behind the main house on the crest of the long knoll overlooking the glorious Rockfish Valley to the east.[71] Ralph Crawford was there to hear Coles give forth. He was forty-six or forty-seven years old at the time and short, about 5 foot 3 inches. Crawford, a man of gracious manners, had accompanied John Coles II and various Coles brothers on their travels.[72] His wife, Kate, forty-three or forty-four years, was there, as were their four children: Betsy, sixteen or seventeen, Thomas, thirteen, and with a weak right arm and leg, Mary, eleven or twelve, and William, nine. Robert Crawford, a little taller at 5 feet 7 inches than his older brother Ralph, was about twenty-five years old at the time. At one time, Walter Coles, Edward's eldest brother, had owned him. (Evidence that Walter owned others in the Rockfish group is not conclusive.)[73] Finally, there was Polly, sister to both Ralph and Robert, about sixteen or seventeen years old. These were the Crawfords. Others were there as well. Thomas Cobb was thirty-eight or forty years of age. Nancy Gaines was sixteen or seventeen. Sukey, who had been purchased by John Coles II just before his death in 1808, had five children, "the oldest of whom was not large enough to nurse the youngest": Frankey, Alfred, Elizabeth, Wilson, and Lucinda.[74] And Sukey was pregnant. Finally, there were two elderly women.[75]

Coles announced that he was moving to Illinois and proposed that they should go with him.[76] He did not desire that they go against their will. On the contrary, going to Illinois would be no favor to him. Coles invited them to discuss the prospect with Ralph, who was familiar with the country from his trip there four years before. If any should decide not to go, Coles said, he would exchange them with another family slave.

All were eager to go. Exceptions were made for the two elderly women, one of whom had an only child, owned by Rebecca Coles, Edward's mother. This eighty-year-old woman was left in the care of Rebecca Coles after Edward's party departed for Illinois. She died sometime between 1819 and 1822. The other, a cripple about fifty years old, had a husband who was elderly and infirm, also owned by Rebecca Coles. She was left in the care of Mrs. Coles. Upon Rebecca's death in 1826, she was left with Edward's brother Isaac and was supported by Edward until her death.[77]

One further complication would be resolved before the group was ready to embark on its western adventure. Sukey's husband, Manuel, owed service to a neighbor living close to Enniscorthy. Manuel was entitled to his freedom in August 1825, according to the will of a former master. At Sukey's request, Edward purchased the time remaining in Manuel's indenture, thereby preventing the breakup of that family. Manuel would join the group.

Why was the group so ready to go? The answer can only be surmised, but Coles's encouragement that they talk with Ralph may hold the key. While Ralph was surely not told of the emancipation plan in specific, he had traveled with Coles. Had the two talked openly about slavery? Had Coles planted hints in Ralph's knowledge, calculated to keep his promise to his family but to subtly advise Ralph as to what he might reasonably hope for? Later, Coles indicated that he felt Ralph knew what the plan was, and this is all we know.

On 30 March 1819, Edward Coles went the fifteen miles from his plantation at Rockfish to Staunton (known then as Beverly's Mill Place), a bustling way station and supply center in the Shenandoah Valley. The Great Philadelphia Wagon Road ran through Staunton. As spring was gaining momentum, the town was coming back to life, supplying those moving south and west to the frontier or north to the great cities and the northern gateways to the west. Coles purchased two horses for $250 and a two-horse wagon with gear for $175.[78]

Packing commenced. Coles reported that personal luggage was loaded into the new wagon, but some tools and travel gear must have been included as well (for minor wagon repairs and the like). On 1 April 1819, a Thursday, this party of seventeen bundled aboard the wagon and left home.[79] Six adults and eleven children left all that was familiar. They left the long, white house that had been home. They left the horses that had been their charge. They left the fields, where labor was endless.

The wagon, horses, and anxious cargo bounced down the little track by the house, westward (roughly) hundreds of yards along a trail by the Rockfish River to the crossroad at Greenfield.[80] Then, bearing more directly west, the group rode along the "Old Road" until it met up with Three Notch'd. Edward Coles was not with them.

The Finest Feelings of Our Nature

Edward Coles left two days later from Enniscorthy with two horses and a small wagon. He had given Ralph Crawford money and papers to cover their security and necessary expenses while on the road. Ralph would captain the little cart taking its human cargo to Brownsville, Pennsylvania, on the Monongahela River. Coles would purchase boats, and they would collectively float down the Monongahela to Pittsburgh. Then they would ride the great Ohio River to Shawneetown. A final overland trek to Edwardsville would finish the trip off. This would be but a baptism, of course, for a new life of work and hardship in Illinois.

Friends and family thought Edward foolish by leaving Ralph in charge of the black party. They were sure that Edward would never see them again. They had money, horses, and papers. They would not follow the plan: they would make off with the money and goods. The party would betray his trust, they said. Coles's relatives laid out the expected objections to providing slaves with all the necessities and sending them on unsupervised travel.[81]

Edward went first to Milton, a trading and transshipment hub just to the east of Charlottesville, in the lee of Jefferson's Monticello mountain.[82] There he left $40 in the care of Mrs. Dawson in satisfaction of an account to his brother John.[83] From there, Coles traveled to Orange County for a visit with the Madisons at Montpelier. Given the miserable weather, they prevailed on him to stay two days. On, then, to a final farewell with friends in Washington. Then to Brownsville.

Ralph and his charge probably traveled the Three Notch'd Road westward to Jarman's Gap, the main route from Charlottesville, over the Blue Ridge to the Shenandoah Valley. It would be slow going. From one wag about Three Notch'd:

I say its not passable;
Not even kick-assable;
And those who would travel it;
Should get out and gravel it.[84]

Spring rains would cut deep ruts in the road, uncovering boulders and washing away dirt that might otherwise smooth the way. The route is mostly uphill, especially the rise to the crest of the Blue Ridge as it winds back and forth looking for the easiest route to Jarman's Gap. At times, the adults might have to get out of the wagon and push, and the kids might, too.

Scarcely five miles from home, Jarman's Gap was under their feet. Before them was the valley of the Shenandoah River, a luscious, greening country whose hills roll along gently before plowing against the Alleghenies twenty miles away. Down the western slope of the Blue Ridge they went, wheel-brake lightly engaged all the way. Then on to Staunton.

The Great Wagon Road at Staunton, running north and south and following the Shenandoah River, was a vital artery of American expansion. It was great only in name and in the numbers of travelers it saw. In parts, it would not easily handle a Conestoga wagon because the track was too narrow. In other places only a horse could get through easily. Some spots were corrugated with logs laid down across the road for a stretch. These spots were few. Travelers fared as best they could over the uneven course, crossing and crisscrossing the cricks, runs, and rills. When horses couldn't make the grade with their wagonload or when boulders got in the way, pushing and pulling and yanking and grunting were the order.

Ralph and his company of emigrants made their way up the Great Wagon Road through little places like New Market and Woodstock. Nights were on the wagon under blankets or maybe under the wagon for some. The route took them north to Winchester, where a western shortcut may have taken them up to the National Road. The National Road had been authorized during the Jefferson Administration. Building commenced in 1811 at Cumberland, Maryland. The first phase was complete as far as Wheeling, on the Ohio River, in 1818. The road, rough and unfinished—little more than a blaze trail in many spots—had quickly become a ribbon for commerce, with little towns and way stations knotting at certain spots along the length of it. Stagecoach taverns and wagon stands flourished, giving service good, bad, and atrocious. So the group went on, over the macadamized portions and the rougher portions, through Frostburg and Uniontown.

Edward Coles caught up with his party on the evening of April 9 just thirty miles east and south of the agreed destination, Brownsville. He found everyone in good spirits. The big news, the excitement, and the fun of the trip, they told Coles, were in seeing maple sugar in the making somewhere along the way. Eager for the glamorous and exotic sweet, they asked Coles, "Are there any maple sugar trees on your property in Illinois?"[85] Coles continued on his way to Brownsville, eager in his own way. He could well use the next day or two to complete preparations for the next leg of the trip.

Brownsville, Pennsylvania, was a frontier extravaganza. Situated both on the National Road and on the Monongahela River (flowing north to Pittsburgh), Brownsville quickly became a gateway to the west for countless families. If going to Pittsburgh from the south, one would go through Brownsville. Or if New Orleans was the port of destination, one would go by river, embarking from Brownsville. Fancy banks and traders were marshaled along the waterfront in splendid brick and stone edifices. The town had a market house, an Episcopal church, eighteen mercantile stores, two tanyards, a rope walk, two tin and copper manufactories, two factories of nails, a printing office (and a weekly newspaper), a post office, a scythe and sickle maker, blacksmiths, silversmiths, tailors, shoemakers, and saddlers.[86] River craft were made at Brownsville. The *Enterprise* (the first steamboat to get to New Orleans and back by its own power) was designed and built in Brownsville in 1814. Dunlap's Creek flows into the Monongahela at Brownsville serving as home to various boatbuilders who made keelboats and flatboats for parties going west by water. Brownsville was a boisterous frontier town, gratefully taking in money from travelers who needed equipment and services.[87]

Edward Coles arrived in Brownsville at about 2:00 P.M. on April 10 and got down to business. Straightaway, he purchased two flatboats for $70. One was twenty-three feet long and would hold the horses. The other, at thirty feet, was for the people. This would be fitted out with a little cabin of two rooms, one for Coles and one for the rest. The price also included a little fireplace. Edward retained the services of a river pilot. The next day, April 11, was a Sunday. He wrote to his brother John: "I have particular pleasure in telling you that however correct you may be in general, you are not infallible in your prophesies. Your predictions as to my man Ralph and his party have proved erroneous, at least so far that I passed them just beyond Laurel Hill, about 30 miles from this, the evening before the last, all safe and getting on remarkably well. I look for them here today between 12 + 2 oclock."[88]

It is grand to be right. Ralph had not made off with the money and the horses and the wagon and the papers.

The weather turned foul. It was rainy, and the road, as Coles knew, was nasty after Unionville. Ralph did not arrive quite when expected. They didn't come into Brownsville until two days after Coles's arrival, April 12 (about eleven in the morning). Tom Cobb had taken ill with pleurisy.

They wasted not a day. Horses and wagon were put aboard. Luggage and provisions were stowed away. Tom was made as comfortable as possible. All was ready. Cast off both boats (chained together). Commence to floating.

* * *

The river from Brownsville follows a roundabout passage through the foothills west of the Allegheny Mountains. It runs northward, one of very few rivers in America that does so. It's not forthright about its northerly course; rather, it sneaks around mountains and coils about as if to tease travelers into believing that it is not going to Pittsburgh at all but anywhere else. The river is comfortably wide at Brownsville, then grows wider still and bolder as it gets closer to its sister river, the Allegheny, at Pittsburgh.

Edward Coles and his fleet of two flatboats made their way down the river. The din of industry in Brownsville would be replaced by the racket of churning waves and maybe the shouting of the men as they tried to get a grip on controlling two boats lashed together. The plan would be something like this: the river pilot would see to getting them down the river safely, the men would provide muscle to steer, and the parents would keep the children from going overboard.

Edward's labor pool shrank quickly. None of the slaves had ever before been on a watercraft of any description. Ralph and Robert were awkward, inexperienced oarsmen. Tom was already ill. Manuel got sick in short order.[89] The river pilot proved to be a drunkard.[90] These were problems enough on the river north on the Monongahela. Nonetheless, they made it into Pittsburgh.

Edward disposed of the pilot forthwith, replacing him with a copy of Cramer's "NAVIGATOR, containing Directions for Navigating the Monongahela, Allegheny, Ohio and Mississippi Rivers, with an Ample Account of the Much Admired Waters, from the Head of the Former to the Foot of the Latter." This book, an indispensable guide for anyone wishing to travel by riverboat on America's principal thoroughfares, was in 1818 already in its tenth printing.

Coles spent one day in the town visiting with friends and some of his "Philadelphia favorites," as he referred to certain acquaintances in his letter to brother John of 11 April 1819. In addition to his copy of Cramer, Edward purchased a third horse ($50), gear for two horses ($15.50), six weeding hoes ($5.32), and four axes ($6.66).[91] He also met up with a Mr. Green, a Virginian, who would travel with them downriver, by prior arrangement through a certain Captain Peyton.[92]

All were loaded aboard, and the boats and their holdings once more joined the river. The water was low that season, so Coles would try to find the channel, as best he and his crew could, by muscling the boats so as to pinch between the two major sandbars reaching from the mouths of the sister rivers as they joined to become a new river: the Ohio. That's what Cramer recommended, anyhow.

Stay close to the left bank for the best water. A few miles down, come to Brunot's Island. Stay also to the left here, taking the chute at the head of the island bar. Coles would pay particular attention to depth for a while, as bars are strewn about (but well described in Cramer's).

The water soon gets easy. The morning is just so. All is sunny perfection.

The morning after we left Pittsburg, a mild, calm and lovely April day, the sun shining bright, and the heavens without a cloud, our boats floating gently down the beautiful Ohio, the verdant foliage of Spring just budding out on its picturesque banks, all around presenting a scene both conducive to and in harmony with the finest feelings of our nature, was selected as one well suited to make known to my negroes the glad tidings of their freedom. Being curious to see the effect of an instantaneous severing of the manacles of bondage, and letting loose on the buoyant wings of liberty the long pent up spirit of man, I called on the deck of the boats, which were lashed together, all the negroes, and made them a short address, in which I commenced by saying it was time for me to make known to them what I intended to do with them, and concluded my remarks by so expressing myself, that by a turn of a sentence, I proclaimed in the shortest and fullest manner possible, that they were no longer slaves, but free—free as I was, and were at liberty to proceed with me, or to go ashore at their pleasure.[93]

Depiction of Edward Coles freeing his slaves, one of eight murals the Phillipson Decorative Company of Chicago produced in 1885 for the first-floor walls of the state capitol's north and south corridors, Springfield, Illinois. Courtesy Illinois Secretary of State.

PART TWO

4

Beginning

Edward Coles freed his slaves drifting down the Ohio River on the craft he had purchased and outfitted in Brownsville. Stillness held the river; it was on a perfect May morning. Flecks of sunlight danced among ripples on this watery highway to Illinois. Coles left several accounts of the event—one to his mother only days later and a later account in his autobiography.

The slaves had assembled on the decks of the boats. In a sentence, Edward Coles washed his hands of owning slaves. It had taken almost twelve years for Coles to settle on his plan and make it real. Yet, the act of emancipation was, in the end, a simple matter. Freedom was given by the turn of a phrase.

[And the effect on the newly freed was] electrical. They stared at me and at each other, as if doubting the accuracy or reality of what they heard. In breathless silence they stood before me, unable to utter a word, but with countenances beaming with expression which no words could convey, and which no language can now describe. As they began to see the truth of what they had heard, and to realize their situation, there came on a kind of hysterical, giggling laugh. After a pause of intense and unutterable emotion, bathed in tears, and with tremulous voices, they gave vent to their gratitude, and implored the blessings of God on me. When they had in some degree recovered the command of themselves, Ralph said he had long known I was opposed to holding black people as slaves, and thought it probable I would some time or other give my people their freedom, but that he did not expect me to do it so soon; and moreover, he thought I ought not to do it till they had repaid me the expense I had been at in removing them from Virginia, and had improved my farm and gotten me well fixed in that new country.[1]

But for Coles, honor and ethics required granting them immediate and unconditional freedom. He would provide each head of a family with a quarter section as a reward for past service and stimulant to future exertions. Coles had thought much on his own duty and on their rights. He laid his vision before them. He surveyed a broad plain of possibilities for their new lives. While gliding down the placid Ohio, he held forth on what they might expect of their new lands. Coles described his great hope that they would acquit themselves in such a way as to bring success and reflect well on their race. His anxious wish was that the descendants of Africa might demonstrate that they were well able to care for themselves and enjoy the blessings of liberty and thus promote universal emancipation. In Coles's view, Ralph Crawford appeared less impressed with his new status in freedom than with the lesser gift, his own land.[2]

Seventeen miles from Pittsburgh is Big Seweekly Creek; then, just a little farther on is Loggstown (Cramer's *Navigator* says it is a jumble of logs that can be avoided if the river pilot first steers to the right, then threads between deadhead timbers to open water again).[3] Crow's Island came into view, then Big Beaver Creek on the north side of the Ohio. The town of Beaver stands below the creek. For the most part, the travelers stayed on the flatboats, rolling past the little settlements and edging around the rough and rocky parts. Floating continued, even at nighttime.[4] They went ashore at Newport, Kentucky, (Cincinnati is on the other side of the river) for a brief visit with General James Taylor.[5] And there were other stops along the way.[6] The horses would need grazing; the children would need a little time to frolic at the shoreline.

At some point while still on the Ohio, Coles prepared a general certificate of freedom for the now-freed black pioneers, providing proof of their new legal status. It gave the names and ages of those receiving their freedom. Coles also prepared an "instrument of writing" covering Manuel, Sukey, and their children.[7] Not wishing to profit from Manuel's situation as former indentured servant, however, Coles proposed that Manuel would receive his freedom as soon as he should repay the cost Coles had incurred for the balance of the indenture. Manuel, in turn, asked Coles to hold Sukey's freedom aside and that of their five children (and, presumably, the one child on the way) in the same fashion. This would provide Sukey and her children with some security: Coles would, by law, be her benefactor (and would support the children if Manuel should die). Coles agreed to this. Sukey and her children remained his property, and Manuel remained, technically, in his service. Coles also stipulated, however, that the family would live as if free.[8] At some later point, he committed in writing to Manuel's freedom, giving Manuel his liberty after five years and making the children free at the ages of eighteen or twenty-one years.[9] Coles believed he had washed his hands of slavery. But slavery stayed with Coles as a continuing ache or sore.

The order of business was floating. It took nine days and nine hours to get from Pittsburgh to a point above Louisville known as the Falls of the Ohio. Coles had proposed to continue down the Ohio as far as Shawneetown, Illinois, 150 miles farther downriver, where the party would then ditch the boats and continue overland by wagon, but he changed the plan.[10] At the Falls of the Ohio were Louisville, New Albany, and Jeffersonville, a little triad of settlements. Discovering that he could sell the boats for $50 (and believing that he would get nothing for them farther downriver), he unloaded the horses and wagon and began the final legs of the journey, overland across the Buffalo Trace (then a major artery also referred to as the Louisville to Vincennes road).

Coles again broke company with the rest of the party, traveling ahead by horseback. The wagon with its paired horses, its tools, provisions, and human cargo began the overland trek through Indiana, leaving New Albany on about April 25. They had been traveling for a little more than three weeks. Thomas Cobb, who had taken ill with pleurisy before boarding the boat at Brownsville, was much improved.[11] Sukey was four months' pregnant.

They passed through Paoli (boasting a new stone courthouse and a few fine wooden buildings). Farther on, they came into a sulfurous region; a traveler of the year before had described the water in these parts as tasting "as Strong as the washings of a Dirty Gun."[12] Then another fifteen miles over hilly scarps to the east fork of the White River. Beyond the White, the lands were mostly flatter, and the land's rhythms slowed to a gentler pulse. A wagoner might clatter along under the canopy of a hardwood forest, sheltered in the cool shadows of a protected grove. Of a moment the scene would open. Breaking upon a prairie section, the line of sight would take wing toward the horizon.

They reached Vincennes on about the first day of May. Vincennes, on the banks of the Wabash River, is an ancient little town; a remnant of French settlement from the days when the trapping of furs, shipped out through Montreal, provided the regional economic base. The little wagon of immigrants presented to the ferryman on the Wabash the papers of emancipation that had been drafted by their former owner; they crossed over and set foot in the state of Illinois.[13] And they pushed on toward Edwardsville, their new home in the western reaches of the free state of Illinois.

Slavery on the Western Frontier

French missionaries and military explorers opened the upper Mississippi lands in the late 1600s. They had discovered, at the southern end of Lake Michigan, a portage of only a few miles in length that took them to a river extending the reach of the King of France to the Mississippi River and then to the Gulf of Mexico. More than this, however, Quebec-based traders and trappers began to use the portage as a link in the chain of trade that would allow them to move beaver and other furs to market via the Great Lakes to Quebec. In due course, a series of villages took root along the banks of the Mississippi.

The French government had approved the introduction of slavery as early as 1689.[14] Philippe Francois Renault brought the first slaves to Illinois in 1719. Renault came from France to develop lead mines in the new territory, acquiring his slaves during a stop in Saint Domingue. Twenty-five years later, he gave up his efforts and left to return to France.[15] He sold the surviving slaves to settlers living along the Mississippi River.[16] By 1750, black slaves made up over thirty-two percent of the population.[17] In 1763, the British took possession of Illinois. French ownership of slaves was confirmed by the Treaty of Quebec in 1774. When Virginia ceded the Illinois lands to Congress in 1783, the French inhabitants were again expressly confirmed in their ownership of property (slaves would be included, of course).[18] During the next decade, however, the legal status of slavery in Illinois turned opaque. Lands northwest of the Ohio River became a territory of the United States in 1787 under the Northwest Ordinance. Article VI of the ordinance stipulates that "there shall be neither slavery nor involuntary servitude in the said territory, otherwise than in punishment of crimes, whereof the party shall have been duly convicted." A plain reading of Article VI seems to abolish slavery, but many folks in Illinois did not see it that way. In their view, slaves in Illinois were legally owned and fully confirmed as property. Territorial Governor Arthur St. Clair set their minds at ease when, in 1790, he stated that Article VI applied only to new slaves brought into the state. Resident slaves were protected, he said, and the courts upheld him. St. Clair was supported, in part, by Article II of the ordinance, which stipulates, "No man shall be deprived of his liberty or" (more to the point) "property."[19]

All legal slaves were descendants of those brought to the Illinois area by the French. Each time the area changed hands, the status of these so-called French slaves was reaffirmed. As southerners moved to Illinois after the Revolutionary War, they found this system of legal slavery untouched by the Northwest Ordinance.[20] Some settlers tried to purchase the descendants of these French slaves in order to enjoy the added security of owning slaves whose status was clearly supported in law.[21] The special status of French slaves became a mooring point for the wobbly argument that slavery was on a sound legal footing. In 1818, at the constitutional convention at Kaskaskia, John Graham of Union County attempted to build a fortress protecting slavery of the French slaves. Fitter men than he, he said,

> mout [must] hev been found to defend the masters agin the sneakin'
> ways of the infernal abolitioners; but havin' rights on my side, I
> don't fear, sir. I will show that [their] proposition is unconstitution-
> able, inlegal [illegal], and forenenst [?] the compact. Don't everyone
> know, or leastwise had ought to know, that the Congress that sot
> [sat] at Post Vinsan, garnisheed to the old French inhabitants the
> right to their niggers, and haint I got as much rights as any French-
> man in this State? Answer me that, Sir.[22]

The Indiana territorial government petitioned Congress in 1796 to repeal the slavery restriction in the Northwest Ordinance. Such was the desire for unrestricted slavery in some quarters. It was denied. Then, in 1800, another petition was sent to Congress. This was signed by 270 inhabit-ants.[23] Another petition was submitted in 1802; others in 1805 and 1807. The federal government rejected each of these.[24]

Slavery (aside from the French slaves) and involuntary servitude had been outlawed in 1787, so voluntary servitude became the subterfuge by which slavery would take on new life in Illinois. In 1805, the territorial government passed an indenture law that was reaffirmed in 1807. Slaves over the age of fifteen could be brought into the territory and then enter into a "voluntary" indenture agreement within thirty days. On refusal, the owner could remove them from the territory within sixty days. Any child born to an indentured servant would serve the owner of its mother (until age thirty if a male or until twenty-eight if female). Slaves younger than fifteen could be imported and registered without recourse. Males served until age thirty-five; females until thirty-two.[25] It was a slavery work-around.

As an organized territory (1809 through 1818), the Illinois legislature passed a variety of laws affecting African Americans and servants. In 1814, for instance, the territorial legislature passed a law allowing slaves to be brought into the state for up to a year without changing their status. The effect might be predicted. For the 1810 census, only 168 slaves were in Illinois. But in the next decade, the slave population mushroomed to 917. This growth gave Illinois the distinction of being one of only two territories north of the Mason-Dixon Line whose slave population had increased (Missouri was the other).[26]

On 10 December 1817, Charles Matheny introduced a resolution in the Territorial Assembly to abolish all forms of indentured servitude.[27] His resolution passed both houses after vigorous debate, but Governor Edwards vetoed it. He was against slavery but felt that the bill impinged on the rights of the judiciary. Three camps emerged in the slavery debate.[28] The Edwards faction contained the antislavery voices, including those of Daniel P. Cook, an antislavery son-in-law of former Governor Edwards, and Jesse B. Thomas, an Illinois senator during the 1820s. Elias Kent Kane, a moving force in the drafting of the Illinois Constitution, led another group that favored some sort of slavery. Finally, Shadrach Bond, who would become the first governor in the new State of Illinois, led a group of older settlers who were primarily interested in other issues, though they also tended to support slavery.

No faction had dominated the constitutional convention when it convened at Kaskaskia in the summer of 1818.[29] The constitution was drafted by a committee that was antislavery but chaired by Kane, who was proslavery. Compromise was inevitable. The final version of the constitution maintained the status quo by keeping a system of "voluntary" indentured servitude and passed the convention seventeen to fourteen.[30] The status of slavery in Illinois was left ambiguous enough to satisfy immediate needs. It resolved none of the underlying issues surrounding slavery. Current slaveholders and indenture owners were protected in their property. Yet, the "introduction" of new slaves was forbidden as was involuntary indenture. Article VI, paragraph 2, of the Constitution of 1818 stipulates that slaves could be hired voluntarily into Illinois for one year at a time. The privilege was reserved to the saline district, and the practice was mandated to end in 1825.

Slavery's Hold on Illinois

Slavery as an economic engine was driven by twin pistons: land and salt. The salty business of slavery was centered in Gallatin County (in the southeast corner of the state, not far from Shawneetown, where the Wabash meets the Ohio). Of 917 slaves counted in Illinois during the Census of 1820, 267 (almost a third) were in Gallatin County, the saline district.[31] Salt springs of the Saline River had been exploited by the Indians for generations. In the early nineteenth century it produced wealth and power energized by slavery. The value of salt lay principally in its ability to cure meats, and the ability to turn profits lay in keeping labor costs low.

Making salt from brine was a simple enough process requiring but a few tools and enormous effort. The key to profitability was the ready availability of slaves as a cheap, steady source for labor. Kettles of one hundred gallons each were laid out in rows over wood fires set into channels that had been dug into the forest earth and lined with sandstone.[32] According to notes made by Edward Coles regarding the business of slavery in Illinois, one Colonel Wight kept forty such kettles going. A Mr. Hay had 120.[33] These were big operations. Roaring fires consumed enormous quantities of wood as the salt water was concentrated by cooking prior to the final boil-off in an oven.

When a forest was worked out and the trees turned to ash, the operation would move to another grove. The water would be pumped to the new location through pipes, hand-fashioned from logs with their centers reamed out and crudely joined by jamming the thin end of one log into the thick end of the next. Up to a hundred miles of pipes were laid through the saline between 1800 and 1873.[34] They carried an enormous volume. A bushel of salt was made from between 200 gallons and 350 gallons of water; 3,000 bushels of salt were produced in the saline each week.[35]

It took labor to turn the salt water into wealth. Dozens of axemen were called for. The work needed drivers for mule teams to get the wood to the kettles, firemen to keep the fires, kettle hands, coopers, and packers. It was hot work, and it was hard. And it was profitable if labor costs could be kept low. Negro slaves were hired in from across the Ohio River in Kentucky at $60 per year or $6 per month.[36] A white laborer cost $10 to $12 per month (paid in salt). Few white settlers wanted the job or any paid job—their eyes were on the land to be bought or squatted on free.

Naturally, Illinois "old money" from the saline wanted to keep slavery. By extension, if slavery was good for the "big" folks, it was good enough for some of the up-and-comers and new arrivals who were struggling to wrestle a living out of hard-packed prairie land. "Old money" was in salt; "new money" was in land. This was the second piston in the economic engine that kept slavery popular in Illinois. Land values would increase so long as westward migration brought new families to Illinois with healthy appetites to buy land. Some Illinoisans worried that immigrants were bypassing Illinois for Missouri, where they could settle with their slaves. It was believed by some that the loss of these migrating families kept the demand for land artificially low and starved the value of acreage.

After 1812, the government sold land in minimum parcels of 160 acres (a quarter-section). The legislated minimum price at government auction was $2 per acre. Terms were a quarter down with payments over four years. In theory, a farmer could pay off the debt in four years from proceeds from the sale of his crops. Success in this was as rare as four successive good years of crops in any brand-new-never-before-tilled country. It was rare indeed. People adopted another strategy: Land would make them rich by sale to future immigrants. The key to making money on land was in maintaining the flow of immigrants. A steady flow of new settlers would keep the demand for land high, and the price would follow.

Credit became the addiction of choice. No one doubted that the land value would rise or that new immigrants would flow in and would be eager to pay. But expectation outran liquidity for two reasons. First, the supply of land at the minimum price remained high. In 1820, that price was set at $1.25 per acre.[37] Second, the Panic of 1819 caused problems throughout the west.

Illinois felt the Great Panic of 1819. It is, according to Murray Rothbard, America's first nationwide economic crisis.[38] The War of 1812 had produced a low tide in the supply of foreign-manufactured goods. After the war, however, goods flowed like never before, and domestic prices dropped. In the face of competition from overseas, many new domestic manufacturers faltered, taking banks with them. And as banks failed, credit was constrained, and money dried up. With money tight, westward migration slowed to a crawl due to lack of hard cash to buy the goods and services to move. And as migration slowed (as new buyers for western lands failed to materialize), land prices dipped. They dipped just enough to make a very big difference to those whose land in Illinois was secured by credit. Hard currency was rare, and bank notes were generally unproven. Those who counted on the rising prices due to the human flood lost their properties and businesses. Hard times took over. And many Illinoisans interpreted the economic lethargy in the young state in 1819 and 1820 as a lesson in the benefits of slavery. Migrants, some believed, were skipping Illinois for Missouri.[39]

Old money wanted cheap labor in the saline. New money wanted rising land values through a steady stream of settlers. Moneyed Illinoisans wanted relaxation of slavery laws to compete with Missouri. The settlers in Illinois knew from their own journeys that the immigrants came from the south (from Kentucky and Tennessee) and with money from the Piedmont of Virginia. So slaves seemed the key and Missouri a logical threat.

Slavery's hold was by no means complete. People had come to Illinois expressly to escape from slavery. Edward Coles was not the only Virginian who came to the state seeking freedom from the deadening venom of slavery. H. H. Hall wrote to the postmaster in Vermillion County, asking for information and "what you deem of interest to a stranger wishing to emigrate from a slaveholding state to a free one."[40] A pioneer missionary from Kentucky, Peter Cartwright, came to Illinois because "I had a young and growing family of children. . . . [B]y chance they might marry into slave families . . . this I did not desire."[41] Though Illinois' rich soil was an asset, its status as a free state was the deciding factor for some southerners. These antislavery southerners came from both the upper and lower south.[42]

The real strength in the antislavery constituency flowed through the Baptists and the Methodists, who dominated religion in Illinois at the time. These two denominations provided social and institutional frameworks within which civil government could develop. They also fought vigorously against the introduction of slavery. Edward Coles would find many friends and allies within the ranks of their leaders. One faction of the Baptist church, the Friends of Humanity, had its origin in Kentucky in 1807 in an antislavery movement.[43] By 1809, these Friends had organized in Illinois and continued to oppose slavery, and by 1818, Friends' leader James Lemen attempted to organize a party to win an antislavery state constitution.[44] Though Lemen failed, the group's membership continued to grow. The group showed marked gains whenever the slavery question was raised in the state.[45] The Methodists in Illinois were more united than the Baptists. By 1824, the group numbered 3,708 white members and 27 black members.[46] Like the Baptists, they were active in politics, warring during the 1820s against slavery and vices such as drinking and gambling. Peter Cartwright, the leader of the Illinois Methodists, was bitterly opposed to slavery. During his two terms in the Illinois House, he fought to destroy the institution.[47]

The Baptists and Methodists and their leaders had a strong impact on Illinois' history in the early nineteenth century. They constituted one of the few organized blocs of votes in the state. Occasionally, as in the case of slavery, the bloc was mobilized. More often, it remained only a potential force. Still, the churches' impact was deeply felt. They worked to create a moral environment by crusading against gambling, drinking, and dueling. They succeeded in beginning a permanent system of education. The churches were a potent force but often splintered Methodist against Baptist and Baptist against Baptist.

The congressional races in 1819 and 1820 show the ongoing potency of the slavery question. Cook won both races. In 1819, he defeated John McLean, in part by accusing McLean of supporting Missouri's admission as a slave state. In 1820, Cook defeated Kane in a campaign that included an exchange of letters in the *Edwardsville (Illinois) Spectator* concerning Kane's position on slavery.[48]

The Missouri Compromise kept the slavery issues bubbling in Illinois politics. Many Illinoisans felt Missouri's status as a slave territory gave it an advantage in attracting settlers. When the Missouri Compromise came to a vote in Congress, Cook voted against it. Both U.S. Senators, Edwards and Thomas, voted in favor of it. The votes of the two major leaders combined with the failure of a censure motion against them in the state legislature bolstered the proslavery advocates' belief that Illinois might yet become a slave state. The failure of a censure motion was viewed as a sign that the legislature favored slavery.[49]

Illinois stood ready for another burst of growth as the Great Panic of 1819 bottomed out. Its population was increasing, and the eastern states were providing an influx of young, aggressive leaders. These men were finding the threads of politics and through the fluid system of factions were spinning the strands that later would be twisted into cords of party. One issue confounded the growth of the political system—slavery. The factions could not coalesce into parties aligned with national groupings until Illinois had declared for or against slavery. For the next five years, this issue bedeviled Illinois and Edward Coles. The slavery issue would cause Coles's rise to prominence, and it would ensure his decline as well.

5

A Rough Land of Great Promise

A week or so into May of 1819, Ralph Crawford and his wife, Kate, and their four children, Robert Crawford and his sister Polly, and Thomas Cobb, Nancy Gaines, and Manuel and Sukey and their five children arrived in the town of Edwardsville, the seat of government for Madison County. Edwardsville is in the northern reach of the American Bottom, a sumptuous crescent of farmland wrapped around a bulge in the Mississippi, starting across the river from St. Louis and going south beyond the mouth of the Kaskaskia River. Edwardsville is six or seven miles from the bluffs of the Mississippi River and twenty-five miles from St. Louis. The prairie started in earnest just to the east of town. The town, which had been laid out in 1816, had a log courthouse, and Lusk's hotel, another imposing structure of logs, went up that year.[1] Four years later, an estimated sixty or seventy residences formed the nucleus of a growing town.[2]

The very day after Ralph, Kate, Robert, Tom, Manuel, and the rest arrived, they were breaking up the prairie and beginning the heavy work of readying new land for corn.[3] The spring had been wet, and much of the land was sodden. Still, the prairie was tough. It took two horses on a plow to get below the surface.[4]

Coles's financial records tell the story of a man setting up a farm in the midst of a small community of families entirely dependent on him. On May 15, Ralph Crawford in St. Louis took on provisions for Coles. He spent $49 on tools and another $2 for expenses (perhaps the cost of the ferry across the Mississippi). Ralph also loaded up on 4 bushels of meal and additional bushels of corn, 2 bushels of salt, and 110 pounds of bacon. Before the month was out, Coles bought another 20 bushels of corn. June and July entries show purchases of still more corn and payments to Mr. Holland, the blacksmith, for a strapping plow and for sharpening services. The toughness of the prairie led to repairs: a payment to Holland to fix a scythe and a payment to Mr. Robertson for woodwork on the plow. Purchases also chronicled the formation of a community. He made payment to Mr. Ringgold for a dress for Kate. He bought primers to help the children in learning to read and write. Journal entries are peppered throughout with small expenses in the names of various members of Coles's newly freed dependents: eight yards of cloth for Bob and Tom, $12.87 "for my Negros shirts etc. etc."[5]

Along with the hard work came exhaustion and illness. Robert Crawford, Edward Coles, and Ralph Crawford were ill at different times during that first summer and fall. Coles was sick in August. Summer was the time of fevers in Illinois. The land along the streams was swampy. The climate—the malodorous air—was widely feared. On November 18, Coles registered payments in his account book to Drs. Todd and DeCamp for services previously rendered to both Ralph and Bob. On August 4, Coles gave Ralph $2.25 for a dose of medicine. On September 4, he gave $10 to Ralph and Kate, $5 to "Bob" (Robert Crawford), another $5 to Thomas Cobb, "Sugar and medicine for Ralph" on September 8. On September 13, the entry was for a bottle of wine from Ringgold's for Ralph. Another bottle of wine paid on account was obtained from Wiggins's hotel for Ralph. Finally, an item appears in the ledger of Edward Coles dated October 14. He paid $7 to Mr. Tollman for Ralph's coffin. Ralph had died of bilious fever.

* * *

The ledger of Edward Coles shows payments totaling $1,550 in June of 1819 for the purchase of two contiguous quarter-sections: one to William L. May for a deed dated 20 May; the other to John Rice Jones for a deed dated 11 June. These parcels formed the basis for Prairieland Farm, Edward Coles's homestead in Illinois. In all probability, the entire group moved to the property, some miles east of Edwardsville, as soon as possible in order to provide a base of operations as the immigrants settled into their new life. On June 25, Coles paid Caleb Shinn $125 for the lease that Shinn held on a portion of the land, and another $6 went for the hire of Shinn's horses and other livestock.[6] In November, $40 went to Shinn for twenty-two pigs and hogs. Coles and his group knew they had to make a crop or the coming winter would be expensive.

Edward Coles appeared at the log courthouse in Edwardsville on July 4. There he registered papers of emancipation for those he had freed on the Ohio.[7] Three days earlier, he had been engaged in a sociable conversation with Edwardsville lawyer Daniel P. Cook.[8] Cook asked Coles if he had recorded the legal papers of those he had freed.[9] Coles replied that he had not so done and did not believe it necessary. Cook explained that an Illinois law (freshly passed but not yet printed) required all free black people to register and show evidence of their freedom. Failure to do this would result, Cook said to Coles, in arrest of those in question, their confinement to jail, and sale under month-to-month indenture contracts for one year. Any person who should hire an unregistered free African American would pay a penalty of $1.50 for each day thus illegally employed. Cook advised Coles to undertake these registrations. An instrument should be prepared for each person or family, and the individuals should be clearly described. Coles questioned the advice, seeing no reason to execute instruments of emancipation for people who were already free. They had entered the state as free people. Coles, himself, had written the document while on the Ohio River. They had shown the document to the ferryman at Vincennes when they entered Illinois. Cook proposed that completing these registrations would be the simplest way to accommodate the new law. Accordingly, on July 4, Edward Coles stood before Justice of the Peace Hail Mason with Jacob Linder, a local farmer, acting as witness.[10] Coles certified the freedom of the Crawfords, Nancy Gaines, and Thomas Cobb. Each document was a manifesto: "Not believing that man can have of right a property in his fellow man," the certificate registered for Polly and Robert Crawford proclaimed, "but on the contrary, that all mankind were endowed by nature with equal rights, I do therefore, by these presents restore to the said Robert and his sister Polly that inalienable liberty of which they have been deprived."[11] The advice had appeared sound, but later events would show it to be misdirected. The fault was inadvertent but would result in a knotty court battle that would take three painful and humiliating years in the untying.

Later that day, 4 July 1819, Coles joined "Washington's March," a patriotic parade down Main Street. Celebrations continued at Wiggins's hotel. Coles enjoyed the excellent dinner. He heard Reuben Hopkins read the Declaration of Independence and an oration by Nicholas Hansen. Forty-three toasts were offered up. One was given by Edward Coles: "To the rights of man! They appertain equally to him, whether his complexion be white, red or black!"[12]

* * *

During September, social reformer Frances Wright paid a visit to Coles's Prairieland Farm. The memoir of her tour of America would become a well-known commentary on social justice. Writing from Washington in April 1820, she reported on her visit to Edwardsville the previous summer and the time she spent at the Coles settlement: "The liberated blacks spoke of their former master with tears of gratitude and affection, and two of them, who were hired as servants by the family with whom [ ] resided never omitted to pay a daily visit to Mr. Coles, anxiously enquiring if there was nothing they could do for him. I envy more the feelings of the man who hears that question than those of Caesar in the capitol."[13]

* * *

Sometime in September, Manuel, Sukey (who had given birth in August), and their six children left Edwardsville for St. Louis. Instead of settling in the Edwardsville area with the others, Manuel's family headed to St. Louis in search of the higher wages and broader work opportunities available in the larger town. Higher wages would bring the possibility of reimbursing Coles for the indenture payment that had allowed the entire family to move west. Manuel obtained work at the Hempstead farm.

Stephen Hempstead Sr. was fifty-five years of age in 1811 when he arrived in Missouri from New London, Connecticut. He set up a homestead farm on the outskirts of St. Louis. On 2 October 1819, his son Thomas sent out to his father's farm a black family, "a man, woman and their small children." Sukey and her family stayed with the Hempsteads until late November.[14] It may have started as a bright and hopeful launch into a new life in a new country, but it ended in sadness and loss.

Hempstead's journal entry for Friday, the fifth of November, reports the weather as very dry and smoky, much damage having been done in several places by the burning of the prairie. On Saturday the thirteenth, the farmhands butchered a beef. Hempstead sent James Baird to retrieve a horse that had been left behind at James Kenney's in July and had finally been located twenty miles from St. Louis. Then, on Monday,

November 15, Hempstead was at home but unwell. His journal speaks: "The Negroe family of Mr. Coles that hath Stopped here for a number of weeks lost their young child a 2 month old and Burried it in my Grave yard."[15] Two days later, Manuel was sent on an errand into St. Louis to see if Baird had yet returned with the horse. On Tuesday of the next week, Manuel and his family left the farm. Hempstead sent a team to St. Louis with Manuel, Sukey, and the remaining children. They left behind the youngest of their family, dead now and laid in the soil of Mr. Hempstead's farm.

The family moved into St. Louis and rented a house. Manuel worked as he might during the next two years. But times remained hard for Manuel and Sukey. Illness overtook them often, and Edward Coles was moved to pay various of their bills and assist them on frequent occasion. They often required the services of Dr. David V. Walker, a St. Louis physician who also provided care to the Hempstead family. At the end of two years Manuel had accumulated a $96.50 debt to Dr. Walker.[16] The responsibility for payment devolved to Coles, of course, as he was the owner of Manuel's indenture.

Manuel, in his despair, approached Coles. He felt unable to gain headway in repaying the indenture fee, so Manuel proposed that Coles give the time remaining on the indenture to Dr. Walker. He reported that Walker was very likable and that this would be a happy resolution to their debt to the doctor. Coles agreed, and the remainder of the indenture was passed on to Walker in trade for the medical bill.

The debt to Walker was erased but not the debt to Coles. Ultimately, Manuel did pay Edward Coles the indenture money as agreed, and the family achieved the freedom that had been promised them on the Ohio River below Pittsburgh.[17] They built a house in St. Louis on a vacant lot owned by Edward Coles and lived on that lot rent-free until at least 1844.[18]

* * *

On 15 October 1819, Edward Coles recorded in his personal account book a distribution of lands: "In consideration of past services, I this day gave by Deeds the following tracts to my late slaves, emancipated on the 4 July last. The North East qr of Sec 19 in T. 12 N. & R. 2 east to Robert Crawford. The North West qr of Sec 23 in T. 12 N. & R. 3 east to Kate Crawford & the North East qr of Sec 29 in T. 12 N. & R. 3 E. to Thomas Cobb." Edward Coles's covenant with his former slaves was being fulfilled. He gave land to each slave over the age of thirty.[19] The properties were located in the Ridge Prairie Township, east of Edwardsville. The area would become known locally as Pin Oak.

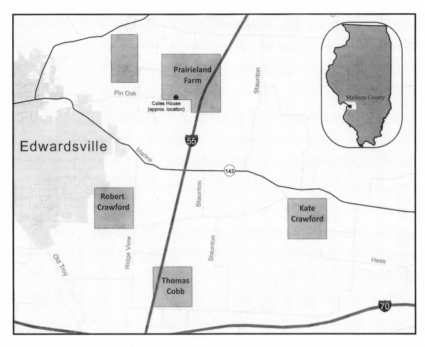

Prairieland Farm and the properties purchased by Edward Coles on behalf of his former slaves.

Ralph, whom Coles believed celebrated his ownership of land almost more than his freedom, had died in September.[20] He died before gaining this heart's desire. His lands went to Kate. Nancy Gaines has been a silent participant in the story. It is known that she died sometime after July 4 (that is, after her emancipation was recorded at the courthouse in Edwardsville). How she died and the date of her passing are lost.[21]

* * *

Coles had been appointed as Register of Lands in March 1819 by President James Monroe just before leaving Virginia for a new life in the nascent state of Illinois.[22] The register of the land office was responsible for administering the orderly sale of lands on behalf of the federal government. It was, in fact, a two-man operation, located in an office on Main Street. The other part of the transaction was handled by the receiver of monies, who collected money and deposited it before transferring it to the U.S. Treasury.[23] Both positions were appointive and were paid on a commission basis. Coles's counterpart was Benjamin Stephenson, a businessman and president of the Bank of Edwardsville.[24]

Stephenson, staunchly proslavery, owned thirty-five slaves.[25] Three months after Coles moved in, Stephenson moved out to an inconvenient office located in "Buncombe," (a new Edwardsville development sometimes referred to as the "New Town"), where he was building a house. (The bricks of his first house in "Old Town" Edwardsville had been made hastily from Main Street mud and were turning to dust.) The relationship between the two men did not improve, and both criticized the other's inattention to duty at various times.

Coles's primary work was to record land sales in the plat books. Each time a new area was surveyed and declared open, Coles organized and conducted the public auction at which the initial sales were made. Coles and Stephenson held such an auction during two weeks in October of 1820.[26] (The Edwardsville land office sold 2,649 acres in 1820, representing 40 percent of all public sales in the state. The next year, sales exploded to 35,243 acres through the Edwardsville office, 70 percent of all Illinois public-land sales.)[27] At other times, settlers arriving in the area stopped at the office to see what land remained available after the auction. The new arrivals purchased land or, perhaps, learned from the register who might be interested in selling land purchased at an earlier auction. Land sold by the government could be paid for on a time-payment plan under provisions of the Land Act of 1820. The receiver and register usually knew who might want to sell some of their land to make the next payment.

The register was also called upon to mediate land disputes. In 1820, Coles spent a great deal of his time arbitrating the French land claims near Peoria.[28] The Peoria claims were frustrating to Coles and the government for several reasons. As Coles noted in his report, Peoria was settled without grant or permission from any government. Title was without document, and the value of lands was never certified.[29] Worse, to Coles's logical mind, he discovered that Peorians believed that if a person left his claim and the land reverted to its natural state, it was assumed that the person no longer owned it. It could be settled and claimed by someone else. These French claims had to be defined, and counterclaims resolved. The law required that legitimate prior ownership, such as the claims from the French period, be recognized and platted before survey and sale of what remained. The Peorians further complicated Coles's task by selling their claims to new settlers. Adding to the confusion, Peoria had been organized in the pattern of a French village in which each inhabitant owned a village lot and an unconnected outlot for cultivation.[30] Coles spent seven frustrating months collecting depositions and verifying claims to determine what land was owned and by whom. He submitted his detailed report to Secretary of Treasury William Crawford in November 1820.[31] Coles held the post until 1822. The job seemed filled with difficulties, complexities, and tedium, and it gave few satisfactions. He was clearly frustrated with the challenges of untangling difficult legal knots that had been tied innocently by simple people over many generations.[32]

Prairieland Farm

Coles's popularity grew despite his frustrations as register of lands. He was seen as fair and honest. However, Edward Coles thought of himself as a farmer, not a bureaucrat. Prairieland Farm became a going concern and remained the object of his enthusiastic attention. His was not a big farm: 474 acres in all (large by the standards of many of the east and Europe, though not by the standards of Coles's experience). About half was in timber and half in prairie. The main property of 400 acres formed an "L." The remaining 74 acres were located one section away. And by the end of the first ten months of his residency, Coles was breaking even when sales of his wheat were added to his meager income as register from the land auctions.[33]

During his years as register, Coles spent little time at his farm, living instead at the home of James Mason in Edwardsville.[34] He was keen to farm but left the labor to those he had hired. Ralph was one of these until his death in September.[35] No doubt Robert Crawford and Thomas Cobb were included, but Coles did not name them specifically. Kate Crawford worked as cook on the farm.[36] In any event, during the second and third seasons, Coles proposed a new arrangement. He furnished stock, tools, food, and all expenses of the farm. Those working on the farm would receive half of all that was sold. The arrangement worked out well as far as Coles was concerned. It was gratifying, he said, to see the excellent crops that came in and to see the cheerful contentment shared among those who lived at Prairieland Farm.[37] Gratifying, yes; profitable, no. Prairieland Farm never showed a profit for Coles during the years it was worked by his freedmen.

In the spring of 1821, the freedmen were attracted to an opportunity to make a good wage at Theophilis W. Smith's brick-making business in Edwardsville.[38] The offer of $20 monthly was altogether tempting. Coles advised them to take the offer if they could be assured of payment and of steady work for a reasonable length of time. The offer would be more lucrative than farming; they all left the farm (Kate and her children remained). Two or three months later, they returned. They complained of being deceived and cheated. Their new employer had refused to keep the agreement, offering them a lower rate of pay and insisting on paying in devalued bank scrip. Coles found that they had not obtained a written contract, as he had advised. The only evidence remaining of the original agreement was their word, inadmissible in court as evidence against a white man. The men were bitter over their treatment, frustrated and angry over the deception. They regretted leaving Coles's employment and asked Coles to return them to work at Prairieland. But he had no work to offer as he had begun employing others in their place. He did offer, however, to reinstate them the next year. The men returned to Prairieland Farm in 1822. Entries in the ledger of Edward Coles for 2 June 1821 show six yards of linen for Kate and payment to Robert for the balance due him on last year's crop after payment for doctors' bills and the like. Thomas Cobb appeared in the ledger as recipient of nine yards of linen. It was the last entry made for Thomas Cobb. He died sometime after this by falling into a public well in the village close to his property.[39] The Crawfords remained there, working for Coles under a liberal rental agreement until 1827. Robert Crawford continued until at least 1843 to act as an agent for Edward Coles in securing renters for the Prairieland property.[40]

* * *

In October of 1819, Coles sent an open letter to farmers in Illinois over the signature of "A Farmer of Madison County." He proposed that they meet on the tenth of November in Kaskaskia for the purpose of forming the Agricultural Society of Illinois. This was a republican invitation in full bloom. Coles was familiar with the Albemarle Agricultural Society in the county of his birth. Formed two years before Coles left central Virginia, the Albemarle Agricultural Society was a vibrant civic organization, albeit made up primarily by wealthy farmers with large holdings. Its members published the results of agricultural experiments and offered annual prizes for the best products.[41] James Madison was its president. No doubt the vision that danced in Coles's head was similar in its tone and aspirations.

The meeting in Kaskaskia convened. Governor Shadrach Bond was called on to chair the assembly. Henry Dodge was asked to be secretary. Rules of the association were prepared by a committee and adopted after the first recess of the first day. Coles was successful in having Morris Birkbeck elected (in absentia) as president of the new association.[42] Coles became first vice president and one member among four on the committee of correspondents.[43]

The society may well have been dismissed by many as a collection of "amateur professors of agriculture."[44] Birkbeck, founder of the English Settlement in Edwards County and an enthusiast of agricultural theory, was held in some contempt when (according to William Faux, who was competing with Birkbeck to develop an English Settlement) his own efforts to farm came up well short one season. Instead of making his goal of one hundred acres of corn from the hard-packed prairie, president Birkbeck had only half an acre of potatoes and a broken plow to show.[45]

The society's most visible authorities, Edward Coles and Morris Birkbeck, recommended radical new methods of farming that were at odds with the accepted practice of clearing and cultivating forest lands. (If the land would support trees, common wisdom held, it had already proven itself arable for crops.) In an 1821 letter to Henry S. Dodge, later published in the *Edwardsville (Illinois) Spectator*, Coles deplored the loss of timber from bottomland cultivation. He advocated corn as a prairie crop, and he argued that the prairies were healthier than the low, swampy river bottoms and thus should be cultivated.[46] He went on to propose a new method of prairie cultivation based on his own experiments conducted in May and June of 1820. One should use two oxen or two horses and plows for breaking up the prairie instead of four horses. Plow with a plain knife coulter (as is usually used to break up rooty land), then plow the land a second time with a small bar shear followed by two harrowings with an iron-tooth drag, he said. Also, he said, use the one-horse harrow of either three or five teeth. He recommended the "Beef's tongue" harrow tooth and described in detail the method of making one from bar iron.[47]

The Agricultural Society was a short-lived experiment (it lasted but six years). Even in its apparent failure, it offers clues about Edward Coles. He is shown to be an aspiring republican farmer, somewhat out of touch with certain elements of Illinois society. Naïve, yes, and faithful to republican ideals of public service and scientific agriculture.

Birkbeck declined running for a fifth term as association president in 1824 with the private aside to Coles that the state was not yet ready for an agricultural society.[48] True, the leadership of the association was made up largely by new immigrants (that is, outsiders) and large landowners at that; true also that Illinois farmers were a rough and independent breed who (for the most part) valued experience over book learning. The Agricultural Society was an experiment before its time.

* * *

In 1820, Illinois was climbing out of the Panic of 1819. Edwardsville had sixty or seventy dwelling places.[49] In March, U.S. Marshal Henry Connar submitted Illinois results from the fourth census of the nation. It showed the state population to be 55,211. Twenty thousand people (more than 35 percent of the population) had settled in the state during the past two years.[50]

In 1818, during the statehood enumeration, Madison County had counted 5,456 persons. Two years later, the federal census showed that the county had grown by almost 250 percent. Madison County, home now to Edward Coles and his household, held almost one-quarter of the total population of the state. And it was thoroughly white. In 1818, 111 servants, slaves, and free people of color lived in the county. The number nudged up to only 127 in 1820, less than 1 percent of the county population.

Free black people in Illinois numbered 457 in 1820; 17 of them lived in Madison County. There were the Crawfords, of course. And a few newcomers: Samuel Vanderberg, Henry Daugherty, Thomas Seton, and Michael Lee. Most of them lived in Ridge Prairie Township, in the community of Pin Oak, found to the east of Edwardsville. This community was destined to attract free black residents for decades to come and would prosper as an agricultural center. Its churches would sponsor a church organization structure that would blossom into a national movement.

In this, a former slave of Edward Coles would take a leading role (see chapter 13 of the current volume).

Edward Coles had freed himself (almost entirely) of slavery. Robert and Kate Crawford and their children were free of slavery. Manuel and Sukey and their children were living as if free of slavery. Life was opening to a veritable prairie of opportunity, and the horizon was broad and bright.

6

Contest and Convention

On 30 October 1821, the *Edwardsville (Illinois) Spectator* announced, "Edward Coles . . . in compliance with the wishes of his friends" would be a candidate for governor in the upcoming election.[1] Six months previous, friends had encouraged him to run.[2] Although equivocation had marked his drawn-out decision to emigrate to Illinois, and self-doubt caused him initially to reject Madison's offer for employment in the White House, neither indecision nor self-doubt impeded this surprise announcement. For Edward Coles, this decision showed clarity of purpose and direction; seemingly, this was a new feature in his personal landscape.

The election would be held on the first Monday of August 1822. There was no need to wait for the incumbent, Shadrach Bond, to declare. The Illinois Constitution imposed the limit of a single term on its governor, so Governor Bond would not be running. The race for governor had begun when Chief Justice Joseph Phillips announced his candidacy in February 1821, fully a year and a half before the election.[3] Phillips, Tennessee-born and proslavery, had been territorial secretary from 1816 to 1818. Edward Coles was the next to enter the gubernatorial political pool. Initially, he made scarcely a ripple. His problem was that as popular as he was inside Madison County and in the few counties making up the American Bottom, few people farther afield knew of him.[4] It is a testament to the fluid nature of western politics of the time that an immigrant from Virginia, only a few years at his adopted new home, might make a serious run for high office.[5]

In March 1822, a third contender entered the election. Like Coles, James B. Moore of Monroe County was unknown to a large portion of Illinois voters.[6] He was homegrown and could point to his exploits as a general defending Illinois settlers against Indians in the War of 1812. By the summer of 1822, the strongest statewide faction (headed by former territorial governor Ninian Edwards) had not yet fielded a candidate. Personal factions were all in frontier Illinois politics. No parties, no cohesive machinery dictated the orderly nomination of candidates, rather, power was gathered in loyal pockets of support around men. The state waited for Edwards to declare, yet Edwards did not enter, and his bloc was slow to offer up an alternative candidate. With only three months left, Thomas Browne, a justice of the Illinois Supreme Court, entered the contest under the Edwards banner.[7] Like Moore, Browne showed little interest in the issues or in campaigning. In the letter announcing his candidacy, Browne took safe positions: he favored expansion of education and business.

Shortly after Coles announced his candidacy, the *Edwardsville (Illinois) Spectator* claimed Coles had not settled in Illinois until 1820 (fully a year after his appointment as register of lands). A writer penning under the name "Justice" immediately challenged the *Spectator*, claiming that Coles had visited Illinois in 1815 and had vowed to make the state his residence. This, "Justice" argued, should be considered the date of Coles's residence. "Justice" further pointed out that papers documenting Coles's appointment as register of lands expressly stated that Coles was "of Illinois."[8]

Hooper Warren, editor of the *Edwardsville (Illinois) Spectator*, agreed that Coles had been in the state in 1815, but since Coles had not stayed, he could not be considered a resident. Warren admitted that Coles had come to Illinois and remained for an extended period of time before 1820. Still, Coles's activities appeared suspicious—buying large amounts of land, long absences in spite of broadcasting his intent to settle there, his actual settlement coinciding with a political appointment. To Warren, Coles was either a nonresident speculator or an opportunist (or maybe both).[9] Coles had no real defense against Warren's attack. Coles asked for forbearance on the matter of his short residency.[10]

In December 1821, Coles set out on a tour of southern Illinois to make himself better known.[11] He made a second tour a few months later. This second time, the *Edwardsville Spectator* printed a satirical sendoff:

Yesterday departed from this place, on a political cruise, the new flat-bottomed boat Edward Coles. It is said she will touch Vandalia, to take on an additional supply of whisky and gingerbread, a description of ammunition essentially necessary to enable her to contend with the barge Joseph Phillips, which it is expected she will fall in with on the Wabash. Much apprehension is entertained for her safe return, as she is thought to have been hastily built, and of the worst materials; and her commander is known to be a mere fresh-water sailor, and has put to sea with a bad compass.[12]

Coles's status as a recent immigrant did not sit well with some. Here was a newcomer who had pocketed one of the best jobs: register of lands. No doubt, many Illinoisans coveted the few available federal plums, and one of the choicest had been placed in the lap of a newcomer. The shadowy, unprincipled, eastern speculator was already part of Illinois frontier folklore by 1821. Ironically, the leading antislavery editor, Hooper Warren, and the leading antislavery political figure, Edward Coles, shared neither affection nor respect one for the other. Warren and Coles could have formed a powerful alliance, but it was not to be.

To Warren, Coles made too much of his Virginia breeding and his friends in high places. Warren gave his impression of Coles as a man who was an incorrigible name-dropper and who chattered without end, mostly about himself.[13] Warren was quickly satiated by Coles's overbearing banter.[14]

It is probable, furthermore, that Warren viewed Coles as political competition for control of Illinois. First, Warren and Coles were on different sides in the emerging Second Party System. Warren supported John Quincy Adams; Coles was a firm friend of William H. Crawford, a Georgia politician who had been born in Virginia just a few short miles from Coles's Rockfish plantation. Second, Warren believed that Coles had come to Illinois specifically to build a new faction in the state. Both beliefs led Warren to oppose any candidacy Coles put forth, notwithstanding their agreement on the problem of slavery. Warren was unfriendly to Coles, but his comments and barbed criticisms ring with a note or two of truth about Coles. Warren grants a credible, unflattering but limited view of Edward Coles; we judge his assessment to be not far from the truth in so far as it deals with Coles's manner, his foibles, and his affections. Otherwise, Warren shows a bias against Coles that lacks generosity and does no service to a fair overview of the man.

Interest statewide in the election was feverish. This was the first gubernatorial race since statehood, and watching it became the sport of choice.[15] Horatio Newhall wrote to his family in New England, "[W]hen party politics were at the highest point in Massachusetts, there was, probably never an election more warmly contested than our next election will be for all our state and national officers. Wherever you go you hear of nothing else."[16] A strongly contested frontier election was not won in the rocking chair on the front porch. The two most active candidates, Phillips and Coles, traveled, stumped, and politicked. Little was reported about the other candidates in the papers.

* * *

In May 1822, with the statewide election in full chase, the remaining members of the Crawford family could be found working on the Prairieland Farm owned by candidate Edward Coles. Three years in Illinois had come and gone. Ralph had died thirty-two months before. Kate had remained on the farm as a cook. Robert had moved back to the farm that year after the disastrous experience of the spring before, when he and others had been cheated of their pay for work in a local brickyard. The Crawfords lived and worked under a rental arrangement with Edward Coles that suited both parties. Coles took particular pleasure in watching how successfully and productively the Crawfords had made the transition to freedom.[17]

In the spring of the year, Polly Crawford married Michael Lee. Polly, the sister of Ralph and of Robert, had been sixteen or seventeen years old when the family made the long trek from the Rockfish plantation in Central Virginia. Lee was one of the first African Americans to move into the Pin Oak area east of Edwardsville. According to Madison County indenture records, Lee had been bound by his mother, Margarette Lee, in Harford County, Maryland, to Rebecca Guest in April 1813 for four years.[18] With the fulfillment of his indenture, Lee had moved west to Ridge Prairie in Pin Oak Township, Illinois. He owned lands located close to those of Edward Coles and to those owned by Kate and Robert Crawford.

Lee was twenty-five years of age when he and Polly married. His indenture record describes him as about 5 feet 10 inches tall, rather slender in person, with a good countenance, with two scars on his left leg, and one on his right near the knee. The Lees had three girls (Mary, born in

1834, Martha in 1839, Susan in 1841). They moved to Decatur, Illinois, sometime after 1850.[19]

* * *

On 4 July 1822, with the election four weeks away, Coles offered up a simple toast in celebration of the forty-sixth anniversary of the signing of the Declaration of Independence. He distilled a republican ideal into three words: "Principles, not Men."[20] It was three years to the day since he had registered freedom papers for all the Crawfords, Nancy Gaines, and Thomas Cobb at the Madison County courthouse.

Whiskey and Gingerbread

It took food and drink to warm the voters to a candidate. If a candidate wanted a turnout to his rally, he had to feed and water the crowd—with gingerbread and whiskey. As Coles and Phillips crisscrossed the state, stump speaking was sweetened at key stops with salvoes of hard drink and sweet bread. There are no descriptions of Coles's performance on the stump, but even hostile reviewer Warren admitted that Coles was a splendid storyteller. He told his readers that Coles could entrance an audience with stories of the White House for five or more hours at a time.[21]

At no time did any party or candidate clearly endorse slavery.[22] The Phillips group got close to it in proposing a constitutional convention. The 1818 constitution could not be amended except by a new convention. Agitation for such a convention began almost immediately after statehood. The complex machinery that produced the Missouri Compromise in 1820, furthermore, was very much influenced by efforts to position Illinois as a slaveholding state and to build a rationale for the state to have an entirely free hand to refashion its constitution according to its own preferences, notwithstanding the Northwest Ordinance and federal law.[23] A constitutional convention, Coles believed rightly, would be a ruse to bring slavery under the protective mantle of the state constitution. This idea had a history that churned quietly but persistently below the surface of Illinois politics.

Phillips's suggestion of a constitutional convention was the first wisp of a gathering cloud that would soon darken the horizon. In time, this cloud would rain down bitterness statewide; it would draw Edward Coles into a stormy battle that would, in the end, settle the basic question of slavery in Illinois. The economic problems that frustrated many

Illinoisans (banking problems, specie problems, the need for roads and canals) were the issues bearing on the election; slavery was (so far) a secondary matter. It would not remain so.

The election arrived. It was Monday, August 6. Coles left for Virginia the following Monday with the election still not finalized. Though a major contender, Coles was considered a dark horse.[24] He waited out the results with his Virginia family, far away from the precincts in Illinois. The results were known by the end of August (although newspapers reported varying vote counts through the end of the year).[25] Perhaps none was more surprised at the results than governor-elect Edward Coles. The *Republican Advocate* of Kaskaskia printed what it claimed were the official final totals in January 1823:

Coles	2,810
Phillips	2,760
Browne	2,634
Moore	598

The election had been as tight as a prairie tick. Coles received 32.29 percent; Phillips trailed by just slightly more than half a percentage point at 31.72 percent; Browne received 29.12 percent, and Moore 6.8 percent. Coles won by 50 votes.[26]

Many years later, Warren recalled his reaction to Coles's victory: "half gratified and half chagrined, I indulged in some editorial remarks on the result of the election, and in reference to Mr. Coles, observed that whenever the president wished to get rid of a useless lackey, he could send him out to Illinois, and the people would make a Governor of him."[27]

Since both Phillips and Browne supported slavery, scholars have considered Coles's victory somewhat of a fluke, resulting from a split in the proslavery vote.[28] After examining the vote totals in the other races, it is clear that the slavery issue was not as simple as that. Illinois had, in fact, elected an antislavery Virginia aristocrat as governor, a proslavery frontiersman as lieutenant governor (Adolphus Hubbard), and an antislavery bourgeois as congressman (Daniel P. Cook). Probably more important than slavery was banking, with internal improvements as a strong minor theme. The leading role of slavery in the election is a persistent theme for many who have written about the contest, but other topics were more central.[29] The dramatic events that followed the election of 1822 have led some historians to cast the entire season as a prelude, but the evidence for this is not strong. Illinoisans were frantic about the rough waters that were swamping Illinois banks. Economic stability, roads, canals, and regional development were the driving issues. Slavery was present, but its main effect was to further muddy the already dense and churning electoral waters.[30]

Shortly after Coles's election, James Madison sent a warm, personal note of congratulations and encouragement. Included was the symbolic gift of a pedometer that Madison offered with the wish that Coles would in his new role walk a straight path with measured steps.[31] Coles acknowledged Madison's gift in a note from Washington at the end of October.[32] Coles returned to Illinois on 1 December (just in time for the opening of the legislature). On the fifth, he was inaugurated at Vandalia, the state's new capital, as Illinois' second governor.

* * *

During the summer of 1818 on a high, uneven bluff on the western bank of the Kaskaskia River (known by some as the Okaw), the new Illinois capital of Vandalia had been laid out in a perfect grid by federal land surveyors. Hills to the north and southwest and stands of timber and patches of the Grand Prairie to the north and east framed the site. The surveyors placed a public square (half a block in size) four hundred feet from the Kaskaskia River. Main Street runs east and west through the square. Sixty-two lots were laid out north of Main in an even grid, the same on the south side. North-south streets were named First through Eighth. East-west streets honored men of the day: Ninian Edwards, Arthur St. Clair, John Randolph, Richard M. Johnson, Albert Gallatin.[33]

Edmund Tunstall of Carmi had won the lowest bid to construct the state house. It went up at the corner of Fifth and Johnson, across from Reavis's Hotel. He began work in the spring of 1820 and finished it a few months later. The basic, two-story box building, just 40 feet by 30 feet, touted the main meeting room on the ground floor. A ten-foot-wide passage downstairs connected with the stairway. The second floor held two, 10 foot by 15 foot council and committee rooms. Two brick chimneys were called for, but because Tunstall did not finish the south one, he forfeited $40 of his $4,732 commission.[34] The state capital was modest. One legislator described it as "primitive and Plain as a Quaker meeting house."[35] No cushioned chairs complemented the rustic setup—delegates and senators sat on long, hard benches. The speaker's chair was placed on a platform just large enough to hold the chair just a few inches high. He worked at a desk, that is, a board supported by four sticks, or balusters. The senate was just as plain, only on a smaller scale still.[36]

Vandalia was the place to be. The Census of 1820 listed 525 people in Vandalia, including 11 slaves. Seventy-five new households had arrived since 1818 to join the original thirteen in Vandalia Township. For all of this, it was still a frontier town. The third legislature, to be led by governor-elect Edward Coles, gathered in the new town on the high bluff by the Okaw.

7

A Prairie Firestorm

Edward Coles arrived in Vandalia on Sunday, 1 December 1822, one day only before the Illinois legislature would convene. He arrived scarcely in time to wind up his affairs at the land office in Edwardsville and move on to Vandalia to undertake his new duties.[1] Travel had been disagreeable. Muddy roads were swollen with rain, and the rough travel had detained him. Coles would be inaugurated as the second governor of Illinois the following Saturday.

Coles was mindful of the princely trappings of the governor's office and rejected them as unrepublican. Shortly after his election, he made very clear his dislike for titles of office. He wrote a sharp letter to the *Vandalia (Illinois) Intelligencer* to complain about their reference to him using the title "His Excellency." The title of governor was, he said, was "specific, intelligible and republican," and he lamented the descent to aristocratic and high-sounding titles.[2] Jefferson would have applauded Coles's stand for republican simplicity. A letter appeared in the *(Richmond, Virginia) Enquirer* thanking Coles for rejecting the title because of its aristocratic overtones.[3] Later in his life, Coles referred often to this incident with great pleasure and perhaps a little crowing.

Two pressing issues were brought to the attention of the legislature. First, the outcome of the election in Pike and Fulton Counties was challenged. Second, the legislature was required to elect a senator to represent the State of Illinois in Washington, as the term of Senator Jesse B. Thomas would end in 1823. These two seemingly harmless matters, when mixed with the inaugural address of the new governor, would form a strange legislative cocktail. The effect emerged as a serious case of partisan inebriation. The house would go to extremes in subverting its own rules in order to set the stage for legalizing slavery. This would lead to political convulsions throughout the state for fully eighteen months. Finally the most basic question related to slavery in the state would be settled, and the influence of a major faction would be broken. Illinois would not witness a more eventful or entertaining term of legislature for many decades. Coles's inaugural speech uncorked the bottle.

The election of a legislative representative from Pike County, in the contest of 1822, was irregular. Nicholas Hansen, a rising star in Illinois politics, representing the new wave of New York immigrants, and John Shaw, something of a prairie outlaw whose cognomen as "the black prince" reflected well-known habits of political chicanery, squared off in a contest that on election day featured spurious polling stations, bogus electoral judges, and phantom voters.[4] Hansen was seated on December 9. The matter rested but not for long.

Edward Coles delivered his inaugural address on 5 December 1822. In the plain little statehouse at the intersection of Fifth Street at Johnson in Vandalia, Coles made a detailed statement of the political views that would shape his administration and ignite a prairie firestorm that would sweep the state. His views paralleled those of his political mentor, President James Madison. He endorsed an active government in areas such as internal improvements, farming, and education. He advocated a cautious approach to banking and money and delivered just what his campaign had promised.[5] And Coles addressed slavery. He made three demands regarding slavery. First was the final abolition of all slavery in Illinois, arguing that the institution was immoral by natural law and illegal under the Northwest Ordinance. "Conceiving it not less due to our principles than to the rights of those held in bondage," he recommend to the legislature that just and equitable provisions be made for the end of slavery in the state. Second, he recommended a general revision of the black laws. And finally, he asked the legislature to strengthen the laws against kidnapping. Coles believed that southerners often came into Illinois, captured free black persons, and then transported them by force south for sale at southern markets.[6]

The match had been struck, and a dry political wind would stir, driving the flame to kindling. Having presented his demands on slavery, Coles turned to the program of legislative priorities on which he had run for governor (though the slavery stuff may have deafened many legislators to the rest). He suggested that Illinois, in light of the problems of neighboring states, should try to establish a stable currency, whether gold, silver, or paper. A stable currency, he argued, would spur the current prosperity to greater heights. He urged growth and expansion in the field of internal improvements, specifically, an Illinois-Michigan canal and better roads. Coles proposed to pay for these improvements from a special fund made up of money from land sales in the military district and rent monies from the saline district. Believing, furthermore, that a democracy must have an educated population, Coles proposed that the government should guarantee the availability of that education. And Coles recommended that the state build a penitentiary. He was the first of several governors to urge this new form of criminal management developed in the east.

Coles's wide-ranging program left both his friends and foes astounded.[7] For once, he had taken decisive action. Coles believed that a convention to endorse slavery would be proposed in any event. He chose to seize the initiative by demanding the abolition of slavery outright.[8] Hooper Warren later criticized Coles's decision to confront slavery as a tactical mistake. He claimed Coles's speech embarrassed the opponents of slavery with its boldness. If Coles had not brought slavery before the legislature, Warren believed, the issue would have died in the legislature, and a divisive and potentially dangerous referendum could have been avoided.[9] Warren's criticism misses the mark, as does the dismissive assessment of politician Coles by James E. Davis. Davis sees Coles as a political stumbler for whom success was founded largely on the weaknesses of his opponents.[10] Not so. Coles was far more calculating and deliberate than Davis warrants. Coles's inaugural speech was not cautious. But it was also not, as Davis would have us think, simple or naïve. Clearly, the convention forces planned to raise the question themselves. Richard Flower, a prominent English immigrant and cofounder (with Morris Birkbeck) of the English Settlement in the southeast corner of the state, pointed to the existence of a proslavery faction already determined to present the question of slavery to the public when the time might be right. Coles's inaugural address sparked forthright action on an issue already gaining momentum.[11] William H. Brown, publisher of the Vandalia-based *Illinois Intelligencer* (and later, president of the Chicago

Historical Society), seemed to concur. He pointed to "a few designing men" who were secretly positioning themselves to ensure that a resolution to hold a constitutional convention would pass.[12]

By 1822, various groups and individuals had proposed changes in the 1818 constitution. Most of the proposed changes were procedural and desired by most citizens. Rumors were thick, however, that a constitutional convention could (and very well might) be used to fully and permanently legalize slavery by revision to the state constitution. Coles was probably right to meet the question squarely. It may be, furthermore, that Coles was pursuing a calculated risk.[13] He brought the question out of the shadows, clothed it in moral terms, and laid it where it belonged: on the docket for public debate. He undoubtedly knew the fears of his former slaves and their friends concerning kidnapping. Without the force of the law Coles proposed, black persons would not be safe from the wiles and clutches of slave owners only a river away in Missouri or Kentucky. Coles had made a major and life-changing decision to move to Illinois. He had cast his fate with Illinois and was not willing to step backward.

* * *

Each house appointed a subcommittee to examine and report on various parts of the governor's speech. In the senate, the committee on slavery included Leonard White, William Boone, Milton Ladd, William Kinney, and Joseph Baird: proslavery men every one.[14] The three-man house committee of Conrad Will, John Emmitt, and Risdon Moore contained a majority against slavery.[15]

The senate committee filed its report in a week. Unanimously, the members disagreed with the governor. The Black Code of 1819, they felt, was the best law for the time. They objected to the claim that the Northwest Ordinance forbade slavery after statehood. Under the ordinance, slaves and their descendants already in Illinois in 1787 remained legally enslaved. Any change from that position, they concluded, required an amendment and thus a convention.[16] A week later, the house committee presented both a majority report and a minority report. Moore and Emmitt, speaking as the majority, concluded that the Northwest Ordinance barred any type of slavery (including indentured servants), supported Coles's reforms, and recommended against a constitutional convention.[17] The minority report by Conrad Will argued that since slavery had withstood thirty years of proscription under the Northwest Ordinance, a resolution from the legislature could not be enough to settle the issue. Will called for a constitutional convention.[18]

The 1818 constitution required two steps for amendment. First, the legislature had to pass a resolution with a two-thirds majority calling a referendum on whether Illinois should hold a convention. Second, if a majority of the voters passed the referendum, then the convention would be held. At the time of the referendum, convention delegates would be elected to serve if the call for a convention was successful. Indeed, the calling of a convention would unleash political winds that could blow in any direction.

Feelings against Coles turned acid among those who were becoming known as the "conventionists." The drive to revise the constitution to suit business tastes and proslavery passions was mounted, and the convention movement began to ride hell-bent for results. Those who had business before the legislature found their measures tabled until their support for the convention could be secured. Threats and denunciations were used like levers to move the great convention, bit by bit, closer to passage. So far, not a word had been said about the convention on the floor of either chamber.[19]

It was soon recognized that the senate held support enough to assure the two-thirds majority needed to call the convention. Support in the house was less certain. In fact, the convention forces believed that they lacked only two votes for passage in the House of Representatives, so the convention party proposed that two-thirds of the combined vote of the house and senate would be taken as constitutionally valid support for calling for a referendum on the convention question. The measure to change the rule was quickly passed in the senate. Much to the surprise of some, it was rejected in the house by a vote of 16 to 20.[20]

On 27 January, Emmanuel West introduced a motion in the house calling for a public referendum to authorize a constitutional convention. Expecting the bill to fail, he hoped to gain an accurate count of the votes. The measure lost by two: 22 yea and 14 nay—a two-thirds majority of 24 was required). West could count on one additional vote because Thomas Rattan of Greene County, a supporter of the measure, had been asked to vote against the bill, allowing him to move for reconsideration as a member of the winning side. West sought the one additional vote he needed from William McFatridge of Johnson County. As a reward, he offered support for McFatridge's choice of the town for a county seat.[21] McFatridge was, according to journalist and historian William H. Brown, a character of kind heart and generous disposition. McFatridge had his failures, of course. He was, for instance, believed to drink more whiskey than his legislative duties actually required.[22]

On the evening of 27 January, well understanding the lay of the land, West and others of the conventionist persuasion met at Kinney's house in Vandalia—John Shaw, the losing competitor in the recent Pike County legislative race, was among their number. This meeting marked a shift in the political tone in Vandalia; a bitter determination seemed to set in, joining this brotherhood in a steely resolve.

On the following night, 28 January, the state bank and land office burned. The buildings were not seriously damaged, but records of the bank's loans were destroyed, as were the land-office deeds.[23] Neither cause nor culprit was ever identified. The cashier had taken pains to vacate the fireplace, so a stray ember can be ruled out. A debtor or land speculator may have had an interest in destroying the records, of course, yet the proximity of the fire to the combustible meeting at Kinney's suggests a possible link (although the motive would not be entirely clear).

It was 10 February when the senate finally brought the convention question to the floor. It passed without a hitch: 12 to 6. The house was next to speak on the matter. On February 11, West, believing, with McFatridge in his pocket, that he had the votes in the house, had Rattan move the convention resolution for reconsideration. This was the culmination of weeks of finagling, wangling, and contrivance. All was in place for a new dawn to arise at the beckon of a new constitution, for the flowering of prosperity in the Great State of Illinois, and for the securing of a people's rights to hold property in slaves.

The question was called; the votes were tallied. The count was 23 to 13. To the utter dismay of the conventionists, the measure was lost. This time, they had not seeded the winning side with a sleeper who could recall the question. The convention question was lost. The resolution was dead. For want of a single vote.

It was Hansen.[24] Hansen had killed the measure. Nicholas Hansen of Pike County had entered the legislature under suspicious circumstances and had been seated over the objections of the black prince. He had changed his vote, siding with the anticonventionists.

Next, J. G. Daimwood moved for reconsideration. He had voted for the resolution (he was, that is, a member in the minority on this constitutional vote). Speaker of the House William M. Alexander called the motion out of order (correctly—the rule against recall by a member on the losing side was clear). An appeal was entertained. It fell 18 to 16. The measure was finished.

Hansen owed his seat to a majority of the house. He had sided with them in earlier votes. They thought he was a conventionist. On the other hand, he had supported Coles, the antislavery candidate for governor. Moreover, his county was considered antislavery. Years later, George Churchill, who as representative of Madison County was present during the events described here, offered the view that Hansen had, in the first instance, voted for the convention to satisfy his debt to the proconvention members who had supported him in retaining his seat. Hansen also was indebted to the majority for having supported his request to locate the Pike County seat in Ross's Settlement. Then, Churchill argued, with his debt paid and with passage of the convention bill a likelihood, Hansen changed his vote, showing his true feelings.[25] The convention men charged that a conspiracy was behind it all, that Hansen was a plant designed to defeat the bill. They were virulent and wild in defeat.

That night, the leaders of the convention movement gathered at Kinney's house.[26] They agreed to convene a rally in the capitol square. People flocked to the square just as the shadows of night began to overtake the little Illinois capital. Speakers warmed the winter's evening with high-minded words about liberty and the rights of the majority. A petition was passed calling for the unseating of Nicholas Hansen. Sixteen or eighteen people signed. The meeting dispersed but two hours later regrouped into a more interesting breed of wild animal. Carrying torches of fire and parading a straw effigy of Hansen, two hundred revelers circled the statehouse square, blasting the little town of Vandalia with rolls of the drum, indignant trills of the fife, and howls from numerous horns. They hooted, "Convention or death! Convention or death!" When the party was ripe, a straw Hansen burst into flames, the gunpowder ball planted in his gut igniting into a sharp complaint in the night air. The roiling assembly advanced to the house of George Churchill, who had vocally opposed the convention, giving "three groans for Churchill . . . and three cheers for the convention."[27]

On 12 February, the day following the defeat of the convention measure, Colonel Alexander Field made an astonishing motion in the first-floor legislative meeting room of the rustic statehouse in Vandalia. He moved reconsideration of the house's decision (nine weeks prior—9 December) to seat Nicholas Hansen.[28] More than just the representative of Union County, now, Field was the defender of democracy. According to Field, friends of John Shaw had set up an election poll where, it was asserted, eighty or ninety men (some from Missouri) had voted. In seating Hansen, the legislators had rejected the results from this poll, effectively denying these men the exercise of their privilege. Field was just warming up. The rights of these good Americans must be upheld. Did not the Constitution confer upon the people the right to vote?[29] For the love of democracy, Field pleaded for the rights of these Missouri voters whose ballots had been discounted by the heartless legislature of Illinois.

Thomas Mather of Randolph County and Churchill of Madison County rose to argue that the house should not alter the decision it had made these many weeks ago. Mather tried to inject a cautionary note: "If a member of this house is to be deprived of his seat upon such testimony, whose seat, let me ask, would be secure?"[30] But Field had set a train in motion, and it was not about to be derailed by two men who were, apparently, insensitive to the great wrong committed against men who were proudly expressing their constitutional right to vote.

What began as a bizarre plea for a long-shot challenge to a seated member emerged, at the end of Field's long-winded sermon, as a viable attack. Should this challenge fail, however, the convention men held another card. A man named Crow was prepared to challenge the seating of John Emmitt.[31] Field's motion to reconsider the 9 December vote to seat Hansen was brought to the vote. It carried. At this point, the legislature received an affidavit of Levi Roberts. The affidavit, dated 29 January 1823, certified that, in Roberts's opinion, Shaw had received a majority of twenty-nine of all the qualified votes of Pike County. Roberts's affidavit was seized upon as the final proof. The vote was scheduled. Hansen had, on 9 December, been seated with the following: "Resolved that Nicholas Hansen is entitled to a seat in the house." A motion was now made to swap out the words "Nicholas Hansen" for "John Shaw."[32] The motion was carried. Hansen was unseated. John Shaw, the black prince, would represent Pike County. They sent a rider to bring Shaw to Vandalia posthaste.[33] In a matter of days, he arrived and was seated.

With Shaw in the house, the conventionists mustered the brute force required to complete the business at hand. By rules of the legislature, a defeated motion could not be recalled for consideration by a minority voter. Speaker of the House Alexander on 11 February had rightly overruled such a request for reconsideration from a minority member. The appeal to Alexander's decision had been defeated. Now, (almost a week later) comes the minority member, arguing that in the situation of a failed two-thirds majority, both sides could be considered the losing or minority side. Thus, either side could move for reconsideration. The call for a referendum on a constitutional convention was reasserted. It passed by one vote. Shaw's. They scheduled the referendum for August 1824.

The conventionists gathered into another giddy meeting on the night of their victory.[34] In an 1865 paper to the Chicago Historical Society, Brown recollected the spirited and vindictive gust of mob gaiety that blew through Vandalia that night. It was, he said, a "grand procession" stimulated by whiskey and punctuated with loud blasts upon tin horns and the crashing music of kettles and pans beaten with iron and wood. The crowd visited groans and derision upon the residences of the governor and certain anticonvention members of the senate and house.[35]

Commenting on the mob scene of 12 February, Horatio Newhall, a Harvard-educated doctor, noted that most of the revelers were Kentuckians and Tennesseans (half-horse, that is, and half-alligators), the most contemptible of beings and the refuse of mankind.[36] Elihu B. Washburne, in his biography of Coles, called the joy taken by the conventionists "indecent."[37] This rampage was a fitting start to an eighteen-month feud that swallowed the state.

Edward Coles, Governor of Illinois, was intent on fulfilling his prerogative by filling the position of recorder in the newly formed county of Fulton. The rancorous state of the opposition, however, would not let him do it. The senate had demanded to see the recommendations of all the people suggested for the post. Coles refused, arguing that the senate had the power to confirm those whom he nominated and not the power to select the candidate.[38] He proposed J. G. Lofton to the senate. Rejected. Coles proposed Pascal P. Enos. Rejected. He then proposed O. M. Ross. Rejected. On 18 February, the senate adjourned the session. They neglected to advise the house. They neglected to advise the governor.[39] Such was the disdain of the proslavery majority for the antislavery governor.

8

The Chasm

Commentators, then and later, have had harsh words for the events in Vandalia of February 1823. Historian and politician Elihu Washburne called the unseating of Nicholas Hansen outrageous and "a measure of revolutionary violence and madness happily without parallel in our history."[1] To historian Wayne Stevens, the legislature showed audacity surpassing belief.[2] Morris Birkbeck characterized the proceeding as "the most unjust and impudently tyrannical, that ever, as I believe, disgraced the legislature of a free country."[3] William H. Brown called the affidavit of Roberts flimsy and worthless.[4] Reviews of the time were not less caustic. The *Edwardsville (Illinois) Spectator* ran a sneering "Epitaph":

> Beneath this cold and earthly pall,
> Sleeps Soft a Legislature,
> Whom all the world, I think will call
> A black, infernal creature,
> His beauty bloomed! Oh what a pink!
> His death, Oh what a chasm!
> But sure the world will laugh to think
> The D——safely has 'im.[5]

But not all of the indignation was poured out on the convention faction in the legislature. A proof copy of Brown's critical review (in the *[Vandalia] Illinois Intelligencer*) of the disturbing and remarkable events of the legislative session was inadvertently circulated before publication. The sneering tone of Brown's review ignited a blast of abuse. Hoping to prevent publication, a crowd formed at the *Intelligencer*'s offices. Threats were hurled; the printing press of the newspaper was nearly tossed into the Kaskaskia River.[6] Still, the number was published, and, as a result, Brown was tossed out of the business by his partner, William Berry, a conventionist member of the legislature. By way of Brown's unvarnished account, the story of the legislature's unseating of Hansen and the late-night whiskey-stewed parades of the conventionist vandals through Vandalia became notorious statewide.

* * *

In the midst of the furor generated by the convention question, Governor Edward Coles pressed ahead on programs for education, the building of a penitentiary, resolution of problems with state and local banks, and construction of an Illinois-Michigan canal. The future prosperity of Illinois and its citizens lay with these measures; the slavery proposals were to clean up old business.

The Illinois River reached to within a handful of miles from Lake Michigan, all but closing a loop connecting the Mississippi River with the great markets of the east. A canal would speed eastern products to the frontier and western raw materials to the manufacturing centers in the east. Illinois' canal would become, many thought, a wealth-producing catalyst for western growth. In 1822, Congressman Daniel P. Cook secured a federal land grant supporting the development of a canal. To keep the grant, Illinois needed to begin surveying the route.

On 4 January, the canal bill easily passed to a third reading in the house by a vote of 27 to 6.[7] The canal bill created a commission of five members charged with laying out the route of the canal between the Illinois River and Lake Michigan. In addition, the committee was to urge the governor of Indiana to help develop the Wabash River into a navigable stream.[8] Some complained that the cost of the bill, when added to other proposed programs, would drive taxes too high. Supporters, including the editor of the *(Kaskaskia, Illinois) Republican Advocate*, countered that the canal would create wealth for the state. Some citizens in Bond County displayed an early case of canal fever. They held a meeting and delivered, in the form of a letter in the *Intelligencer*, an ultimatum to their state senator—vote for the canal or be thrown out of office.[9] On 10 February, the canal bill passed the state senate with only three negative votes, all from proslavery men.[10] Two days later (after the convention bill had passed the house), the canal bill achieved house approval and final passage. With the commission approved, Coles hastened to appoint the commissioners so work could begin.

Like the proposed canal project, banking in Illinois remained a hot topic before the legislature for years. Money in Illinois was shadowy stuff. Banks printed and distributed their own scrip. All manner of paper and scrip circulated but rarely at face value. Instead, the true value of a bill rose and fell with the reputation of its bank. If a person's money happened to be scrip from a bank fallen on hard times, that person might have a hard time making a purchase, or paying taxes, or even paying an installment owed at the land office. To make change for a purchase, a holder of the scrip might just snip a little piece off his bill and make the correct amount. These shreds of paper circulated, trying to work like coinage. Banks from Missouri, banks from Illinois, banks from Kentucky, the Bank of the United States—all of their notes vied for value and general acceptance.

The Bank of Edwardsville provides a relevant, if melancholy, little story. In 1818, it was made an agent of the federal government for the purpose of completing land-sale transactions. It also joined with the Bank of St. Louis in various dealings and suffered mightily when its sister bank failed. The Bank of Edwardsville, as the land-office depository, was never permitted the luxury of deciding for itself what paper it would accept in trade, so it was at a disadvantage in managing the value of its holdings.[11] Bank President Benjamin Stephenson (who doubled as Coles's reluctant and antagonistic partner in managing the Edwardsville land office) had difficulty in keeping the federal-land-receipts account above water. Stephenson struggled to convert the bags of scrip circulating as money into varieties deemed acceptable to the Bank of the United States. At the same time, he needed to gather capital pledged by investors and make loans so the bank could earn money and profit. The bank failed in 1821, taking with it a large account payable to the U.S. government and innumerable smaller accounts of farmers, speculators, and depositors statewide.

The Bank of Illinois got off to a rocky start. First authorized in 1819, the bank was unable to raise the capital to get off the ground. It was reauthorized in 1821 with capital of $500,000, $300,000 of which was to be loaned out to the counties. Residents were to avail themselves, if they so pleased, of unsecured loans up to $100. This program was, to no one's surprise, wildly popular. Residents dutifully made time in their busy schedules to get their loans without fail. The faith of the General Assembly had been pledged to the redemption of these loans in ten years (one tenth in each succeeding year). Obviously, problems were in a plan like this, but the people were for it. The bank was in need of more money from the legislature in 1823. Some people were paying back their debts, but many were not; a large percentage simply could not. The request was before Governor Coles and the legislature for a further $200,000.

Governor Coles recommended that the bank not be extended this transfusion. The select committee of the senate followed his recommendation that the additional $200,000 in notes not be issued.[12] The house approved the same recommendation by a wide margin (24 to 9).[13] The *Intelligencer* praised these actions as supporting the credit worthiness and general interests of the community.[14] Coles and the legislature would have welcomed both a stable currency and a stable banking system but achieved neither. Stability for the banks was decades away.

Distinct from his duties as governor, Coles found himself involved in a lawsuit that William Crawford, secretary of the treasury, had instituted against the Bank of Edwardsville to collect the land-office funds that were lost in the failure of the bank. The suit had proceeded very slowly. Coles had recommended the suit to Crawford when he had been register of lands; he had found the bank officials to be uncooperative. Moreover, he had found inconsistencies in the records of the land-office receiver (his proslavery and estranged land-office colleague, bank president Benjamin Stephenson). He had urged that a suit be brought quickly, before the bank's assets could be sold off.

The suit against the Bank of Edwardsville brimmed with politics. It lay at the beginning of a snarling match between Senator Ninian Edwards and Secretary Crawford that became known as the AB Affair.[15] Edwards, in support of the Edwardsville Bank, had published some blunt letters criticizing the secretary of the treasury. A feud between the two men erupted and then spun out of control. It ended up in congressional hearings, with Edwards ultimately suffering considerable loss of prestige.[16] Coles was impugned by Edwards for his supposed alignment with Crawford, based on Coles's earlier investigations of the bank and of land-office receiver–bank president Stephenson.[17] Coles returned some flak. He criticized Elias Kent Kane, prosecutor in the suit, for dragging his feet to suit the agenda of Edwards. Kane got it from the other side, too. Horatio Newhall complained that Crawford was using the suit to maintain Kane's support and loyalty.[18] The AB Affair, in the churning and bubbling stew of Washington power-cookery, was a tidbit, a minor scrap that all but destroyed Edwards's reputation. Fortunately, Edward Coles's involvement remained minimal and peripheral.

Governor Coles took steps to guarantee for Illinois some federal support for education. This entailed selecting federal land that would then be ceded to the state and sold to support the school system. Coles appointed a commission to select the thirty-six sections Illinois was entitled to receive. By the end of his term the selection process had been completed. Coles left office believing public education had a firm financial base.[19]

In the Name of the Injured Sons of Africa

On the very evening of conventionist victory, after Shaw had been seated in the Illinois legislature, and the motion to reconsider a call for referendum was rammed through, Governor Coles invited opponents of the convention to meet with him in his rooms at the local boardinghouse. They appointed a committee to raise funds for the battle to defeat a call for a constitutional convention. Money was collected that very evening from the committee to publish and circulate an address to the people of Illinois.[20]

The address was certainly under the pen of Edward Coles. It phrased the primary argument against the convention (and thus against slavery) in moral terms, arguing that slavery violated higher law, both natural and man-made. The address gave five reasons why the admission of slavery into Illinois was ill-advised: slavery was against God's will; the Northwest Ordinance had decided the issue in 1787; the institution of slavery exploited one person's labor solely for the profit of another; admitting slavery would slow the flow of immigrants, not speed it up as the proponents argued; and finally, slavery would not be a panacea for Illinois' economic woes.[21] These five points remained at the core of the anticonvention argument. They were expanded upon and restated but not revised.

This first salvo denounced the movement for a convention as a proslavery ruse. It declared that whatever the convention supporters claimed, their true aim was the introduction of slavery into Illinois. The address ended with a call for action. Coles invoked "the name of unborn millions who will rise up after us, and call us blessed or accursed, according to our deeds." Coles pleaded, "[I]n the name of the injured sons of Africa, whose claims to equal rights with their fellow men will plead their own cause against their usurpers before the tribunal of eternal justice, we conjure you, fellow citizens, TO PONDER UPON THESE THINGS."[22] It was signed by fifteen members of the General Assembly and was published three days later.[23]

On 15 February, three days before the senate's adjournment, the conventionists had met to begin preparation of its own statement for publication throughout the state. It was released in the *Edwardsville Spectator* on 1 March and was reprinted one week later, 8 March 1823, in the *Illinois Intelligencer*. Most of the address defended their actions in the legislature. At the end of the address, seemingly as an afterthought, they published their reasons for needing a new convention. The Constitution of 1818, they argued, contained aristocratic features borrowed from eastern constitutions. The list continued: the lower courts of the state needed reorganization, the tenure of appointed officials was too vaguely defined in the 1818 Constitution, and the conventionists pointed to a need for annual rather than biennial sessions of the legislature. It said nothing about slavery.

Thrust and parry became the business at hand. On 5 March, a dinner was mounted in Edwardsville to show support for the governor. Coles gave his own assessment of the conventionist program in a toast after the dinner: "The Crisis is big with the fate of Illinois, and requires every friend of freedom to rally under the banners of the constitution." On the following night, the conventionists threw their own Edwardsville dinner, complete with toasts. Senator William Kinney of St. Cloud County parried Coles's jab: "The Crisis: it is big with the fate of Illinois, and requires every friend of freedom to rally around its constitution and amend it so as to promote their prosperity, safety, and political happiness."[24]

Coles became a key player in the campaign to defeat the call for a convention. He became the clearinghouse for antislavery information. He sent pamphlets and articles to any who could make good use of them in the battle under way. He was a skilled writer and researcher and a well-connected and energetic organizer. He fully committed both energy and money to the campaign. A view presented early in the twentieth century that Coles had done little for the effort but act as a reference service is not borne out.[25]

He poured out his views over four pen names: "One of Many," "The Voice of Virtue," "Wisdom and Experience on the Subject of Negro Slavery," and "Aristides."[26] As "Aristides," Coles attacked the issue of apportionment. The delegates to the constitutional convention would be elected by legislative districts, but the state's rapid growth had left the districts' boundaries out of sync with their populations. Illinois' electoral districts were malapportioned. Coles and other anticonvention men believed that the convention forces had wanted to convene the convention as quickly as possible so as to benefit from existing district patterns. The southern part of the state, where the conventionists had their strength, had an artificial advantage over the more rapidly growing north. "Aristides" argued that the slavery issue could not be decided fairly until the state was reapportioned to represent its true character. Thus, any convention should wait until the lines had been redrawn.[27]

In another letter, "Aristides" opened the question of the economics of slavery. He argued that free labor was more efficient than slave labor and that land values in free states were higher.[28] This theme was widely discussed in the campaign. Many slavery advocates believed that if slavery was legal, thousands of rich plantation owners would migrate to Illinois and cause the sagging land prices to rise.[29] Coles specifically asked Roberts Vaux, a wealthy Philadelphian and ally in the fight, for information about land values and productivity.[30] By May, Coles was arguing in strong terms that northern land values were higher than southern land values. He concluded that prohibiting slavery was more likely to raise land values. Slavery was inefficient because the landowner who depended on slaves became lazy, he said: "Emigrants from the South will bring us idleness, vanity, luxury, and the slow but fatal disease of slavery—things we do not want."[31] Coles (the republican true-believer) warned against slavery as a tyranny that will undo all freedom.

The anticonvention group, under Coles, recognized the political challenge before them and aggressively mounted a campaign to organize. They formed antislavery societies; first, at the end of May, in Monroe County; then, on 4 July, in Madison, Sangamon, Edgar, Pike, Greene, and Morgan counties. Groups later were formed in Lawrence, White, St. Clair, and Bond.[32] Secretaries and financial committees kept up lively programs of communication and fundraising. They held meetings, distributed pamphlets and tracts. They wrote to the local papers.

John Mason Peck, a Baptist missionary, traveled widely through Illinois bearing the holy word and nurturing antislavery sentiment. He was six feet tall and more, muscular, athletic and blue-eyed. His head was large and, according to friend and biographer John Reynolds, well-developed "according to the laws of phrenology."[33] He was a ramrod in the pulpit, but when walking, he would lean forward, pressing into an aggressive, no-nonsense gait. John Mason Peck had energy. He invested it in preaching, distributing Bibles, and carrying the antislavery torch.

Historian Merton Dillon views Peck as crucial to the antislavery effort. Peck was out in front, organizing the St. Clair County antislavery society with thirty citizens in March of 1823.[34] Using this as a base, Peck extended antislavery and anticonvention groups to fourteen other counties. As a circuit-rider, he kept the groups viable and connected. He preached the antislavery cause wherever he went. He sold Bibles for very little and gave away countless copies to the poor. And he paved Illinois trails and tracks with his Bibles and, thereby, was a respected emissary of the anticonvention movement. But Peck's own description of his work in 1824 was more modest: "Illinois was then [1823–24] shaken to its center with the harassing and distressing question of the introduction of slavery." He wrote to the secretary of the Massachusetts Baptist Missionary Society: "And though I had avoided mingling with the politics of the day, my sentiments on that question were well known. Concealment would have been criminal." The secretary probably did not want to hear that an agent and minister had been too directly involved in politics.[35] The truth probably sits midway between these two versions. Peck was well known in his opposition to slavery. He probably tried to maintain a line between his work for the Baptists and his efforts in the campaign in 1824. In referring to the earlier debate in Missouri in 1820, he wrote in a newspaper, "I have had too much regard to the cause of religion, the interests of the country, and my own public and private reputation, to preach on slavery or any other subject of party politics."[36]

Peck played a significant role in the campaign, but his public statements may have been moderated by awareness of the dangers of overtly mixing politics with preaching the Word. Perhaps he adopted something like the approach of another legendary circuit rider, Peter Cartwright, who introduced politics into services by announcing a stump speech for the next day but only at the very end of his sermon.[37]

The work of some churches ensured that the anticonventionist/antislavery mission reached into every corner of the state. In addition to Peck's Bible Society Baptists must be counted the Baptist Friends of Humanity, a small sect from Kentucky, led by the formidable James Leman and influential well beyond their numbers. Also in the phalanx of churches working to defeat the convention: the Covenanters of Randolph County and the Cumberland Presbyterians in Bond and White Counties.[38] Whether as individuals like Peck and Cartwright or as church communities, religion became a force opposing slavery in 1824.

Morris Birkbeck was another whose untiring work contributed greatly to the anticonventionist cause. Birkbeck, the wealthy idealist republican from Surrey County in England who had immigrated to eastern Illinois in 1816, supported the antislavery cause with conviction. Birkbeck was a hooty-owl-looking chap, with a long, refined beak of a nose and frilly, feathery hair cresting his head like a wild nest protecting a big bony egg in the middle. Coles had written to Birkbeck in the spring of 1823, pleading with his friend from Surrey to take up his pen in combat against those who would protect slavery under the state constitution. In July 1823, he published a nineteen-page pamphlet, "An Appeal to the People of Illinois on the Question of a Convention." He laid out the case against slavery on many fronts: he celebrated the splendor of the U.S. Constitution, he worried over the encroachment of slavery as reflected in the 1820 census, and he preached the economics of land values. "Freedom, if it exists in reality," Birkbeck wrote, "extends to all—it is the right to do every thing but injury, and the enjoyment of protection from being injured. Without this restraint, on the one hand, and the protection on the other, liberty is an empty sound. Difference of color makes no difference in the nature of oppression, or in the crime of inflicting it; and that only is a country free where every man in it is protected from oppression."[39] A second pamphlet appeared soon after. He was also the author of a widely read series of letters in the *Illinois Gazette* under the pen name "Jonathan Freeman." At other times, he used his own name or "Q."[40] His letters and pamphlets found their way into homes; they became the stuff of public argument and discussion.

In April 1823, Coles assessed the course of the campaign against the convention. He realized that the slavery dispute was splitting Illinois and that such a split could have long-lasting detrimental effects. Yet, he remained steadfast in his commitment to stop slavery at the Ohio

River. His faith in the higher law of God and nature, crystallized in his wholesale acceptance of the Jeffersonian republican ideal, won out over his own indecisiveness. He lamented to James Madison that this convention business will certainly give "a very stormy time."[41] In April, he wrote the editor of the *Genius of Emancipation* to order a complete run of the journal. He added this to his large and ever-growing collection of clippings and excerpts from books and articles against slavery.[42]

Coles recruited among the influential people he had known in Washington to gather the information used in the battle. He wrote, for instance, to Bank of the United States president (and close personal friend) Nicholas Biddle requesting help in finding allies in the east.[43] With the Bank of the United States reaching the zenith of its power, Biddle pleaded he had too little time. He placed Coles in contact with Roberts Vaux, whom he described as "a gentleman of education, talents, fortune, leisure, and high standing in the community."[44] This was the beginning of a friendship that would become a foundation in the struggle. And here was the beginning also of a connection to a family that would become Coles's own in less than a decade.

Roberts Vaux came from Philadelphia's upper crust and spent all of his life working at philanthropic endeavors. His energies were spent on temperance, prison reform, and abolition. Vaux, like Coles, would become a victim of the Jacksonian party system. Siding with the Workingmen's Party against Biddle's bank in 1832, he would be stripped by Biddle's machinations of all his honors and chairmanships.[45] In 1823, however, Biddle felt little hesitation in recommending Vaux to Coles. He did caution Coles to hide Vaux's association with the abolitionist society in Pennsylvania from the voters of Illinois.[46] Biddle feared that Vaux's abolitionist leanings and eastern connections would inflame Illinoisans against the anticonventionists cause. He was probably correct.

Vaux agreed to help, fearing that an unthinking populace might well "pollute your soil with the blood and tears of slaves."[47] Vaux sent three sets of pamphlets to Illinois for Coles to distribute. The first pamphlet discussed the unprofitability of slave labor. The second covered the horrors of the slave trade, and the third dealt with the moral and constitutional questions of slavery.[48]

Heeding Biddle's warning, Coles and Vaux carefully concealed the origins of the pamphlets by sending them to a friend in St. Louis. He then sent them on to Illinois in different wrappers. The ruse was not completely effective. The conventionist *Kaskaskia Republican* charged that "foreign" pamphlets were circulating in the state. Because the pamphlets had been, by this time, reprinted, the anticonventionist *Intelligencer* retorted that all the pamphlets had been printed in the state and noted that the pamphlets circulated publicly: "Not so with the secret [conventionist] committee letters, that are actively making the rounds of the State."[49] The committee letters were informal newsletters containing information, gossip, and arguments for use in campaign debates and speeches. The *Intelligencer* was taking a moral stand noting that the anticonventionists made their sources public while the conventionists hid theirs by keeping the letters secret.

Coles feared that strong antislavery stories in out-of-state newspapers could hurt the campaign in Illinois.[50] Particularly he worried about stories in papers like the *(Washington, D.C.) National Intelligencer*, which were widely reprinted in Illinois. One such item in this "outsider paper" from the nation's capital scolded Illinoisans: The introduction of slavery in Illinois would be "suicidal" in its effects and unworthy of a free people.[51] Coles feared that strong pressure from these outside papers would rebound. Illinoisans, Coles believed, might embrace the convention scheme if only to demonstrate their independence from the east.[52] Coles was overly sensitive on this issue. The Illinois papers carried no letters complaining about the foreign reports they printed. In the case of the pamphlets, his concern appeared more justified. If it had become known publicly that an outside abolitionist had written them, the reaction might have been more negative. The pamphlets smelled more of a conspiracy perhaps led by the outsiders.

Coles's stature in Illinois rose considerably during this period, but he took little pleasure in it. At one point, Coles wrote to his niece Rebecca, to complain of the low level of pay and high level of party feeling. Overall, he groused, the office of governor was a disappointment.[53] His farm was not very profitable, and while he was governor, his lifestyle had been cramped because of lack of funds.[54] He found nothing in Vandalia to relieve his boredom and melancholia. He bemoaned his bachelor status.[55] This mood of despair and melancholy hung as if a dull fog over most of his administration.[56]

* * *

In the fall of the year, the conventionists recognized that they had lost the initiative. They met in Vandalia on 3 December and appointed an organizing committee of eighteen men to direct the battle. Subcommittees of five were appointed in all counties; each of these appointed committees in the townships.[57] By the end of the year, as many as fifteen men (on average) were active recruiters in each county. At times, the numbers swelled as work progressed in preparation for local meetings.[58] The conventionists held dinners, meetings, and rallies.

The constitutional referendum election was an all-out contest. Historian James Simeone's review of newspaper accounts of these local efforts identifies forty-five county meetings that were held by both camps during the eighteen months of the campaign.[59] All contemporary writers agree that business halted, and a state of virtual civil war ensued. The *(Louisville, Kentucky) Public Advertiser* reminded readers in July 1823 that the admission of slavery, though probably good for Illinois, was still a matter of policy and not of life or death.[60] But many in Illinois thought otherwise. Conventionist John Reynolds, who was to become governor in 1831, believed that the boisterous excitement stirred up by the convention question was without precedence.[61] Politician Thomas Ford, who could campaign with the best of stump speakers, was astonished at the oratorical violence.[62] William Brown later declared that the election divided neighborhoods and families and sundered friendships. Pistols and dirks were in great demand, he said.[63] For eighteen months, Illinois lived politics; there was no escape except to leave the state.

Simeone makes a case for major social disruption during the period. He cites increased murders (thirteen between 22 July 1823 and 12 June 1824, including those of two prominent anticonvention supporters) and increases in divorce as tangible indicators of stress and social discord.[64] Simeone's argument is thin, but the plain point is taken: the state was convulsed in political worry, anxiety, and division.

The Time of Fire

The statehouse burned down six days after the conventionists energized their movement with meetings to organize throughout the state. Once again, land-office papers were destroyed. Edward Coles was worried that the loss of the statehouse might work to the benefit of the conventionists. Among the professed reasons for calling a convention was the removal of the state capital from Vandalia; with the statehouse destroyed, he surmised, the need for a constitutional convention to settle the question might compel some to support the conventionist position.[65]

A plan for the rebuilding of the statehouse was quickly put in place by the conventionists. The plan called for private subscriptions, thus placing influence for the design and location in private hands. Edward Coles was asked to subscribe to the program. Believing the plan to be another subterfuge and its specifics to be bad public policy, he refused and offered up an alternate plan that he believed to be more responsible.[66] That night, Vandalia was witness, again, to a mob adventure. Coles and his supposed refusal to support the rebuilding of the statehouse were winds to the flame. An eyewitness account of the scene was printed in the *Edwardsville Spectator*. The reporter was awakened from a sound sleep by the glow of a fire brightening his chamber. A straw man fashioned to look like the governor was in flames outside his home, and a mob was chanting "statehouse or death!"[67]

Two weeks later, fire once again lit the night sky. This time, it was a prairie fire, tearing across lands east of Edwardsville. It destroyed much of the governor's Prairieland Farm. He lost two-thirds of all the enclosures and buildings on his farm, two hundred apple trees, and the same number of peach trees.

On January 7, Edward Coles received the following from the sheriff:

The People of the State of Illinois

To the Sheriff of Madison County, Greeting:

You are hereby commanded to summon Edward Coles to be and appear before the Circuit Court for Madison county, at the next term to be holden at Edwardsville at the Court House thereof, on the 4th Monday in the month of March next, to answer the County Commissioners of the County of Madison in a plea of Debt Two thousand Dollars which to them he owes and from them he unjustly detains to their Damage Five Hundred Dollars And have you then there this writ.

Witness Joseph Conway, Clerk of the said Court, at Edwardsville, this 7th day of January in the year of our Lord one thousand eight hundred and twenty-four and of the Independence of the United States of America the forty-8th.

[signature] Joseph Conway[68]

The law in question was part of Illinois' 1819 Black Code. It required that the owner of any slave brought into Illinois and freed post a $1,000 bond. The intent of the law was to dissuade the freeing of slaves whose support might devolve to the public purse. Coles, having brought twenty slaves into the state, should have posted a $20,000 bond (or so held the plaintiff).

The summons of Edward Coles. From Edward Coles, Miscellaneous Papers, Illinois State Historical Library, Springfield.

The suit against Edward Coles had been initiated in September of the prior year, when a "worthless and malignant partisan" (Coles's own words) had contacted the commissioners of Madison County and accused Coles of freeing slaves without giving the required bond to ensure that they would not become dependent on the county.[69] The complaint might have remained at rest on the table of the county commissioners, but the complainant returned to argue before them in person. The commissioners must, he said, take action against this man who had so clearly violated the laws of the state. No immediate action was then taken by the commissioners, so the complainant made his appeal publicly through the newspapers.

The complainant was Andrew Banks.[70] In an 1827 recollection of the matter, Coles described Banks's standing in this matter before the court. The complainant was not a property holder; he paid no taxes. The man had no direct interest in protecting public taxes as he was not a contributor. In the same breath, Coles noted that those he had freed were, in fact, *payers* of tax (resulting from the fact that they were land-owners), *not wards of the county.*[71]

It was Coles's view that he did not owe a bond to the county of Madison. His lawyers agreed. He objected to making such a bond. Still, to avoid the suit and its embarrassments, he posted the bond soon after the charge was made. But a few days later, Coles was visited by a friend and clergyman who, on the advice of Hail Mason, recommended that Coles withdraw the bond, as the county commissioners would discontinue the suit with the end of the election.[72] Coles withdrew the bond, taking what he believed to be a safe route consistent with his own belief that the bond had been unnecessary. The law was addressed to those who might be emancipated in Illinois. Coles, of course, had freed his slaves on the Ohio River while in Kentucky. He had brought free black persons into the state. The law did not apply to his situation, so a bond was not required.

It must have been a nasty awakening for Coles when a new complaint was filed in circuit court against him. The court date was set for March 1824.[73] The suit demanded that Coles be fined $200 for each former slave in addition to the bond.[74] Hail Mason, less a friendly adviser than a duplicitous adversary, had apparently engineered Coles's withdrawal of the bond to keep the issue alive in the courts, hoping the embarrassment of the suit would slow Coles in his steady march to defeat the convention. Coles concluded that his enemies, having slandered his name, were trying to bankrupt him as well.[75]

The wounds carried by Edward Coles at this time were fresh and raw. His farm had been torched, the freeing of his slaves had been dragged before the court, and the burning of the state house had produced charges impugning his patriotism. Coles's letter to Morris Birkbeck (29 January 1824) shows how this growing vine that bound him in trouble and difficulty was giving flower to something deeper and more positive. Coles saw through his hard times and gave thanks to Providence for placing in his hands a great work of justice.[76]

The March term of the Madison County Court was called to order. Edward Coles was in attendance. Hon. John Reynolds, the proslavery candidate for Congress who had lost to Jesse B. Thomas during the recently completed state legislative session, presided in the court. The defendant pled the statute of limitations and added several special pleas beside. A demurer was filed by the plaintiff in response to these special pleas. Reynolds wished to consider these matters at his leisure, so the case carried over to the September session of the court.[77] The leader of the anticonvention movement was forced, consequently, to continue the battle to defeat the proslavery call for a convention, while the propriety of his own act of emancipation was now under a cloud of doubt.

Then a ray of light. During the spring of that year, 1824, the *Illinois Intelligencer*, based in Vandalia, became "financially embarrassed." David Blackwell was joint owner of the paper with William Berry (a member of the legislature and proconvention activist). When Coles learned of the paper's difficulties, he quietly loaned Blackwell money to buy out Berry and settle the debts of the paper. In return, Coles would have editorial control of the paper through the end of the contest in August. Coles placed management and editorial direction in the hands of Blackwell.[78]

This adventure had been the culmination of a carefully orchestrated effort by Governor Coles. March 1823: the first of the antislavery societies was taking form, and William H. Brown had just been forced out of his position at the *Intelligencer*, having published his review of the scandalous turning out of Shaw by the conventionists. Judge Samuel D. Lockwood resigned as Secretary of State. At a late-night meeting with John Mason Peck in Coles's rooms at the house of James Mason, the men stewed over a replacement of Lockwood. The qualifications were of a strange mix. The candidate must have sufficient knowledge of the law; must be an anticonvention supporter; must also be able, should the opportunity present, to manage the editorial department of a newspaper. Peck recommended a Mr. David Blackwell, Esq., residing in Belleville. David was brother of Robert Blackwell, who had edited the *Intelligencer* with Elijah Berry for a time starting in 1817. "He is the very man; why did I not think of him," exclaimed Coles, bounding out of his chair, according to a description of the events by Peck.[79] The next morning, following a late breakfast at a log cabin in Rock Spring, Reverend Peck made his way to Blackwell's office, in Belleville, and presented him with an offer and a mission that was no doubt an astonishing surprise to the recipient. In short order, Blackwell occupied the office of Secretary of State and became part-owner of the *Intelligencer*. Blackwell became Coles's mole at the proslavery newspaper. When financial difficulties overtook the paper one year later, Coles was among the first to learn of it. With some months to go before the election, Coles handily, and in all secrecy, took control of the paper.

This was a stroke, a well-timed triumph. The convention forces were dismayed, the anticonventionists elated. Coles had reduced the voice of the conventionists from four Illinois newspapers to three and had expanded the reach of the anticonvention effort from one newspaper to two.[80] Coles insisted that the paper be delivered to all the old subscribers without fail. If they discontinued their subscription or refused to pay, no matter. They received the paper and its anticonvention reporting.

The expense in purchasing the paper is, to some degree, a measure of the extent to which Coles was committed to the outcome of this struggle. Consider this: Edward Coles also contributed the entirety of his income as governor ($1,000 annually) for each of the four years of his tenure as a means of funding the anticonventionist–antislavery cause.[81] Others gave generously; Coles was not the only one by any means. Tracts and pamphlets were printed and shipped to every town and hamlet in the state. The cost of this effort was borne by men of means in the anticonvention group; Edward Coles was foremost.

* * *

In the summer of 1824, two months before the election, Coles published a series of letters as "One of Many." He reviewed all the arguments against the convention and slavery. The letters comprise a summary of the anticonvention campaign and appeared in time to guarantee adequate circulation before the election. In the first letter, in May, Coles complained that the convention men told different stories to different counties and often implied promises of rewards for the county if the convention was held.[82] Prizes were available, since Illinois had been discussing the development of a prison, a college, and several canal routes. Coles promised that his letters would offer the truth about the convention and refute any arguments favoring it. Of course, to Coles and his friends, that meant refuting arguments favoring slavery.

Two weeks later, Coles published a long, formal letter about the effects of the geographic dispersion of slavery. Convention men had argued that decreasing the density of slavery would improve their position and lead ultimately to the demise of the institution because farmers would not depend entirely on that source of labor. The convention men argued that slavery would become too expensive.[83] Using the facts and figures he had gathered, Coles demonstrated that slavery's expansion into the southern frontier had not decreased the slave density on the east coast. He also noted examples from elsewhere in the world. Finally, he pointed out that density had very little effect on the condition of the individual slave, which was why the system was evil in the first place.[84]

The next week, he expanded on the negative effects of slavery's legalization. He argued that expanding slavery to Illinois only strengthened the institution in the south by increasing its power on the national level. Thus, expansion would prolong slavery's existence rather than cut it short. He also complained that any expansion of slavery (geographic or otherwise) would tarnish the image of the United States as a symbol of liberty in the rest of the world.[85] This was an idea he had developed during his European travel and was probably reinforced by his friends Morris Birkbeck and Richard Flower. Following the same argument he had made in his 1814 letters to Thomas Jefferson, Coles pointed out that slavery's existence would accelerate the moral decay of American society and plunge the republic headlong toward tyranny.[86]

On the thirteenth of June, he contributed a sketch of the historical context of slavery in America. He reminded his readers that the founding fathers had expected slavery to die a natural death because it violated the fundamental natural laws on which the Declaration of Independence and the Constitution were based. Like Jefferson and Madison, Coles did not believe that the two races could ultimately live peacefully together. And like Madison (especially), he advocated colonization to prevent revolution or civil war after emancipation.[87] Unlike Jefferson and Madison, Coles did believe that the races could live peacefully for a short time. Emancipation did not have to wait until there was a workable plan for colonization. Coles believed firmly that all African Americans would want to emigrate to Africa. They would readily embrace that homeland. And emancipation would allow them to work toward this goal.[88]

"This Ignorant, Immoral, and Degraded Race"

Edward Coles was an ardent supporter of the American Colonization Society (ACS). Here was an organization transparently rooted in its own time: equally propelled by virtue and fear and limited in its vision by the biases of its day. Edward Coles believed in the "natural law" of equal rights for all people; he did not believe that the races were otherwise equal. He did not believe that black persons and white persons could live together indefinitely in harmony. He didn't think this was possible.

The Reverend Robert Finley, a Presbyterian minister from New Jersey, organized the American Colonization Society to return large numbers of free black persons to a "homeland" in Africa. The society was formed in December 1816 at a series of meetings held in Washington, D.C.[89] The intention of the society was to accomplish two things: to benefit free black persons by providing them with a homeland settlement in which they could better enjoy the blessings of freedom and to benefit the nation by removing from its midst a dangerous and pernicious element. The society was funded by private subscription, and there was no want of donors at the outset. Free African Americans were invited to emigrate from America to the new colony of Liberia. A joint project of the government and the American Colonization Society was mounted to begin moving free black people voluntarily to Africa in 1820. During the next fifty years, the American Colonization Society sent thirteen thousand Americans to Liberia in an experiment in social justice that is fascinating in its idealism, tragedy, and telling biases. The call to form a democratic colony of free black individuals came from a voice deep inside the conscience of the times; still, it was a voice shaped by white interests and by misunderstandings reflecting the racial gulf separating the races. Especially during its early years, the cardinal principle of the colonization society was, as Henry A. Wise of Virginia asserted, "Friendship to the Slaveholders."[90] The overall goal was to preserve the republic by preserving the white civilization that was its basis.

Still, the American Colonization Society was one of very few platforms on which slaveholders, abolitionists, and all shades between could gather to discuss "the slavery problem." And it should be remembered that the colonization society was a significant factor in the emancipation of many thousands of slaves. The judgment of history has tended to agree with William Lloyd Garrison's assessment of the American Colonization Society that it was a racist organization that accepted and reinforced slavery.[91] Coles, Madison (who was president of the American Colonization Society beginning in 1833)[92] and Jefferson shared the basic view of the ACS: the free mixing of white and black societies in America was no answer at all. They must be separated.[93]

Edward Coles's Fourth of July toast in 1827 reflects his abiding affection for the colonization ethos: "Liberia—Destined to rid America of Negroes and to give to Africa civilization and Christianity, it claims the support of every patriot, philanthropist and Christian."[94] Coles repeated his enthusiasm in the *Illinois Intelligencer*, the paper Coles had purchased in 1824. The evil of slavery would be eradicated he reasoned, without infringing any but future rights.[95] Three years later, an Illinois branch of the ACS was formed in Vandalia at the beginning of the legislative session.[96] Coles may have had a hand in this, but no evidence remains of his direct involvement.

While Coles advanced a plain reading of the republican ideal and took its essence to heart, he was also heir to a racist paternalism that marked his station and his time. Coles wrote Thomas Jefferson Randolph, Virginia legislator and grandson of the third president, on 29 December 1831 (a letter that propelled Randolph to a feat of great political courage described later), lamenting the condition of slaves in Virginia and forecasting a future of growing civic danger from this "ignorant, immoral & degraded race."[97] In this view, Edward Coles appears to be one with Thomas Jefferson. And yet, this language seems quite out of character with representations that Coles makes elsewhere, so the letter must be read with care. Coles describes the lamentable condition of the slave; he may or may not be giving his own view of African Americans' status. The term *degraded*, for instance, was a term of art used in these times to point less to the nature of the individuals than to the pernicious effect of slavery upon them. This "degraded" race was not degraded by nature but by the existence of the institution of slavery. It points to black persons as victims.

Notwithstanding affectionate support and long-standing encouragement he offered to "his" freedmen, Edward Coles appears to have retained a durable semblance of paternalism. As later interactions with Robert Crawford indicated, Coles believed that African Americans "should" want to leave the country that had enslaved them. They should, that is, want to "return" to a more hospitable and a more ancestral country or homeland. For Coles, that meant either Africa or the Caribbean.

All Emotion Spent

The campaign's tempo increased as the election day drew near.[98] As the campaigns for various offices began, the convention's influence was seen in them. The anticonvention party held rallies and meetings to select candidates for the various offices.[99] A letter-writer in Gallatin County asked the candidates to "publically declare your views and sentiments on the various questions which now agitate the publick mind, particularly that of the Convention."[100] In response to this request came two letters discussing the views of Colonel Grable, a candidate for the legislature.[101] Voters saw the issues of the convention reaching well into the future of the state; candidates were obliged to declare themselves.

Oddly, the election day was quiet and anticlimactic for all the emotion that had flowed so freely during the campaign. The Reverend Thomas Lippincott remembered the election as a "hot time."[102] The weather was warm, and the people heated with excitement. But, he said, the defeated party submitted quietly. And the triumphant party rejoiced without noise or show. All the emotion had been spent in eighteen months of contortion, trouble, scheming, and campaigning.

The anticonventionists polled 6,822 to the conventionists' 4,965.[103] The 16 percent margin would be considered a landslide today. There was no doubt that the convention advocates and slavery had been dealt a decisive blow. Illinois' constitution remained as it was until 1848, when another convention movement succeeded. At that time, despite concern on the national level about slavery and the Mexican-American War, nothing was said about slavery.[104]

* * *

The election was as complete a repudiation of slavery in Illinois as could be hoped for. Daniel P. Cook, the antislavery incumbent, easily defeated former Governor Shadrach Bond, who supported slavery and the convention. Cook received 5,981 votes, or about 61 percent, to Bond's 3,841 votes. The anticonventionists, furthermore, made substantial gains in the legislature: they now controlled the house (but were still a minority in the senate).[105] Sam Butler, a zealous opponent of slavery, offered his sincerest congratulations to his Illinois friend Jacob Harlan. And, he said, if all good men would go round the state and shoot all in favor of the convention, then Illinois might be worth living in.[106]

The election was not without its political stories. In St. Clair County, the county clerk was proconvention while the county went against it. John T. Kingston, an early Illinois pioneer, remembered that when the clerk refused to deliver the returns to Vandalia, the settlers converged on the clerk's office. In a scene reminiscent of the rise of the Minutemen, Kingston remembered the settlers, rifles shining in their hands, determined that the clerk would deliver the correct vote at the right time. The clerk quickly saw the light and turned the tally over to a messenger.[107]

The convention vote is a window on Illinois settlement patterns and the impact of those patterns on attitudes to slavery. Although Illinois' culture during this era is generally characterized as southern, much of the population north of Vandalia was from northern states; their people entering Illinois via the Great Lakes. The election returns from 1824 suggest a north versus south split in the voting. Every county supporting the convention by 60 percent or more of the vote was in the southern part of the state; every county rejecting the convention by 60 percent or more of the vote was in the north.

Why did the anticonventionists win this contest? Among the foremost reasons was Coles's commitment and energy. He provided the base that allowed other factors, such as the growing strength and reach of the churches in Illinois, to come to the fore. John Mason Peck's energy in gathering the churches into a voting block and his efforts (covert as they may have been) in nurturing their support in a moral crusade against slavery were critical ingredients. Birkbeck's inspiring writings added energy and an important voice to the movement. And a case can be made that immigration from New England had accelerated in the past two years, giving an advantage to Coles and his faction.[108] Edward Coles's resources (the contribution of his entire income as governor and his purchase of the *Illinois Intelligencer*) and his aggressive organizing of an anticonvention resistance were central factors in the victory. Edward Coles addressed and advanced the conflict, developed the battle plan, and funded many of the key skirmishes. The churches formed regiments on the front lines, but it was primarily Edward Coles who prosecuted the contest and gained the victory. He demonstrated his adherence to the political ideology he learned as a student. He based his views on the belief that republicanism reflected fundamental natural law. Any action that deviated from natural law must be immediately identified as a threat to the republic. Such actions were those of selfish men bent on gaining power. If unchecked, Coles believed their selfish actions would lead to tyranny and the destruction of the republic.[109]

9

The Complaint

In August 1824 the victory seemed complete. Horatio Newhall rejoiced after the election: the conventionists were so defeated as to be almost ashamed to show themselves in public.[1] Newhall was all for casting out the proconvention office holders and electing good New Englanders like Sam Lockwood. In August 1824 it all seemed possible.

Edward Coles considered the convention fight the high point of his career. He cherished the affirmation. And he pointed to the success of the venture time and again with pride.[2] Though he considered 1824 his finest hour, Coles was deeply disturbed by the attacks upon his character and his principles. Years after the election, he complained of the unjust treatment that was returned for the honorable, consistent, and fully transparent positions he expressed publicly during his election as governor.[3] Coles's plea was simple: he had done just as he said he would. He could not understand why the conventionists had attacked him personally. The point of the dispute was slavery and the convention; personalities should never enter into such a difference. He could not understand the new politics where debate of ideas involved attacks on their sponsors. The two, idea and sponsor, were separate in his mind. His belief in the distinction made it impossible for him to understand the concept of party loyalty that developed in the next eight years. The Jacksonian lion cub was quickly maturing to become king of political beasts; soon it would rule the prairie and much else besides. Political parties were growing muscular, and political attacks were growing ever more personal. Coles was not of this era; he belonged to an era in which honor-bound public discourse was a common ethic (a Jeffersonian ethic). This personal attack for political gain took him into territory in which he was, proudly, a foreigner.

After the referendum and election of 1824, the legalization of slavery was a dead issue in Illinois. Enthusiasts kept their views hidden. Almost everyone was exhausted by the very topic. Yet, slavery clung like a leech to Coles, draining from him much of the joy he had gained from his victory.

Bond in Arrears

The convention issue was laid to rest in August of 1824, but convention-ists had started a court proceeding against Coles at the beginning of the year, and now they stirred the embers of that trouble. The Illinois' 1819 black code required that the owner of any slave brought into Illinois and freed in the state was obligated to post a $1,000 bond; failure to do so would incur a penalty of $200 for each person freed. The charge as-serted that Edward Coles had brought twenty slaves into the state and had neglected to post the required bond for $20,000. The defendant, at the court's March session in 1824, had pled the statute of limitations and brought various objections to the bench. The plea held, in essence, that as the alleged offense occurred on 4 July 1819, and as the charge against Coles was recorded on 7 January 1824, the commissioners were late by six months in keeping to the three-year statute of limitations. The commissioners, acting as complainants, filed a demurer to the plea; the court took the summer to ponder these matters.

In September 1824, the Madison County Circuit Court was brought to order. *County of Madison v. Edward Coles* was heard in the court of John Reynolds, a proslavery candidate for Congress who had lost to another proslavery man, Jesse B. Thomas, eight months earlier. Reynolds sustained the plaintiff's demurer to the statute of limitations plea. The defendant further pled *nil debit* (denying, that is, that he owed either the bond or the penalty). The case began in earnest. A jury was seated, and the combatants rolled up their sleeves for the heavy lifting.

James Turney, a private attorney in this case (otherwise, the state's attorney general), was brought in as prosecutor on behalf of the county commissioners. The arrangement with Turney was intended to inspire a great performance: no win—no fee.[4] The potential fee was set generously at $500. Hail Mason, a Madison County Commissioner and one of the plaintiffs (and formerly the Madison County Justice of the Peace who, in 1819, had recorded Coles's certificates of freedom), insisted on taking a direct hand in supervising the prosecution. He sat at the prosecution's table and held forth when it pleased him.

As the case opened, Mason objected to certain of the jurors, especially those known to be on friendly terms with the governor. Coles, represented in this proceeding by Henry Starr of attorneys Starr and Lockwood, offered no objection to the jury. Indeed, Coles refused to take exception to the proceeding in any way. His case would stand or fall solely on the merits of his honorable behavior.[5]

It was not until the case was well begun that Edward Coles discovered that the jury foreman, John Howard, was, in fact, a member of the Madison County Board of Commissioners. The setting, then: a proslavery judge on the bench, one plaintiff who was also a proslavery antagonist directing the prosecution, and another plaintiff sitting as foreman of the jury. Was ever a deck more neatly stacked?

The plaintiffs demonstrated the existence of certificates of emancipation dated 4 July 1819 and registered with the circuit court in Edwardsville. When Coles had arrived in Illinois in 1819, Daniel P. Cook warned him that each slave had to have his or her own certificate rather than just a copy of the general paper Coles had written on the Ohio River. Coles had followed this advice, making out new certificates and registering them on Independence Day. This date, then, was the recognized and recorded date, certifying (by implication) that Coles had brought slaves into the state and that freedom had been granted in Edwardsville, Illinois.

Coles tried to argue that this was only a technicality. He could prove that the people in question were freed in Kentucky on the Ohio River and that they were already freed when the certificates were registered in Edwardsville on the Fourth of July. He had registered the certificates as a formality and only after consulting with three lawyers. Ample witnesses could, in fact, attest to the actual date of emancipation.[6] The court turned a deaf ear.

Witnesses came and went for the prosecution. The defense was silenced. Literally, scarcely a word was permitted in court on Coles's behalf. Cook was sworn in but allowed to give no testimony. Madison County resident and state legislator Emmanuel J. West was prevented from taking the stand. Clerk of the Court Joseph Conway was called to testify as to the deaths of Ralph Crawford, Nancy Gaines, and Thomas Cobb. (And if the liveliness of the slaves is not relevant to the case, then, as historian Elihu Washburne says in his review of the events, the court could find it necessary to hold the county harmless from the support of dead men and women.)[7]

The defense offered to prove that these black people had entered the state as free persons and had exhibited documents to that effect at the border and that they were fully documented and had in all ways been treated as free persons in Illinois. Thus, the defense would show that the law was falsely applied in this case. Reynolds would not hear the argument. This would be oral testimony and (according to Reynolds's entirely unique and unfounded theory of evidence) could not be offered to explain a written document.[8] Cross-examination of prosecution witnesses by the defense was cut short by the bench. In sum, no point was permitted to be made to the jury on behalf of the governor. Hardly a word was spoken on his behalf.

The jury returned its verdict for the plaintiff. Penalty imposed in the amount of $2,000 ($200 in penalties for each slave emancipated) plus court costs.[9] Court was adjourned. The jury submitted a bill to the county for $27.00 in expenses.[10]

* * *

John Reynolds was a frontier breed of judge. He had been elected a judge of the Illinois Supreme Court in 1818 at the Kaskaskia Convention, which organized the new state of Illinois. At the time, he was a young lawyer in Cahokia, visiting Kaskaskia with friends and entirely disinterested in politics. He thought little of the emergence of the new state of Illinois. The General Assembly was embroiled in the appointment of officers; Reynolds was asked to run for a position as judge. He did so and walked away with one of four spots on the supreme court.[11] He was scarcely qualified. Historian Theodore C. Pease describes Reynolds as a "pantaloon peeping from behind his mask" and as having the fulfillment of "mental slovenliness."[12] His shortcomings proved no barrier to success. Reynolds would be elected governor of the state in 1830; he went to Congress in 1834 as a representative.

* * *

On 22 September, Coles requested a new trial. He had been falsely convicted, he argued. The court, he said, had rejected the testimonies of Cook, West, and Conway. The court had seated a plaintiff in the case as juror. Coles had been convicted of breaking a law that had not been published at the time of the supposed offense (thus it was not, according to the convention of the time, in effect). Finally, the verdict was contrary to law and evidence.[13] The request for retrial was continued to the March term of the court.

Life went on in Vandalia. On the day of the continuance, Edward Coles wrote to his friend Morris Birkbeck.[14] In the letter, he noted the resignation of David Blackwell as secretary of state. With pleasure, Coles offered this position to his trusted friend. Birkbeck accepted the offer and immediately traveled to Vandalia. He wrote to Coles from Vandalia, accepting the position on 9 October.

On 15 November 1824, three months after the election of legislators and defeat of the convention proposal, the Illinois legislature gathered in Vandalia for the political season. Governor Coles delivered his annual message on the next day. The legislature had been assembled early in order to finalize the selection of electors to represent the state in the nation's electoral college according to the federal timetable. Delicately and indirectly, he celebrated the results of the August convention contest. He went on to ask for progress in improving the state's contract law. He called for a thorough examination of the state bank. He then called for the final eradication of slavery in Illinois, revision of the Black Code, and tightening the laws against kidnapping (especially of free black people into slavery).[15]

Slavery in Illinois would not let Edward Coles alone; and he would not leave slavery alone. The list of miseries that opposition to slavery had visited on Coles was by now extensive. Yet, he continued to poke the wasp nest of slavery—he would rattle that nest as best he could, and if he got further stung, Edward Coles might rattle the nest some more.

Birkbeck had been at his side since October and, as secretary of state, was turning confusion and disorder in that office into a picture of order and arrangement.[16] Yet, confirmation by the senate was still required. The question came to the floor on January 15. Understand that the senate had not been transformed by the August election; it retained a proslavery majority. Here was Governor Coles, then, somewhat high and mighty in victory over the convention question, offering up for approval one of his strongest lieutenants in the slavery struggle. Birkbeck received a huffy and sneering rejection from the senate, providing dark satisfaction for the proslavery men. Birkbeck was rejected as secretary of state, having held the position under appointment by the governor for just three months.

A few months after this, Birkbeck attended court at Albion, county seat in his home county of Edwards. With court business done, Birkbeck joined with Judge James O. Wattles and certain lawyers in a visit to New Harmony, Indiana, the community experiment set up twenty miles away by well-known reformer Robert Owen. The visit provided a few days of pleasant socializing. Birkbeck and his son left the community shortly after a heavy rain. Crossing the creek opposite New Harmony on the west side of the Wabash River, Birkbeck, his son, and their horses were swept away in the current.[17] Morris Birkbeck was sixty-one years old when he died.

* * *

The legislature passed a law, during its 1824–25 term, removing penalties imposed by the March 1819 manumission law (including penalties already in suit). The law provided relief for defendants already joined in a suit on the condition that a bond would be submitted guaranteeing that any black person in question would not become a charge of the state. Any person wishing relief must also, by the terms of this act, pay court costs and damages. Furthermore, the legislature set aside, in specific, the verdict and judgment against Edward Coles.[18]

On 31 January, Coles paid the bond called for by the act of the legislature. He appeared before Conway, still clerk of the Madison County court, who witnessed the paying of this bond of $1,000. Coles went to the plaintiffs, offering to pay the costs of the court to date. He was turned down.[19]

The term for service of the Honorable John Reynolds, judge of the circuit court, had recently expired, so the legislature was called upon to consider reappointment. They turned Reynolds away. In his place, they installed Samuel McRoberts, who, according to Coles, was a violent advocate for slavery and harbored even more bitterness than his predecessor.[20] In March 1825, the circuit court of Madison County was brought to order with Judge McRoberts presiding. Coles submitted his plea based upon the legislature's recent action. The court was also considering the governor's request, submitted in September, for a new trial. Judge McRoberts overruled the request for a new trial, and he overruled the plea, based as it was on the legislature's recent act setting aside the verdict and judgment against Coles. The judge held that the legislature could not make a law to bar the recovery of the penalty in this case.[21] Washburne regards the findings of the McRoberts as "outrageous and indefensible."[22]

Coles called for a bill of exceptions to be sealed, which McRoberts did in a two-paragraph statement certifying that Coles had offered to prove that three of the immigrants identified in the suit had died and that the testimony had been prevented by the court; that Joseph Conway, witness for the defense, was not permitted to testify; that Daniel P. Cook had been called to testify for the defense, but his testimony was not permitted.[23] Coles appealed McRoberts's decision to the Illinois Supreme Court. The case was now fourteen months old. It would take another fifteen months before the question would finally be settled.

Following the trial, a verbal and written debate broke out between Coles and McRoberts. First off, McRoberts had his opinion in the case published in the newspapers; Coles responded with letters of his own pointing out errors of fact and of law in the judge's opinions.[24] During the summer of 1825, McRoberts lambasted Coles in the *Edwardsville (Illinois) Spectator*. Coles responded in measured fashion, but McRoberts was galled. He sued Coles for $5,000 in a private action and compelled the grand jury (of his own court) to indict Coles for libel in a second, public suit.

The Supreme Court of the State of Illinois sat in the spring of 1826 to hear the appeal of Edward Coles. The court found that the legislature was entirely competent in releasing Coles from the penalty imposed by the circuit court. That court had erred in declaring the law unconstitutional. Judgment was reversed. Coles was relieved from further penalty. The circuit court was instructed to receive the defendant's plea regarding the paying of court costs and the like.[25] McRoberts abruptly dropped both of his legal actions.[26]

The heat of the struggle gave way to a cool prairie breeze of vindication that settled happily on Edward Coles. For the rest of his life, Coles used the suits as evidence of his sacrifice in the cause of freedom. There is no doubt that the trial was a simple case of political harassment. He chewed with some bitterness on the challenge to his integrity represented by the charges leveled against him by the Madison County Commissioners. But he also took the manner of the circuit court in baldly denying him his own fair defense as a measure of the biases playing out in the system at the time. Yet, Coles did not try to use his vindication to turn the tables on his opponents as other politicians might have done. Edward Coles lacked the instinct to attack the jugular that marked later successful party politicians.

Lafayette in Illinois

In January 1824, President James Monroe asked Congress to extend an invitation to Marie-Josef-Paul-Yves-Roch-Gilbert du Motier, Marquis de Lafayette to visit the United States as a guest of the nation.

Lafayette's career had overflowed the Revolution in America. By 1824 he was a much-beloved enigma in France. He had agitated for democracy in France through the Revolution and the Napoleonic era. He had been a thorn in the side of the powerful and was a moderating counterweight to the dangerous excesses of the radicals. In France, he was a celebrity, but his influence was hemmed. He was an object of suspicion in the court of Louis XVIII, yet his readiness to defend the monarchy made him no *ami* to radical republicans. He was loyal to ideal, not to faction. It had cost him his fortune. Lafayette, now sixty-nine years old and no longer wealthy, sold off some cattle and borrowed to make the voyage to America.[27]

Americans harbored no equivocation about Lafayette. They loved him deeply and truly and thoroughly. He was, after all, a symbol. In this patriot-by-adoption, Americans saw themselves at their very best. In 1824, when Congress extended the nation's invitation to visit, Lafayette was regarded as second only to Washington in representing the ideal of American virtue. His visit to America in 1824–25 was a procession in triumph. It was a moment of national celebration, a moment of solidarity, a moment of excess. Illinois shared in the moment. And Lafayette's visit to Illinois was a time of sunshine in the otherwise mostly cloudy second half of Coles's administration.

Lafayette and his small entourage stepped off the packet ship *Cadmus* at the wharf in New York harbor on 16 August 1824. Lafayette was met at the wharf in New York's Battery by a jubilant throng of thirty thousand people. The parade up Broadway to City Hall drew fifty thousand. He stayed in New York until late September (with excursions to Albany and Boston) and then went on to Philadelphia. He toured the United States through every one of the nation's twenty-four states for thirteen months, the recipient of accolades, salutes, parades, honors, testimonials, and gifts. The tour became an industry. An endless stream of merchandise bearing the distinguished portrait of the nation's guest: plates, teapots, flasks, badges, flashes, silk ribbons, doilies, gloves, scarves, banners.[28]

In November, he went to Monticello. Madison came to him there. Madison, Jefferson, and Lafayette dined and talked, rekindling the warm feelings, and shared history that had tied them together, in sundry ways, through the decades of revolution and national development. Madison offered the toast: "Happy the people who have virtue for their guest and gratitude for their feast."[29]

By March 1825, Lafayette was in Raleigh, North Carolina. From there, he traveled south as far as Savannah, Georgia, then west to New Orleans, Louisiana. He wrote to Governor Coles from there on 12 April, saying that he would in all likelihood complete his visit of St. Louis, Missouri, on 29 April and was due to visit with General Andrew Jackson in Nashville and hoped, therefore, to be in Shawneetown, Illinois, by 8 May.[30]

Illinois was, of course, jubilant that Lafayette had accepted the official invitation extended by the Illinois General Assembly in November and the more personal invitation from Governor Coles in December.[31] Coles was acquainted with the marquis, having met him in Paris in 1816 during his European tour. Plans commenced for the welcome, but time was short, and details as to the general's itinerary were nonexistent. Two weeks were available between acceptance of Lafayette's letter and arrival of the great man. In the midst of the confusion and haste, Coles received word that Lafayette was arriving early. He stayed up the entire night writing a speech, only to find out that it had been a practical joke.[32]

Unwilling to be made a fool twice, Coles sent his aide-de-camp, Colonel William S. Hamilton, to St. Louis to receive Lafayette. (Hamilton was the son of Alexander Hamilton.) From St. Louis, Hamilton was to advise Coles as to the guest's proposed route of travel and exact timetable.[33] Coles apparently altered his plan, joining Hamilton in St. Louis for the momentous arrival. Lafayette's steamer came into sight and then streamed up to the wharf at St. Louis on 29 April. Coles shared with other dignitaries in the ceremonies and celebrations.[34] On the following morning, 30 April, Lafayette and his small party, together with Coles, Hamilton, Dodge, and others boarded the steamer *Natchez* bound eighty miles downriver for the Illinois town of Kaskaskia.[35] The *Natchez* arrived at about 1:00 P.M.

The people of Kaskaskia had not been advised as to the time that Lafayette would be arriving, and judging from the letter of introduction provided by Coles for use by Hamilton in meeting Lafayette, the itinerary was entirely unknown until the very last minute. When the *Natchez* docked at Kaskaskia, the Committee on Arrangements was hastily assembled. A carriage was commandeered, and citizens gathered frantically to process Lafayette to the house of General John Edgar, a soldier of the Revolution, who opened his house to the community for the occasion. Governor Coles delivered his speech of welcome on behalf of the people of Illinois.[36]

During the afternoon, while Lafayette was resting at the home of William Morrison, a prominent merchant, Auguste Lavasseur (Lafayette's secretary) and Lafayette's son were conducted to a nearby Indian camp. There they met a Native American girl who produced a letter of 1778, written by Lafayette to her father, a chief of one of the Six Nations, in thanks for his service during the revolution. The woman asked to see the writer of the letter.

The men returned to town and proceeded, in assembly with all the influentials whom Illinois could muster on short notice, to Sweet's Tavern, where a dinner was given and toasts offered up. After the dinner, as guests were moving to Morrison's home for a ball to honor Lafayette, Lavasseur went back to the Indian camp, returning with the woman he had met. She spent a half-hour with the marquis. No doubt, the ball soaked up whatever remaining energies were left to the town and its guests.

The next morning, Lafayette, his small entourage, and Governor Coles boarded the steamboat *Natchez* and continued the landmark tour of America's wilderness. At the Ohio River, the *Natchez* was replaced with a boat of narrower beam and generally of greater suitability for travel on the Ohio: the *Mechanic*. For the next week, they steamed up the Ohio. On 7 May, the *Mechanic* appeared below Shawneetown; she received a salute of twenty-four rounds as she drew up to the landing.

Folks from all around rushed to town; not a soul wanted to miss this unique experience. The crowd at the dock formed into two long lines from the edge of the Ohio all the way to Rawlings' Hotel; Lafayette passed though this citizen honor guard to Rawlings'. At the hotel, Lafayette was welcomed in a speech by James Hall, judge of the circuit court. A banquet and toasts followed. And Lafayette was back to the *Mechanic* by way of a similar honor guard of adoring citizens of Illinois. The steamer cast off. Another twenty-four rounds were fired in salute. Lafayette left the state.

Although a minor event in the glittering parade of honors heaped upon Lafayette in his remarkable tour of America, the visit of Lafayette was truly a high point in the administration of Edward Coles. It was an affirming event for the state and for Coles. It was also an expensive event for the state. The State of Illinois appropriated $6,475 for Lafayette's entertainment and transportation on the steamer *Natchez*. This amounted to almost one-third of the tax receipts for the year.[37]

The story of Lafayette's visit to Illinois held one more incident, however. At about midnight on 8 May, twenty-four hours after leaving Shawneetown, the *Mechanic* struck a log on the Ohio River and sank. No life was lost, but virtually all the luggage was lost to the river. Lafayette spent the night unprotected, drenched, and shivering in a hard rain. He emerged from this not much the worse for it, however. Ultimately, he passed on to Nashville, Tennessee, and kept his appointment with Andrew Jackson.

The Madisonian Republican

At times, the tenure of Governor Edward Coles seemed filled with stereotypes of frontier-style politics. In June 1825, a month after the departure of Lafayette, Governor Coles advised Adolphus Hubbard, his lieutenant governor, that he Coles would be away from the state for some months after 18 July.[38] Hubbard would act as governor in Coles's absence. Coles visited with his ally Roberts Vaux in Philadelphia during the summer, returning to Illinois on 31 October via Louisville. While in Louisville, Coles heard through a friend that Hubbard had settled nicely into his responsibilities as acting governor these past ten weeks and was proposing not to budge from his new perch.[39] Hubbard would claim that Coles had, in effect, abandoned the office of governor by his absence from the state. He had been encouraged in this by Coles's proslavery opponents. Presumably, they were eager to gain some small victory even in the final year in the tenure of the governor.

Governor Coles arrived in Vandalia and without hesitation or difficulty took up his governorship, but Hubbard would not cease. Two days after Coles's arrival on 2 November, Hubbard forced the issue by appointing William L. D. Ewing as paymaster general of the militia, an appointment that was a privilege reserved to the governor. Hubbard called for a ratifying countersignature on the commission from Secretary of State George Forquer. When Forquer refused, Hubbard went to the supreme court demanding that a writ of mandamus be issued, requiring Forquer to fulfill his office by signing the order. The petition was heard during the December 1825 term of the court. Hubbard was turned away by unanimous finding of the court; the writ was not issued.[40]

Hubbard was tenacious in his attempt to wrest the government from Coles. He went to the General Assembly during its session, requesting that it recognize him as the governor. He was turned away. Finally, he made separate presentations to each house, arguing the merits of his case to assume the governorship. These requests went nowhere. Hubbard's efforts faltered for want of support; his attempt to oust Coles stalled in tatters. This was inept buffoonery. The proslavery cause had sunk to pathetic theater. Hubbard, according to Theodore C. Pease, the "butt and jest of Illinois politics,"[41] was a minor but entertaining accomplice on the Illinois political stage. Hubbard included this in a stump speech during his unsuccessful run for the governorship in 1826 against Ninian Edwards:

> Fellow citizens, I offer myself as a candidate before you for the office of governor. I do not pretend to be a man of extraordinary talents; nor do I claim to be equal to Julius Caesar or Napoleon Bonaparte, nor yet to be as great a man as my opponent Governor Edwards. Nevertheless, I think I can govern you pretty well. I do not think that it will require a very extraordinary smart man to govern you; for to tell you the truth, fellow citizens, I do not think you will be very hard to govern, no how.[42]

Edward Coles seems not to have been very far off the mark in referring to Hubbard as a "simpleton."[43]

In 1826, the winds of national influence blew strongly through the race for governor. Whether it was the divisiveness of the convention issue, the bankruptcy of the caucus system, or just the ensuing confusion after 1824, politicians in Illinois began to talk about party discipline and national parties. Patronage began to have ties to party loyalty rather than to individual friendship. From these changes, the Jacksonians rose to power. But in the election of 1826 this new trend had not yet solidified in Illinois. Illinois had not yet transitioned to a modern party system.

The constitution forbade Coles from a second term so the office was contested among Edwards, Thomas Sloo, and Hubbard. Edwards's non-partisan appeal based on nostalgia and past service was successful. When the votes were counted Edwards had won a narrow victory—6,299 (49.2 percent) to Sloo's 5,940 (46.4 percent). The remaining pittance went to Hubbard. Though the margin was not as close as in the previous election, it was not a mandate from the people, either.

* * *

In 1826, Sukey and Manuel were struggling to build a secure life in St. Louis, living in a house located on a lot owned by Edward Coles. Presumably, the entire family had been freed by this time. Coles and the family had amended the terms and timing of emancipation several times. Coles's original arrangement with Manuel had anticipated repayment of the indenture price Coles had paid seven years earlier to keep the family together when they all left Virginia for a life in freedom. Repayment, according to the arrangement, would produce freedom for all. Coles also had created a document freeing Sukey in five years and the children at ages eighteen and twenty-one years in any event. Either way, the family would have been freed by the time Coles's administration ended in 1826. Coles noted with satisfaction in his 1844 "Autobiography" that Manuel did fulfill his agreement with Coles, paying back all that was owed.[44]

For the Crawfords, however, slavery was a state they had left behind some seven years before. Kate had remained at Coles's Prairieland Farm, and Robert worked by her side as a tenant on the farm, paying their former master in the amount of ten bushels of corn per acre, apparently a normal level of rent. Coles wrote that the productivity of the farm was expected to be fifty or sixty bushels per acre or eighty to one hundred bushels for Indian corn. The tenants were left a good income for their effort.[45]

Kate's eldest daughter, Betsy, had been about sixteen years of age when they first set foot in Illinois. Now, at the age of twenty-three, she married Jesse Price. The wedding certificate was dated 8 October 1826. Then, on 30 December 1826, Kate married Robert, her brother-in-law. They were married by Austin Sims.[46] Kate was fifty or fifty-one years of age; Robert was about thirty-two. Twelve months later, they all left Prairieland Farm. In 1827, Coles reported that two families had purchased improved farms of eighty acres each, possessing good houses, stables, barns, and fruit trees and would move to these farms in preference to the unimproved acreage he had purchased for them in 1819. In all likelihood, the two families were those of the newlyweds, Betsy and Jesse Price, and Polly (Robert's sister) and her husband, Michael Lee, who had married in 1822.[47] At some point, both of these families left the area for Decatur. Jesse Price became the "city scavenger" and grew quite wealthy from his work.[48]

Robert and his bride, Kate, moved from Prairieland also. Kate was now the owner of a farm of 400 acres, 320 of which had been given to her by Edward Coles in 1819; she had purchased another 80 acres. Coles describes her holdings as including horses, oxen, cows, cattle, sheep, and hogs. In short, he said, it was a farm as well stocked and with a house as comfortable and as well furnished and as neatly fixed as most of her white neighbors.[49]

Robert and Kate had two children: Ferdenand (born in 1831) and Richard (born in 1835).[50] Robert remained associated with Prairieland Farm, acting as Edward Coles's agent in arranging for renters of the acreage until at least 1843.[51]

* * *

The legislature assembled in Vandalia in December 1826. Ninian Edwards would be sworn in, and Edward Coles would fade from public service. Coles delivered his annual address (his valedictory, in fact) on 5 December. In it, he drew attention to the deaths of Thomas Jefferson and John Adams on July 4 the previous summer, and he called upon the legislature to assist the estate of Jefferson, as the author of the Declaration of Independence had died deeply in debt, such was Jefferson's generosity in entertaining the many friends and dignitaries who had imposed on his hospitality to the very last.

Coles called for revision of the Illinois criminal code. Again, he called upon the legislature to abolish slavery in the state and revise the Black Code. He drew special attention, this time, to the Black Code's presumption that a black person is to be considered a slave unless he or she can prove otherwise. Coles pleaded with the legislature to afford all black persons the presumption of freedom under the law.[52]

Coles echoed the traditional republican virtues—harmony, order, rationality. He then listed the problems still faced by the state. He pointed to the vast number of prairie properties in default for failure to pay taxes. To alleviate this, he recommended that the redemption period be extended and that taxes be cut by 25 percent. Coles believed that the state bank was stable. If the bank cut expenses, it could become a sound, profitable institution. Finally, Coles again requested that money be appropriated to construct a prison. He pointed in despair to counties that had pardoned criminals simply to save the expense of maintaining county jails.[53]

Coles's final message continued his efforts to make Illinois into a republican paradise. He advocated a tax cut to prevent the government from becoming too large a burden to the people. He demanded that individual rights be safeguarded. The only proposal that did not belong in the ranks of negative liberalism was his request for a penitentiary. Yet, given the developing interest in penal reform and its prospect for reforming the individual into a productive citizen, this, too, fell neatly into the realm of republicanism.[54] Coles's vision of republicanism had matured into a view that would accept positive government action. His recommendations for the penitentiary, the canal, the support of education, and bank regulation suggest a more active government than many early republicans wanted. This was no Jacksonian vision of the republic. Coles was in the line of his mentor, Madison, who led an executive branch in which government activity was allowed. This vision saw America growing prosperous and strong without falling into the trap of corruption and greed because the "Americans were to be active, diligent, and industrious, but not avaricious."[55]

The Want of You Is Felt

Coles left the governor's seat a popular man. One legislator wrote home that Coles, a man of business, could be elected again, no man in the state could beat him.[56] Nicholas Hansen wrote to Coles before Christmas that no man would refuse Edward Coles the character of an honest man and consistent politician. In short, Hansen said, "The want of you is felt."[57]

Coles's rising popularity came in some measure from Ninian Edwards's inaugural address. Edwards, having campaigned as a reformer, continued that stance in his address, attacking Coles. Some, like William B. Archer, cried foul: since Coles could not by law run again, he had no ready platform from which to defend himself against Edwards's attacks. Archer may have reflected many others in a letter to his friend Jacob Harlan when he criticized the indecent manner of Edwards's assertion of duplicity and corruption in the Coles administration.[58]

Coles's popularity was resilient and remained so for some years. When his name was included in the Fourth of July toasts at Vandalia the year following his retirement from the governor's office, it received nine cheers.[59] Throughout 1827, letters appeared in the newspapers praising Coles. The *(Vandalia) Illinois Intelligencer* credited him with a steady hand and granted him a public reputation for honesty.[60] Archer asserted that Coles was the best politician and, in his opinion, by far the most honest man in the state.[61]

But as politician Adam W. Snyder later pointed out, Coles never developed a personal faction or political following.[62] Except for Archer, no one mentioned Coles's political prowess. Coles seemed to have no interest in forming a party organization when he had the advantage. If he had come forward shortly after Cook's congressional defeat in 1826 and his own victory in the courts, he could have constructed an anti-Jackson force. Instead, he seemed unconcerned. He did not want to be a professional politician; he wanted to be a gentleman politician. The latter was a dying breed.

* * *

Through 1828 and 1830, Coles's name hovered on the fringes of politics. His staunch supporter Archer lamented to Harlan that John McLean instead of Coles had been elected unanimously to the senate.[63] Again in 1830, Coles's friends hoped for a bid, but he did not enter the fray. In fact, despite his popularity, Coles's position was relatively weak. He was supported by no major faction or party—national or statewide.[64] From 1828 through 1830, support from one of the blocs and a tie to the national party were vital for success. Had he sought such support and built such ties, he might well have gone far, but his image of the virtuous politician placed such self-service well outside the realm of propriety. Coles was not averse to further political adventures, but the governorship had been a painful experience. His political ideal was of the Jeffersonian republican sort with more than a dash of Cincinnatus tossed in. His old-fashioned view of politics as a personal gesture of public service was quickly giving way to the more powerful forces of Jacksonian party machinery.

One might view Edward Coles as hopelessly behind the times; he was a lonely champion of a bygone era. But the political circumstance was neither clear nor consummate at the time. Historian Gerald Leonard makes a convincing case that the emergence of Jacksonian "partyism" was both glacial and accidental in Illinois. The strength of national-party energy was neither assured nor anticipated during the 1820s.[65] Looking backward and with the comfort of leisurely study, Jacksonian politics has come to represent a Rubicon of American politics, but few saw it this way at the time. Coles was not the only one to miss the change. Illinoisans in droves resisted the Jacksonian call to party, and Coles was in good and plentiful company in not seeing the national-party system as the wave carrying American political power into the future.

The 1832 election marked the last time the race for Congress was statewide. By February 1831, the papers talked of a field of five candidates: Turney, who had prosecuted the case against Coles; Joseph Duncan, governor from 1834 to 1838; Judge Richard M. Young; Judge McRoberts, who sat as judge in the Coles case; and Charles Dunn.[66] By April, Young and McRoberts had dropped out. Within a month, Judge Sidney Breese had announced.[67] On 20 May 1831, Coles placed his name before the people. He came before them as the enlightened, best man, prepared to lead the citizens toward a moral, virtuous republic.[68]

In June, another man, William L. D. Ewing, joined the herd as a firm Jacksonian of the "whole hog" variety.[69] The race, in the end, was crowded with eight candidates.

* * *

Since his term as governor, Coles had made long trips out of the state. Some were on state business, selling canal bonds; others were merely social calls. To many, his absences signified weak ties and a lack of commitment to the state. Was he an Illinoisan at heart or just a part-timer? The issue that had slowed his rise in 1822 returned in 1831.

At this time in Illinois, most politicians identified themselves as Jackson men. Coles firmly repudiated all that the second party system was coming to stand for. His announcement revealed that he had not altered his campaign style or his political philosophy. The election of 1831 represented for Coles a final effort to prove, to himself at least, that the moral republic was alive in Illinois. In his campaign statement, Coles pointed with pride to his apprenticeship with Madison and his years as governor. Coles opposed many of Jackson's programs and made that clear. But he also presented several items that appealed to Illinois voters. He advocated the sale of public lands in blocks as small as forty acres. He endorsed the concept of federally supported internal improvements by calling for liberal land grants. He called on Congress to cede to the states the public lands still unsold within their borders. Coles laid out a program that demanded a more positive role for the central government but still placed eventual authority in the hands of the state. The federal government was to help with grants and exemptions. But the help was limited to stimulating the private or state sectors to carry the task to conclusion. Coles rejected the Jacksonian platform. His positions aligned him with much of the National Republican platform, yet he did not claim it as such and persisted as an independent.[70]

Edward Coles ran a dismal third behind Breese and Duncan. Duncan, the incumbent, won handily with 12,769 votes. Breese managed 4,522, and Coles 3,304. Further behind were Alexander P. Field (1,757) and Turney (1,115). Considering that Duncan had served two terms in the house and was well liked, his victory was not a surprise. The *Kaskaskia Advocate* called Duncan's victory a Henry Clay victory.[71] It was more Duncan's victory than Clay's, of course, but the election did show that an attachment to a national party or incumbency was necessary for a victory. Breese was a young man on the way up and had linked himself with Jackson. For both, the top contenders' party affiliation had a defining effect. For Coles, the defeat was traumatic and marked his political decline.

Coles was unwilling to accede to the emerging lure and compulsions of party. He was in the trailing, but still significant, cadre whose suspicions of party remained strong. True, he was marginally behind the times, but as historian Gerald Leonard points out, the emergence of party loyalty was a slow-moving political force in Illinois and did not have the state in its grip for some years to come.[72]

Coles had appealed to the people as the old hero and statesman and had been rejected. He had gone to them citing his past record, his association with the founding fathers, and had been rejected. He had gone to the people repudiating the cancer of partyism and Jacksonianism and had been rejected. To Edward Coles, Illinois had rejected him totally. Coles returned home to tend his wounds and contemplate his future—a "best man" rejected for a mere creature of party. The election defeat in 1831 ended Coles's permanent residence in Illinois. Throughout his Illinois residence, Coles had regularly returned to the east. After the lawsuit ended in 1826, the visits had become longer and longer. A break from Illinois seemed to be coming. Coles enjoyed all his visits to the east. His letters are filled with descriptions of parties and happy people. In 1831, after a winter away from Illinois, he wrote to Madison, "I remained in New York, where my acquaintance has become very extensive—visiting about 130 families and I enjoyed myself very much, the City having been unusually gay."[73]

After the election, he returned to Philadelphia; he left the state in October of 1831, just two months after the election. The move marked the end of Coles's life of service in politics. Never again did he run for elective office; never again did he hold an appointive office.

10

The Emancipator

Edward Coles returned to Philadelphia in the fall of 1831. He was forty-five years of age and single. He was well connected to Philadelphia society through frequent trips and extended stays in the city during the past fifteen years. Philadelphia had been a second home. He knew the Biddles and the Vauxes intimately. He knew many other families in the upper currents of Philadelphia's social pool. Coles had developed a taste for smart living twenty years before in Dolley's vibrant Washington salons and more recently in Biddle's party circuits in Philadelphia. Despite his republican protests, Coles had cultivated a taste for high society. Philadelphia, with its salons and clubs and the whirl of a lively society crowd, fulfilled him in ways that Illinois never did.

Here were diversion, business, and culture. Here could be a fresh start. He could turn his attention to managing his assets: western lands in St. Louis, large tracts and smaller parcels in Illinois (Prairieland Farm was still his and currently managed by Robert Crawford) as well as properties in Ohio and Kentucky. One might expect him to turn away from the things that had bruised him so in Illinois. The battles over slavery had exacted a price. So, too, had the exhausting convention struggle and the three-year case dragging him through the circuit and supreme courts as political punishment for opposing Illinois' slaveholders. The final insult (his rejection by the voters) was enough to propel him out of the state of Illinois toward a new life in Philadelphia. One can sympathize if Edward Coles wanted an entirely new life. It happened, however, that white society in Virginia was reeling from a racial emergency. The Virginia legislature would convene in December 1831 with good reason to believe that it would debate emancipation, finally. Coles could not, would not, stay out.

Fight against the Serpent

The impetus for breaking a legislative taboo in Virginia originated on Joseph Travis's farm. His was a small farm at Cross Keys, a remote, sparsely populated community in the scrublands of Southampton County (south of Richmond and about thirty miles from the North Carolina border). His slave Nat Turner was convinced that he had received messages from the Holy Ghost, sending him on a sacred mission to take up the yoke of Christ and "fight against the serpent" of slavery.[1] A solar eclipse in February 1831 convinced Turner that the time to fulfill his compact with the Holy Ghost was arriving. A second eclipse (a seeming trumpet calling Turner to action) occurred in mid-August.[2] Turner put his plan into motion one week later on 20 August. Turner and six others, in the depth of night, climbed a ladder and entered the home of his owner through an open window. In short order, all five members of the family were axed in their sleep. The insurgents grabbed guns, powder, and horses. They rode into the night toward the little town of Jerusalem. Other slaves joined up. In that night, the band would kill almost every person in a twenty-mile radius around Travis's farm at Cross Keys—fifty or sixty people.[3]

By morning, the word had spread throughout the landscape and well into Richmond. A dreadful fear began to seep into the populace, choking the sunrise with a realization that no white person might be safe from the marauding slaves. In Appomattox, Fannie Berry, a slave about ten years in age, was just clearing her master's table. In her own words, she reported that her mistress ran up to the dining room window, hollering, "De niggers is arisin', De niggers is arisin', De niggers is killin' all de white folks—killin' all de babies in de cradle!"[4]

By afternoon, a small militia located the troupe of more than twenty armed slaves in a cornfield just a few miles from Jerusalem. The insurgents were dispersed, and those not quick enough to flee were killed on the spot. In the next three days, a small army of three thousand troops was assembled and dispatched to the area. Most of the insurgents were caught and jailed, and in all likelihood a hefty sample of innocents joined them. Forty-eight were crammed into the county jail to await trial. But Nat Turner still ran free. For some weeks, Turner could not be found.

The white population, transforming his mysterious disappearance into a looming evil, was consumed by dread. Some left their homes; some sought refuge in neighboring counties; some took protection in local shelters. Rumors of supportive uprisings in other parts of the state fanned the anxieties of the white countryside. The trials of insurgent black slaves began on 31 August. Nat Turner still ran free. On 30 October, the searchers found him in an underground hideout near the Travis farm not far from Cross Keys. He surrendered without resistance.

On 5 November, Jeremiah Cobb, presiding judge in the Southampton Circuit Court, sentenced the slave Nat Turner to be hanged the following Friday. On Friday, he was hung at one o'clock. Fear and despair, like a fog, had settled on Virginia's farms, plantations, and towns. The execution of Nat Turner did little to relieve it. Repressed fears about the dangers of slave insurrection burst above the surface and flowed like a river over its banks. Nobody felt safe. Was the time ripe to address the problem of slavery head-on? Were the dangers to family, farm, and wealth just too high? What kind of life is it to live always in the grip of fear? As the legislative season dawned in the waning days of 1831, Virginians knew that a debate on slavery would emerge out of the shadows and take center stage.

In late December 1831, having arrived in Philadelphia only weeks before, Coles wrote an impassioned letter to Thomas Jefferson Randolph, grandson of the third president and current Albemarle County representative in Virginia's House of Delegates. Nat Turner was dead just forty-nine days. It was a directive plea, a substantive proposal encouraging Randolph to work for the emancipation of Virginia's slaves (much as Coles had pleaded, unsuccessfully, with his grandfather in 1814): "For God's sake step forward & put a stop to this downward course [i.e., the evil of slavery]—hold out the inducements to the Whites to remain, and not by emigrating increase the more rapidly the relative number of the Blacks—restore to the one colour their rights, to the other their consistency—and to the dear 'Old Dominion,' our common Mother, that station to which she is justly entitled."[5]

There was no need, in fact, to convince Thomas Jefferson Randolph of the necessity for emancipation. As manager of Monticello for many years, Randolph had witnessed firsthand the economic disaster that was slavery on his grandfather's plantation. Following Jefferson's death, Randolph, as executor of the estate, had sold his grandfather's slaves and managed his grandfather's monumental debt. Slavery was a gaping sore in Virginia that Randolph felt keenly. Both his mother (Jefferson's daughter Martha) and his father (former Governor Thomas Mann Randolph) had expressed deep opposition to the institution of slavery.[6] Randolph's wife, Jane, was deeply troubled by the Nat Turner affair. None of those close to him provided any drag holding back Randolph from taking an active, if politically risky, role in pushing emancipation forward.

Coles, having made contact with Randolph's antipathies toward slavery, then proposed a concrete plan. It involved setting a tax on the black population for the purpose of building a fund to transport free blacks out of the state. Children born after a certain date should be transferred by sale to the state for rearing and then work to pay off their debt and the cost of their transport out of the state.[7] If the legislature is unwilling to act, said Coles, then let a referendum on the matter give voice to the people.

Coles shows the product of much experience in the business of resisting slavery. He was well aware of the fears. He had willingly sacrificed some of his wealth in the pursuit of emancipation of his own slaves. Still, he understood that uncompensated emancipation was not a formula that would work generally. Slavery represented too large a portion of the wealth held by Virginians. The economic disruption would be colossal. Resistance would be resolute. He knew slave owners would have to be fully compensated for emancipation.

Coles pointed to the declining value of slaves as laborers in Virginia. Timing was right for action to remove slaves from the labor pool. Virginia had a surplus of labor. From an economic point of view, the chief value of slaves in those days was in their sale to the cotton lands in the deeper south, he said. The value of labor in Virginia, meanwhile, was generally depressed so long as slavery dominated the supply.[8]

Coles proposed a *post-nati* plan that was designed, it seems, to be acceptable to the white population.[9] Emancipation would occur without cost to white Virginians: slaves and free African Americans would shoulder all (or most of) the costs through taxation and required labor. Clearly, the plan was to rid the state of slavery, not to create racial equality. All African Americans would be compelled to participate whether they approved of the plan or not. Free black persons would not be free to refuse deportation and resettlement.

* * *

Virginia's legislators gathered in Richmond early in December; the weather was unusually chilly: high winds whisked up a light snow, hiding slushy ice under little drifts on the cobbled roads and cartways. The House of Delegates convened in the old capitol designed by Jefferson. Straight-backed narrow benches were too few for the growing membership of the General Assembly so additional seats had been nailed to the floor to accommodate the expanding numbers. Governor John Floyd presented his annual message on 6 December. Primary on his agenda was the "melancholy subject" of the trouble in Southampton County. Black preachers must be silenced; religious assemblies must be banned. Slaves must be restricted to their plantations. In short, all slave laws must be revised to ensure that slaves would have no response to their "due subordination."[10]

The speaker of the house appointed a thirteen-member committee to review various responses to the "insurrectionary movements" of recent weeks. Proposals, petitions, and memorials began to flow in. Many called for the colonization of free black persons. Support for colonization and its intent to empty Virginia of its black population had gained ground. Others called for greater controls (barring, for example, both free and slave black persons from mechanical trades).

Two weeks later (on 10 January), Delegate William O. Goode asked for a report on progress of the special committee. Chairman William H. Brodnax reported that the memorials and petitions had been organized into two categories: those dealing with the removal from the state of free black people and those regarding the "gradual extinction of slavery." Next day, Delegate Goode rose. He couldn't wait the week. He moved to discharge the committee from further consideration of the emancipation question. The General Assembly had no right, said the delegate, to confiscate private property. On the other hand, funds were not available to compensate owners. As the state was, in effect, powerless to act, let it not proceed with this game.

Freshman Delegate Thomas Jefferson Randolph of Albemarle County took the floor. The proposal he countered with opened a chasm, and the legislature fell right in. He proposed, in short, that this question of emancipation be submitted to the voters of Virginia. Allow the people, he said, to determine slavery's fate. If a majority of the people supported emancipation, the legislature would act. Let all slaves born on or after 4

July 1840 become state property at the age of eighteen for females and twenty-one for males. Until that time, he proposed, they would be hired out so that their labor would contribute to the cost of "removing them beyond the limits of the United States."[11] Randolph pointed out that this approach satisfied the major objections of those opposed to emancipation. Slaveholders could sell their slaves in the cotton states before 1840 to receive full market compensation. And emancipated slaves would be colonized at no cost to white society.

The effect of Randolph's motion was to open a floodgate. Edward Coles's plan (bearing a strong resemblance to the strategy proposed by Jefferson in his "Notes on the State of Virginia") joined with the well-timed effort of Randolph in cancelling a long-standing unspoken political taboo. The spell of silence had been broken. Open debate about the possibility of emancipation was made not just possible but even necessary. The question would play out on the floor of the legislature. For two weeks, the debate raged on the floor; the gallery was filled to capacity each day. Speakers took the floor to defend conservative claims of constitutional rights to property, and *post-nati* abolitionists to promote public safety and the greater good. Without exception, the debate revolved around identifying what might be the greatest good for white residents of Virginia. The interests of the slave and freed black populations saw not even the dimmest light of discussion in those winter days at the capitol in Richmond. Still, the capacity to discuss the future of slavery had been enlarged by a prescient letter from Edward Coles and the application of its contents by a courageous and resolute freshman delegate from Albemarle County.

On 16 January, the house endorsed a report by the special committee headed by Delegate Brodnax. It was "inexpedient" for the house to enact any legislation regarding the abolition of slavery. Added to this finding, however, was a preamble, voted on separately, proposed by Delegate Archibald Bryce, proclaiming that emancipation and removal of the black population would await a more propitious time. Virginians would look forward to final abolition at some time in the future, the preamble said. Never before had the Virginia legislature adopted a view that slavery might not be permanent. It would (indeed should) be ended some day.

This action/nonaction of the legislature was celebrated. White Virginians of every tone in the political spectrum could claim some form of victory. But those opposed to slavery demonstrated their rather large constituency. Virginia was not a single-minded block of slavers, after all. Internal regional differences figured large in the landscape of opinions on slavery. Even eastern and "southside" conservatives were not all of a single mind on the virtues of slavery. The debate over slavery exposed the divisions between those counties with few slaves and those with large slave populations. As such, the debate also became part of the larger debate over representation and the qualifications for voting.[12] And the antislavery voice was heard in Virginia. It registered as it had not done before.

11

The Devastating Truth of Madison's Will

As the Virginia House of Delegates was in the midst of its debate on the proposal Coles had sent to Randolph, Coles was undertaking another project for emancipation. Edward Coles and James Madison were in frequent communication during 1830 and 1831. A series of letters from Coles made demands on Madison's time and judgment regarding whether federal lands within state borders might be considered state assets for the purpose of making internal improvements. They corresponded on the nullification controversy with Coles supporting Madison's efforts to counter nullification, recoiling over the dangers presented by President Andrew Jackson's subversive influence to exalt the states (and critical of Madison's unwillingness to publicly condemn Jackson).[1] Notwithstanding the warmth shared in the relationship between Coles and Madison, this string of letters betrays a growing shortness of patience by the increasingly frail Madison.

* * *

Christmas 1831. James and Dolley Madison were at Montpelier. Madison, now eighty years, was harassed by rheumatism. Edward Coles was there for part of the season. During this visit, Madison confided in Coles that he wished to arrange for the emancipation of his own slaves through his last will and testament. Together the two men reviewed the difficulties of restoring Madison's slaves to freedom.[2] How to do it was not obvious.

Foremost was the controversial and precipitous manner in which George Washington had freed his slaves: a model of emancipation that Coles and Madison each found wanting. Washington was eager to free his slaves for moral reasons. He also recognized that his plantation was oversupplied with laborers. His hastily prepared will had specified that his own slaves should be granted freedom upon his wife's death. In effect, the barrier to freedom was reduced to Martha's life. Both Coles and Madison perceived dangers in Washington's plan. Martha Washington sensed the problem directly and freed the family slaves early (in 1801) as a means of avoiding the threat. Neither Coles nor Madison felt that Washington had got it right, yet this very approach was initially the mode proposed by Madison to Coles.

Madison's priorities seemed to begin with the comfort and safety of his beloved wife. The two discussed problems of emancipating the slaves during her lifetime. She was, after all, accustomed to the routine and comforts of slave service. And she was used to the responsibility of managing a household through a large coterie of "servants." Without slaves, Dolley might have a very difficult time managing Montpelier at all. But other problems figured, too—practical problems beyond the comforts and direct needs of Dolley Madison.

Elderly slaves (of which Madison owned a large number) would have difficulty in providing for themselves once freed. Freedom for these, with no employment or other means of support, was consignment to poverty after a life of service. (Honor to a Virginia gentleman was more than the taking of comfort. It was tied to fulfilling obligations of providing for those "under" one's care—the elderly, infirm, and the young.)[3]

Consider also those married to slaves on neighboring plantations (a common occurrence and in many cases a preferred strategy, according to Madison, who points out in a 28 March 1823 letter to Dr. Jedediah Morse that slaves often preferred a spouse on another farm as it afforded opportunities to "go abroad," providing a sense of geographic flexibility). Emancipation would often force a choice between love of freedom and the bonds of family. For a quarter century, the law in Virginia had stipulated that freed slaves must leave the state within twelve months or risk reenslavement. This provided families with difficult choices where only some members were to be freed.

Moral and ethical questions persisted, and financial difficulties needed answers. Madison and Coles recognized that in freeing Virginia slaves, one must add to the cost of casting assets to the wind additional costs of transporting these now-freed slaves to any distant land that would accept free black immigrants. Within the United States, the list of possible states was short and growing shorter. The door for free African Americans had closed shut in many states and territories; it was closing rapidly in others.[4]

Or were one to transport them to a foreign country, consider the difficulties and expense of providing transport and settlement costs for entire families, some of whom would have members on neighboring farms who might not be made free. The emancipation of slaves required more than the setting of pen to paper. Virginia's Black Code infused emancipation with a wooly knot of challenges logistical, financial, and moral. Coles reports that these messy issues were covered in his discussions with Madison.[5]

When Coles left Montpelier, no final agreement was in place. Madison had not declared how he would proceed. But they had agreed that emancipation could and would be achieved for Madison's slaves. Coles did not abandon the conversation. On 8 January 1832, Coles wrote to Madison and encouraged him to commit to a scheme to free his slaves through his will. Were the slaves not to be freed, Coles asserted, Madison would suffer in history's judgment of him. Coles proposed to Madison that after a certain number of years following his death, slaves younger than a certain age should be freed. Those older would remain slaves, and their support would be the responsibility of Madison's heirs. Setting the date for the emancipation would be determined by the condition of the estate (Mrs. Madison's need for support versus the costs of emancipation) and by the need for the younger slaves to earn enough to transport themselves to Africa and support themselves after arrival. Satisfying the problems of intermarriage among slaves on different plantations, neighbors could be persuaded to exchange slaves as necessary to keep families intact. Otherwise, the slaves themselves might make a decision between "the natural love of liberty and the endearing ties of family." In general, however, Coles believed that the complications and pain associated with emancipation were small when compared with the blessings of liberty. Indeed, as time goes on, he reflected, the complications increase (as marriages continue to occur and children are born, complicating the networks of families and the painful decisions of leaving family members behind for freedom elsewhere), leading to the need to emancipate sooner rather than later.[6] Coles clearly believed that Madison's slaves would be freed.

James Madison died on the morning of 28 June 1836, some 5½ years after he had, seemingly, committed to freeing his slaves by his will. His will said, in part, "I give and bequeath my ownership in the Negroes and people of colour held by me to my dear wife, but it is my desire that none of them should be sold without his or her consent, or in the case of their misbehaviour; except that infant children may be sold with their parent who consents for them to be sold with him or her, and who consents to be sold."[7]

* * *

Edward Coles was fifty years of age when Madison died. Coles fumed with incredulity when he learned of the terms of Madison's will. In fact, he smoldered for some years, chewing bitterly on Madison's failure to emancipate his slaves. Coles had squared all of Madison's concerns about posthumous emancipation, or so he had believed. And Madison had agreed to it, or so Coles thought. Yet, nothing came of it. No freedom granted. No bondage renounced. Not a soul freed. Not one.

The failure was more than distasteful to Coles. The blame, he came to believe, rested with one of his own family. Coles's frustration in the summer of that year howls from the pages of his letters. Through his sister Sarah Coles Stevenson, he leveled (on 28 July) a remarkable accusation at her husband, Congressman Andrew Stevenson. "His slaves not emancipated! For this Mr. S.[tevenson] will have much to answer," he fumed. "And I am grieved by the reflection that I should have contributed to it by my indiscretion in communicating to Mr. S. what Mr. M.[adison] contemplated."[8]

Sarah (Sallie to her family) was one month into her husband's appointment as envoy and minister to Britain's Court of St. James.[9] She was younger than her brother Edward by two years, and she was a favorite niece of Aunt Dolley Madison, as familiar as any of the Coles with the rambling plantations at Montpelier and Monticello. In 1816, she had married Andrew Stevenson, a Richmond lawyer whose rise began quickly with election to the Virginia legislature. By 1821, Stevenson was a member of the House of Representatives in Washington. In 1827, he succeeded Henry Clay as speaker of the house, where he presided with considerable skill over a tumultuous Congress for seven exhausting and eventful years. With his resignation as house speaker in 1834, Stevenson was nominated to the key diplomatic post in London by Andrew Jackson but was rejected by the Senate. Edward Coles had worked energetically and would continue to assist his brother-in-law in securing the appointment through 1835.[10] The appointment was pressed once more in 1836 by the White House and passed by a close vote in the senate.

Coles's letter to his sister in July of 1836 was prickly with the suspicion that he had been betrayed by Andrew Stevenson.[11] Coles, in recalling the confidence he had shared with Stevenson about Madison's intentions, leveled a remarkable charge. At the feet of his sister, he lay the angry allegation that her husband had taken the initiative in talking Madison out of manumitting his slaves at his death. How else to explain the devastating truth of Madison's will?

Stevenson had, it is true, spoken with Madison and in general conversation condemned individual manumission. He especially faulted eminent southerners of status and position who freed their slaves. Madison reacted later by confronting Coles and charging him with betraying to Stevenson the confidentiality of their earlier conversations. Madison then asserted that Stevenson's arguments had not changed his mind. But now, with the slaves not freed, Coles was forced to consider that Stevenson had been successful in turning Madison from their plan of emancipation, undoing carefully laid plans to affirm the republican ideals that he shared with Madison.[12]

Coles was not so deeply buried in recrimination, however, that he could not suppose a final salvation for the slaves of James Madison. Perhaps a second will exists somewhere. Could there be a miraculous deliverance for the hundred souls left in bondage?[13] But Coles was well off the mark, and it took him almost twenty years to satisfy himself as to what had happened and to reconcile Madison's will with his own knowledge of the man.

Coles's letter of 28 July 1836 to his sister, accusing her husband of dissuading Madison from posthumous emancipation was the first in a series of awkward family letters. Sallie wrote back denying the accusation. Andrew was at a loss on the matter. He had no recollection of any discussion with Madison that might have been so misunderstood. Edward wrote again to his sister on 12 November 1836 with more painful news; he recoiled with horror from the scene of slave traders he witnessed at Montpelier during his visit in August. It was, he said, like the hawk among the pigeons. Madison had died without freeing one of them. And in so doing, Coles wrote, Madison's widow was now saddled with the painful task of managing a declining household oversupplied with slaves.[14]

In the end, Coles came to settle the blame for the continued enslavement of James Madison's human property on Dolley Madison. As time went on (as various willed legacies flowed from the Madison estate and as the historically priceless papers of James Madison attracted little commercial attention), Coles came to better appreciate the plight of his cousin. Yet, he never forgot the plight of Madison's slaves and the role that his cousin (daughter of one of the first Virginia Quakers to voluntarily free all of his slaves) played in perpetuating slavery in the Madison household. Coles came to this view after time, and chance delivered clues to the mystery of Madison's intentions.

It may have been by happenstance that Coles found William Taylor (kinsman of Madison and buyer of sixteen of his slaves in 1834) at Warm Springs thirteen years after Madison's death. There, in the pampered environs of one of the more fashionable retreats in the mountains framing Virginia's Shenandoah Valley, Coles uncovered a critical tidbit. William Taylor told Coles that it was Robert Taylor of Orange County who had drawn up the last will of James Madison. According to Nellie Willis (favored niece of Madison), Taylor went on, Madison had mentioned his wish to free his slaves but felt the difficulties were too great in doing so while his wife was alive. Madison had assured Robert Taylor that Mrs. Madison well knew his wishes "and would carry them into effect at her death." Back in Philadelphia, Coles spoke with Henry Clay about his recent conversation with William Taylor. Clay confirmed it: Mrs. Madison had said to him that her husband expected her to emancipate the slaves at her death.[15]

On 10 December 1855 (six years after the chance meeting with William Taylor and nineteen years after the death of Madison), Coles wrote to Willis (now seventy-four years of age), asking her straight out (after initial pleasantries, standard in all well-bred letters) if she knew her uncle's wishes and intentions as to the freeing of his slaves, and why he did not do it in his will.[16] Could she confirm Robert Taylor's assertion that Mrs. Madison well knew her husband's wish that she should emancipate the family's slaves?

Willis's fingers were stiff and painful from rheumatism; she called upon her son, John, to respond to Coles's letter. She confirmed Robert

Taylor's view. Taylor had told her that Dolley had received her husband's instructions to emancipate the family slaves at her own death. She went on: Madison was committed to freeing his slaves, but certain "difficulties" prevented him from fulfilling this object. Madison considered the slaves to be essential to Mrs. Madison's comforts, given that Madison's property was generating but little profit in agriculture. And Madison, recognizing the error committed by Washington in emancipating his slaves not by his own will but at the death of Mrs. Washington, decided that he could not effect the emancipation himself but must leave it to Dolley to emancipate the slaves in her own will. This would be the safer mode.[17]

Not only had Madison an expectation that Mrs. Madison would free the slaves, Mrs. Willis believed that Madison had left written instructions on the subject. John Willis, for his mother, elaborates: "On the day of Mr. Madison's burial when his body was carried to the grave, Mr. Conway and my mother remained with Mrs. Madison in her chamber. She then took from the drawer two sealed papers, the one endorsed 'My will, opened and resealed by myself' the other endorsed 'To be opened only by my wife should she be living at the time of my death.' The last paper of which nothing more was ever heard was thought to have contained written directions on the subject of the slaves."[18]

The evidence that James Madison left clear instructions regarding the disposition of his slaves is strong but not conclusive. Perhaps they *were* written down in so many words. It would have been like the trusting Madison to feel safe in the belief of her loyalty. She had supported him always. And Madison was ever slow to recognize the limits of a person's fidelity.

What was the final act in this slavery drama? What was the fate of Madison's slaves? Did Madison's approach to emancipation in any way whatsoever serve interests beyond his own?

Those slaves sold by Mrs. Madison immediately after the death of her husband (and referred to in Edward Coles's letter to his sister of 28 July 1836) may have been few. Paul Jennings and a few others (probably about four in number) entered into the service of Mrs. Madison. In a brief commentary published in 1865, Jennings attests to purchasing his own freedom from Mrs. Madison.[19] (Evidence shows, however, that Dolley sold Jennings to Pollard Webb for $200 on 28 September 1846. After this, Daniel Webster paid $120 in a second transfer. It was Webster who allowed Jennings to work under contract for his freedom at the rate of $8 per month.)[20] Mrs. Madison's state so declined, Jennings related, that he transferred gifts of money from his own pocket to that of his former owner.[21]

And the rest? By the fall of 1844, all but thirty were sold. For the slaves of James Madison, as much as for Dolley Payne Madison and John Payne Todd, 1844 was a year of despair and loss. It was the final undoing of Montpelier and the unraveling of James Madison's legacy to his wife. At least a few score of the Madison slaves were sold under circumstances that James Madison had not anticipated. Surely, he could in no measure have imagined that his wife's worldly wealth would take such a dramatic plunge. And surely, we speculate, he would not have stood in the way of his wife's selling the slaves had he but known what her circumstance was to be.

Dolley and Payne sold off Montpelier and most of the family slaves in late 1844 to Henry Moncure of Richmond. This flurry of action and the final disposition of all but thirty of the Madison family slaves were necessitated by debts coming due, a lack of cash on hand, and the threat of seizure of assets created by a case in chancery court, *Madison v. Madison*. The case was brought by executors of the estate of William Madison (James Madison's younger brother) over business more than forty years old related to a disputed debt of $2,000 from the estate of Colonel James Madison, father of both. The suit petered out in 1846 with an injunction freeing Dolley of the debt. The loss of Montpelier and the sale of the slaves were arguably necessary expedients in the midst of this trouble. And it prevented a worse fate from overtaking the slaves of Montpelier: outright sale at open auction leading almost certainly to the splitting of numerous families.

Dolley Madison passed away on 12 July 1849. She held in her possession five slaves, and they were not freed by her will.[22] Payne Todd passed away just three years later. His will stipulated, remarkably, that all of his slaves should be freed.[23] He gave freedom in death (freedom for all and $200 for each), having generated only misery in life. It was a singular, shining gesture of his life and quite out of character. But his estate was not solvent. As slaves are assets, freedom by will is granted only after estate debts are satisfied. In all likelihood, any slave not sold by Todd in life was sold by the sheriff after his death in 1852 and not freed.

And so, we conclude, they were all sold. Dolley Madison did not honor the wishes of her husband. One question lurks inside this observation, and, in fairness, it can remain in the background no longer. Is it more correct to say that she *could* not free the slaves or that she *would* not free the slaves?

James Madison would scarcely have foresworn what she did in selling the family slaves to protect her very solvency. Madison would have been saddened, surely, but he probably would have done the same. Had he known that his notes from the Constitutional Convention would be unsuccessful in providing her with the remuneration contemplated in the will, had he known that his brother's estate would girdle her with a troublesome and embarrassing court case, had he known the desperate straits that she would weather year in and year out . . . he would surely have relented. He would have sold the slaves. This is speculation, yet it is consistent with the priorities he brought to bear in setting out his will. He held the comfort of his wife to be primary and the freedom of his slaves to be, perhaps, next. Still, the question of Dolley's culpability cannot be dismissed quite so easily. It is in her ready sale of slaves in 1836, as referred to in Edward Coles's letter to his sister of 12 November 1836, that one sees Dolley's apparently willful disregard of her husband's instructions to emancipate the slaves (or, at the very least, not to sell them against their wishes, as stipulated in the will). It is in the sale of slaves in 1836, when her finances were not under great strain, that one sees Dolley Madison's apparent disinterest in (or perhaps even contempt for) the virtue of emancipation.

Madison had set before his wife certain duties to accomplish after his passing. One was the publication of his notes on the Constitutional Convention, and the other was the freeing of the family slaves. She embraced the first and repudiated the second.[24] Edward Coles was correct. The failure of James Madison to emancipate his slaves rests to a great extent on the shoulders of Dolley Payne Madison. Of the sales occurring in 1844 and thereabouts, one may have considerable sympathy for her circumstance and may even assert that her actions were successful in keeping families together when a sheriff's sale would surely have torn them apart. Of those sold in 1836, however, one must surely recognize her entire lack of sympathy for the cause of emancipation.[25] In passing control of his slaves to Dolley, Madison made the mistake that

Washington had not. Washington had ensured that his slaves would be freed (at some reputed risk to his wife). Madison had ensured the safety of his family, and for that, he had unwittingly sacrificed the freedom of his slaves. It is fair to confirm the sentiments of Edward Coles: Madison's escutcheon is not spotless.

12

The Aging Historian

F anny Trollope visited Philadelphia in 1827. She went on and on about the market. It is, she said, the very perfection of a setting for the serious householder to engage in the important office of caterer. Every aspect of it (the dairy, the poultry yard, the spoils of forest and river) produced the effect of rhapsody.[1]

The Philadelphia city market was, in the 1830s, a well-groomed celebration of abundance. It started almost at the public landing on the Delaware River and ran seven blocks up the middle of High Street (later named Market Street) to Eighth Street; almost a mile of open-air stalls. Ann Newport Royall was every bit as complimentary as Mrs. Trollope: "Nothing can exceed the whiteness of the benches and stalls. . . . The butchers wear a white linen frock, which might vie with a lady's wedding dress."[2]

This Philadelphia was home to Edward Coles during his final thirty-seven years of life. It was a gay and exuberant urban hub, the very picture of plenty and industry, especially for those close to the top of the social order. The bustling city of 189,000 people in 1830 grew commerce, government, and salons. A few streets west of the market area, where the noise and dust were not quite so overwhelming, fine homes surrounded a smaller market, a diverse collection of churches and the U.S. Mint at Penn Square. In this neighborhood, Edward Coles first made his Philadelphia life.

Edward Coles's two-decade search for a wife ended when he married Sally Logan Roberts, a cousin of Roberts Vaux. Probably Coles met her after 1826. They were married on 28 November 1833 by Bishop William

Heathcote DeLancey. The couple then toured the Atlantic coast where Coles introduced his bride to friends and relatives.[3]

Portrait of Edward Coles by J. Henry Brown, 1852. Courtesy Winterthur Museum.

Portrait of Sally Logan Roberts Coles (1809–83) by J. Henry Brown, 1853. Courtesy Winterthur Museum.

Sally Roberts was the daughter of Hugh Roberts of Pine Grove, a suburb of Philadelphia.[4] The family was firmly tethered to the luminous upper reaches of Philadelphia society. Hugh Roberts's sister Elizabeth, for instance, married William Rush, the son of Dr. Benjamin Rush, a signer of the Declaration of Independence, originator of the first anti-slavery society in America, and one of the best-known physicians of the time. Hugh Roberts's aunt (his father's sister) had married Richard Vaux, whose son was Roberts Vaux, the busy Quaker philanthropist who had assisted Coles in the struggle in Illinois and who was a leading citizen of the city. His son, Richard, would become mayor of Philadelphia.

Sally Roberts was a sixth-generation Philadelphian; in 1682, her great-great-great grandfather, Hugh Roberts, had come to America with William Penn, settling at Merion, Pennsylvania, just a few miles from Philadelphia. The Roberts's rested firmly and comfortably, close to the top of Philadelphia social strata.

Rise and Decline

Coles was restless in Philadelphia. For a few years, his letters hinted at returning to Illinois.[5] He had business interests in land and would make occasional trips to Edwardsville to protect those interests. But his political prospects had evaporated, and his friendships in Illinois had withered especially after Morris Birkbeck's death in 1824. His connections with Illinois began to fade. With the birth of his first child, in 1835, all thoughts of returning to Illinois vanished.

Mary Coles was born on 2 April 1835. The Coles were living on Chestnut Street, directly across from the U.S. Mint.[6] It was a busy part of town. Services of all types were close at hand: shops, churches, and liveries. All manner of lively enterprises provided an animated setting for a family in the city. The main city market was a short walk, six blocks, from their doorstep.

Sally gave birth to Edward Coles Jr. on 26 March 1837. The Coles family had moved just a block away, a little closer to the market, to the northeast corner of Thirteenth Street and Clark Street. One more Coles joined the family: Roberts Coles on 14 November 1838.

The domestic scene surrounding Coles was a hive of family warmth and activity. Coles provided a rare glimpse of domestic arrangements in 1846 (Mary now eleven years of age) when he wrote to Matt Singleton about the accessibility of local schools and the various music, dance, and art instructors he retained for a busy schedule of children's activities in his home.[7] The following year, Coles wrote with some pride to his brother-in-law John Rutherfoord. The family had completed one of its frequent trips to Virginia, this one involving an extended stay at family plantations on Green Mountain. The trip caused a delay in the children's start of school. Still, Edward Jr. very quickly moved to within one position as head of his class; Roberts moved to the very head of his.[8]

Sallie's father, Hugh Roberts, died in 1835. Three years later, the Roberts estate was transferred to Edward Coles, increasing the holdings of the family by great measure. Coles was now managing real estate in Virginia, Missouri, Illinois, Ohio, and Wisconsin, plus a few properties in Philadelphia.[9] The majority of his income was coming, now, from entire blocks he owned in downtown St. Louis. The family income increased at this time from $11,889 in 1838 to $17,266 in 1859; the Coles family was financially secure and well able to provide generously for the children: dancing classes, singing classes for Mary, a new school situation for Mary in 1847, extended family vacations in Virginia's White Sulphur Springs and the Saratoga Springs in New York, yearly treks back to the family plantations of Green Mountain. For Edward Coles, family remained the center of his life. So it had ever been. Edward Coles's opposition to slavery had done nothing to weaken his ties to the rest of his slaveholding family. Excursions to Enniscorthy were met with return visits by nephews and nieces who would stay with the family in Philadelphia for weeks at a time.

* * *

The decade of the 1840s was, for many, a time of financial gloom. Dark clouds of monetary panic rolled over much of the northeast in 1837. Many people blamed this Panic of 1837 on President Andrew Jackson's Bank War that all but destroyed the Second Bank of the United States. The Second Bank of the United States did suspend operations in 1839, and it failed in 1841. State and local banks were thereby freed from the controls the central bank had exerted to stabilize banking in the country.[10] The resulting deflation concentrated economic storm clouds through the scarcity of specie, but more ominous clouds still were on the horizon. The supply of money tightened further to a trickle. The deflation and economic contraction that followed produced a decade of woe in many sectors. Railway, canal, and banking stocks withered as their primary investors, the states, entered a period of serious contraction. In 1841 and 1842, nine state governments defaulted on their debts. The economic contraction was serious enough to motivate two-thirds of state governments to revise their constitutions between 1846 and 1856 to prevent any such future disaster.[11] This contraction reached well beyond the northeast into the state economies of the south and southwest. Edward Coles held banking and railroad stocks. By 1842, his losses led to concerns serious enough to warrant job-seeking.

After President William Henry Harrison died (of pneumonia) just weeks after taking office in 1841 and John Tyler became president, Coles wrote a series of letters on behalf of friends and associates seeking one position or other with the government. Tyler was an old school friend, a classmate from the College of William and Mary.[12] Having intervened with Tyler for his friends, Coles swallowed his pride and wrote a letter offering his own services and confiding his financial embarrassment. He listed as his qualifications his old friendship with Tyler and his life of public service. Tyler remained polite but unhelpful.[13] Nine months later, Coles turned to another old school friend, Winfield Scott (then general-in-chief of the army), asking for intercession in obtaining the position of treasurer of the mint if the position should open (as he had some reason to believe it might).[14] Once again, he pointed to financial strains brought about by the failure of the banks and depreciation of railroad stocks. The position would be ideal, of course. The mint was located in Coles's neighborhood in Philadelphia, just a short walk from his house.

Scott wrote back in disbelief.[15] Scott was the major contender to replace Tyler as the Whig candidate for president and could not fathom why Coles thought he could help. Coles's reply mirrored his total incomprehension of the new political realities.[16] Both Tyler and Scott were old friends. They were school chums. Coles was mortified that he should approach either for a patronage position. His mortification deepened by rejection. Coles retired forever from actively seeking a political appointment.

The 1850 census listed the value of Edward Coles's real estate at $20,000. This was not a great deal more than what he had realized thirty years earlier when he sold his plantation.[17]

* * *

Prior to leaving Illinois, Coles had presented the Historical Society of Alton, Illinois, with all the documents he had collected regarding the State of Illinois. These he left it in their care for use by James Mason Peck, the rock-jawed frontier preacher who had provided much antislavery muscle in support of Coles's struggle to prevent Illinois from enshrining slavery in its constitution.[18] In due course and under agreement with the terms set down by Coles, Peck removed this collection to his residence at the Rock Spring Seminary to write a long-promised history of Illinois. An entry in his journal of 1852 tells the fate of many of Coles's personal and historical papers left behind in Illinois.

Peck's son, working in the lower story of the building, had a fire in the fireplace. A shift of wind was all it took to light the combustibles in Peck's work area. In minutes, the flames took hold and shortly reached the ceiling. The alarm was raised but too late to save more than a sampling. Lost in the disaster was the product of thirty years' work by John Mason Peck. His files, papers, periodicals, and pamphlets were reduced to ash, and with them went the records of Edward Coles.[19] Only the fire sprites know in detail what was lost.

Biographica Americana

With the death of James Madison in 1836, the generation of founding fathers had passed. But with the passing, public interest in the early history of the republic and its actors blossomed. The age of the founding fathers gave way, in fact, to a golden age of *biographica Americana*. Prescott, Parkman, Ingersoll, Sparks, Bancroft, Gorham, Palfrey, Hildreth, and Parton jointly produced a parade of historical scholarship in an era that has come to be known as the Middle Period. In the midst of the parade were Hugh Blair Grigsby, Henry Stephens Randolph, and William Cabell Rives, associates all of Edward Coles during the 1850s.

Edward Coles was a link to America's postrevolutionary past. His personal connection with Jefferson and his political and familial links with Madison opened a new role for him. He became an adviser to historians and an amateur historian in his own right. Not surprising, the advice he provided reflected his own past and present and his loyalty to republican ideals and to the founding fathers he knew so well. As a historian, he did the same.

Coles took upon himself the obligation to preserve the memory of James Madison as a republican hero.[20] Coles saw himself as a member of the administration. He was a republican throughout his life. Edward

Coles took his defense of Madison further than this. Edward Coles conceived of the republican ideal as including the end of slavery. He insisted to the end that Madison was an emancipator (at least in intent), a true republican, and a complete champion of human rights. How deeply he held this view is not known. But this was the view he presented without fail to any public audience.

* * *

The second and final installment of the papers of James Madison were finally acquired from Dolley Madison by Congress shortly before her death in 1849. Seven years later, Congress engaged William Cabell Rives to organize the papers and prepare them for publication.[21] No doubt this would also assist in completing the biography of Madison assigned to Rives by the Historical Society of Virginia in January of the same year, 1856.[22] Rives was well situated to undertake the work: Castle Hill, his home in Albemarle County, spread like a rich carpet from the base of Monticello Mountain. His was the patrician family. In wealth, influence, and social connection, Rives and Coles were on a roughly equal footing. Rives had served in Virginia's House of Delegates before moving on to Congress. He gained prominence, rising to the upper levels of the Democratic Party and ultimately was considered for the vice presidency in 1835. He retained a seat in the U.S. Senate into the 1840s and had grown especially close to James Madison in the final years of his life.[23]

Rives contacted Edward Coles early in 1856, announced the Madison biography project, and requested Coles's help in interpreting certain matters.[24] Coles was delighted to help in any way. During the next three years, in letter after letter, Coles interpreted James Madison and (on rarer occasion) Thomas Jefferson. He commented on the virtues of Madison that had made him slow to declare war on Britain; he remarked on a recently published anonymous letter defending Jefferson's behavior in the election of 1800.[25] Together, Coles and Rives discussed the deliberations between Madison and Washington concerning the regulation of commercial intercourse between Virginia and Maryland, the possible role played by Madison in writing speeches for Governor Patrick Henry, and the veracity of Washingtonian James C. McGuire and the authenticity of certain published elements from his personal collection of Madison letters.[26]

Consider Coles's advice to Rives regarding a Madison letter to Robert Walsh, dated 2 November 1819. He quotes McGuire's version of the letter suggesting that Congress did not view slavery as "among the needful regulations contemplated by the Constitution; since in none of the territorial govts created by them is such an interdict found."[27] The closing of slavery to the Northwest Territories was not constitutionally "needful"? Coles had too much respect for Madison, his letter to Rives asserted, to believe that this was a true quotation of Madison. It flew in the face of the Northwest Ordinance of 1787, which had been passed unanimously by Congress and had been recognized and sanctioned by President Madison. Its prohibitions against slavery were well known. Surely, there is a misreading here, Coles was certain. Coles remained highly suspicious of McGuire, citing discrepancies in published versions of his own correspondence with Madison. He pleaded with Rives to examine the authenticity of McGuire's published versions of Madison materials.

Coles is clearly acting as a steward on behalf of Madison, whose credentials as an antislavery republican might be tarnished by this suspicious letter. Coles was unaware, apparently, of the context of the letter in the debate preceding the Missouri Compromise. Madison was responding to confusions surrounding the intent of Article I, Section 9, of the ordinance and the constitutional meaning of this section restricting "migration" of slaves. This question and Madison's unexpected response to Walsh would grow into a rich vein of scholarly dispute. Coles's own confusion in reconciling his own beliefs about Madison's antislavery convictions (on the one hand) and with the Walsh letter (on the other) is understandable. Others shared his confusion, and many have taken on the daunting task of resolving the apparent contradictions embodied in the Walsh letter.[28]

Coles was mistaken. The McGuire version of Madison's letter was not in error. And Edward Coles's motive seems clear. He believed, deeply and without reservation, that James Madison was a champion against slavery. He would not abide a legacy of Madison that held otherwise.

Jefferson and the Northwest Ordinance

On 9 August 1852, Senator Charles Sumner, Democrat from Massachusetts, rose from his bench in the senate chamber just as adjournment was to be proclaimed. He launched into an item for the obituary regarding Representative Robert Rantoul Jr., who had passed away unexpectedly two days before, a victim of erysipelas, a skin infection usually caused by *Streptococcus*.[29] In his brief remembrance of Rantoul, Sumner recalled that the place of his birth was also the home of Nathan Dane, author of the Northwest Ordinance.[30]

Sumner's speech was reported the next day in the *Daily National Intelligencer*. Edward Coles was apparently astonished. He wrote to Mr. Sumner taking great exception to the idea that Dane had written the Ordinance. Coles cited facts, as far as his recollection would serve him (based on readings and conversation with those who were party to the events). Jefferson had been appointed chair of a committee to propose a scheme for governing the new territories that had come to the nation by deed from Virginia. Joining with him on the committee were Jeremiah T. Chase (of Maryland) and David Howell (Rhode Island). The report was submitted in the handwriting of Mr. Jefferson. The proposal was discussed but not disposed of by vote. When it came back for consideration at a subsequent session, the words used by Jefferson in the earlier draft were retained in a new draft. This draft, too, was discussed and discussed more, then laid over and referred to a committee chaired by Edward Carrington (of Virginia) and also including Dane as a member. Whatever his action in the committee, Coles asserted, Dane can in no way be credited with the Northwest Ordinance.[31] Surely Sumner will correct this error, as a matter of justice both to Jefferson and to history, in a manner equally public as it was made.

Sumner was not convinced. His letter of 23 August to Coles gives not an inch in the dispute. Sumner observes that Dane's treatise, the eight-volume encyclopedia on American laws published in 1824 (while Jefferson was still alive and could, presumably, have spoken up if it was in error) claimed that the author was the source of the ordinance, which was based primarily on the laws of Massachusetts (Dane had been involved in the rewriting of the Massachusetts code). Daniel Webster, in fact, had recognized Dane's authorship of the ordinance. Jefferson's earlier efforts, Sumner went on, are not reduced by Dane's crowning achievement.[32] Jefferson held the honor of initial effort in prohibiting slavery in the territories; to Dane belonged the honor of completing the task in his own hand in 1787.[33]

This would not be the end of it. Coles gathered historical materials and organized his recollections. In January of the next year, he dispatched a five-thousand-word essay to the *National Intelligencer* on Jefferson's just claim to authorship (and Dane's proper station as a northerner of minor celebrity and modest accomplishment).[34] During the next four years, he developed a presentation (later to be published in booklet form) detailing his assertion that Jefferson was the antislavery patron of freedom in the Northwest Territories. He presented his findings to the Historical Society of Pennsylvania at its meeting of 9 June 1856. His remarks ran to thirty-three printed pages when it was released as a publication of the society.[35]

Edward Coles's review of the Ordinance of 1787 must be considered a personal missive. His life as governor of Illinois was, for some years, bounded by his own view (shared by many, refuted by others) that the Northwest Ordinance made all slavery illegal in Illinois. Coles's history of the ordinance celebrates the views that he held closely and had acted on in his youth: the Northwest Ordinance was the law of the land. It was a good law. It was Jefferson's law.

He described the cession by Virginia and Connecticut in early 1784 of lands north and west of the Ohio River to the United States and the subsequent formation of a committee to develop policies for the governance of new lands. Included in the committee were Jefferson (chairman), Chase of Maryland, and Howell of Rhode Island. The presentation of the committee's report (in the handwriting of Jefferson) stipulates, "That after the year 1800 of the Christian era there shall be neither slavery nor involuntary servitude in any of the said States [formed from the new territories], otherwise than in punishment of crimes whereof the party shall have been convicted to have been personally guilty."[36]

Coles argued for the pedigree of the later Ordinance of 1787 as clearly derived from this language. He does not pursue a chain-of-evidence review to tie the 1784 language prohibiting slavery to Jefferson. He acknowledged the removal (by a single vote) of the slavery paragraph from the final text of the 1784 law. And he acknowledged that Jefferson was in France when the Northwest Ordinance of 1787 was passed by Congress. Still, he says, the ordinance bears "kindred political features to its older brother, the Declaration of American Independence."[37] Coles's primary focus was on disputing that Dane had any claim to authorship of the ordinance. He asserted that the pedigree of language in the Northwest Ordinance of 1787 was derived from its earlier version of 1784. He showed that Dane had not taken his seat in Congress until 17 November 1785, more than eighteen months after the 1784 Ordinance had been written. And he argued that the Ordinance of 1784, written in the hand of Jefferson, points in every way to Jefferson as its source.

Coles's *History of the Ordinance of 1787* gallops over the early slavery histories of Indiana, Missouri, Ohio, and, especially, Illinois during the first few decades of the century. His view could scarcely have been more straightforward as regards slavery in Illinois while he was governor. It existed, its eradication was resisted, it was illegal. The proslavery arguments that had been pervasive in 1824 did not alight in the pages of Coles's report of 1856. The rights claimed by the French (awarded first by the English, ratified by Virginia) to retain their (slave) property were given no place. (No doubt he would never endorse those rights in any event.) Slaveholding was illegal in Illinois after 1800. Coles was, of course, certifying and affirming the view he had held thirty-two years earlier, when as governor of Illinois, he had battled against the proslavery conventionist elite.

Coles's work on the ordinances of 1784 and 1787 is remembered principally for its refutation of Dane's (and affirmation of Jefferson's) claim of authorship. The paper was soft scholarship. Coles acknowledged as much in the opening paragraphs. That he was in error in giving Jefferson credit as primary author of the ordinances is unfortunate but forgivable. Historians until recently have sided with Coles, presuming Jefferson's authorship primarily on the strength of the handwritten report submitted by his committee. There was no challenge to this view until 1972, when Robert F. Berkhofer Jr. presented a careful and detailed examination of the making of the ordinance.

Berkhofer documented that much of the discussion relating to governance of the Northwest Territories had coalesced and was nearing consensus before Jefferson took his seat in Congress in November 1783.[38] More to the point in terms of Coles's assertion of Jefferson's credit for the antislavery provisions of the Ordinance of 1784 (and, by extension, for the reinstatement of a similar provision three years later) is the recognition that Timothy Pickering had earlier proposed the prohibition of slavery in new states after 1800 (the central tenet of the fifth article) and that committee member Howell of Rhode Island was at least as likely as Jefferson to have been the source of the antislavery section. Either way, much of the evidence rests on conjecture. Records of the proceedings of the Jefferson-Chase-Howell committee do not exist. Coles acknowledges this in his booklet.

Coles was probably mistaken about Jefferson's authorship. The error was not intentional. His agenda was partisan rather than political. His understanding of the facts was incomplete. He did help to perpetuate a worshipful mythology of Jefferson that survived (indeed, survives still). This sin was repeated thereafter by an army of Jefferson biographers. Jefferson's authorship of the Ordinance of 1784 (and its successor of 1787) became common, unquestioned orthodoxy.

* * *

Coles wrote his history of the Ordinance of 1787 at a time when the chords of its argument were resonant in public discussion. In the past, federal statute had set the terms and prescribed the balance of slaveholding and free states, but with the passage of the Compromise of 1850, the question was left more to the settlers of each territory to "popular sovereignty." The battle for and against slavery in the territories had shifted away from a delicate balance in senate voting power to a series of high-wire agreements opening the expansion of slavery to referenda in the territories.

A plan for Kansas and Nebraska arrived from the Committee on Territories to the senate floor on 4 January 1854. It was presented by committee chairman, Stephen A. Douglas, whose brilliant tactics and thunderous efforts had produced the Compromise of 1850. The new bill would create the territories of Kansas and Nebraska, formally repeal the Missouri Compromise, and call for the settlers to decide for themselves if their territories would be slaved or free. It was this last point that loosed a gale of controversy on Douglas. Although surprised by the galloping strength of feeling on a subject he had thought had been brought to stable, Douglas lost little time in rising to the battle. Legislative combat was his sport of choice.

Senator Douglas took the senate floor again on Monday, 30 January 1854, and conducted a heated dialog with Senator Salmon P. Chase of Ohio, although Douglas contributed a torrent of invective to Chase's trickle. The entire debate was published in the *National Intelligencer* on Thursday, 2 February 1854, and Edward Coles was among readers who took great exception to some of Senator Douglas's speech.[39]

It is not surprising that Coles took a strong interest in the debate. He would view this shift to "popular sovereignty" as a threat to the end of slavery. Had not Coles met this very battle in Illinois? Had not a referendum been used to attempt to move Illinois from a free state to a slave state? And now arguments reminiscent of those he had defeated in Illinois were gaining the national stage. On 18 February 1854, Coles entered the Kansas-Nebraska debate by way of a letter to the *National Intelligencer*.[40] He attempted to weaken Douglas's hold on the matter by addressing a subject with which he had extensive battle-hardened experience in Illinois and freshly minted views: the Ordinance of 1787.

Douglas had argued that slavery existed in fact if not in law in Illinois and did so under the approving eye of the Illinois populace and that the federal law had been ineffective and was not a reliable means of managing the spread of slavery. Let the people decide locally was his main point. Douglas's position, wrote Coles to the *Intelligencer*, "cast a mortifying reproach on our country [of Illinois], its Government, and citizens. If faith is given to [Douglas's assertions,] the history of the country is made ludicrous."[41]

The Ordinance of 1787 was perfectly clear: The existence of slavery in the face of an explicit and strong law was due to local, not federal, failures. Congress had done its duty in passing laws restricting slavery, local failures to enforce notwithstanding. Coles was in some measure sarcastic and taunting: "When behold, a new luminary [referring to Douglas] appears in 1854 in the political firmament of the Senate of the United Sates, and unfolds the astounding fact to a benighted people that slavery was never abolished or prevented by Congressional enactment from one inch of American soil!" Coles went on to relive and refute arguments he had met before. Douglas had reduced the Ordinance of 1787 to a bald affront to state sovereignty. Coles praised the ordinance as the brave antislavery manifesto of Thomas Jefferson.

Douglas responded to Coles by private letter.[42] Coles's sarcastic tone was met with scorn and inflated sarcasm that upped the ante. In a blast of wind, Douglas cited rhyme and verse in the ordinance and other territorial laws. He laced the review with sarcasm and otherwise poured page after page of discussion and complaint on Coles's assertions.

The dispute was, on the surface, mostly semantic, but deeper down, it may have conjured memories that were disquieting for Coles. He viewed the Ordinance of 1787 as clear law generating a bright line forbidding slavery. He was sensitive to any reading of the Ordinance of 1787 that challenged his steadfast view of its virtues and its qualities as a republican contract (that is, a virtuous product of an enlightened leader, Thomas Jefferson). Once again, Edward Coles took a fleeting place on the stage of public discussion, pressing forward (that is, with a backward gaze) to the ideals of the republican era. He then receded back to the shadows of private life.

The Devil or the Itch

Another project taking wing in the 1850s was a biography of Jefferson by Henry S. Randall. A devoted Democrat (living in a decidedly Whig/Republican district in New York, Cortland County), Randall was an enthusiastic Jeffersonian. He was repeatedly nominated for statewide and national offices and gained distinction as an advocate of public education in New York. But it is principally his three-volume biography of Thomas Jefferson that has earned him a laurel or two in the hall of American letters of the Middle Period. Although not a definitive work, Randall's *Life of Thomas Jefferson* continues to attract interest among those who mine the rich vein of early Jeffersonia because of the pains he took to corroborate the biography through personal remembrances by those who knew Jefferson well. More than a hint of his devotion to personalized authority is found in his correspondence with Hugh Blair Grigsby, a scholar of the Virginia constitutional conventions of 1776, 1778, and 1829–30, journalist, and member of Virginia's House of Delegates. Grigsby (who knew Coles via their mutual connections both to Virginia and later in Philadelphia) commended Coles to Randall.

An early letter of 18 February 1856 from Grigsby to Randall shows an Edward Coles not met before. Coles's anecdote relates to Thomas Jefferson in a state of discomfort on returning from travels. Jefferson's physician, Dr. Robley Dunglison, declared that the patient had "the itch," treatment for which was a preparation of mercury. Jefferson complained, according to the story, that the effect of the mercury in producing salivation was an annoyance he could well do without, but "Mr. J added with warmth I would rather have the devil than the itch."[43]

Grigsby and Randall drew Edward Coles and others (such as Nicholas P. Trist, Dunglison, George Woodward, and Henry D. Gilpin) into a warm and friendly society of Jefferson admirers.[44] Dinners and occasional evening discussions in Philadelphia were eagerly augmented by letters. A second letter draws one further into this odd realm of Edward Coles the flamboyant storyteller. Coles related the history of a chance meeting by a Kentucky visitor of a tall stranger on horseback by an Albemarle stream. Unable to cross without assistance, the rider obliged the Kentuckian a spot behind him on the same saddle. The crossing was completed, and the two gentlemen parted. But the stranger soon discovered that his benefactor had been President Jefferson. The Kentuckian, amused and somewhat chagrined, pleaded that the story should never reach his home as he would never hear the end of it, according to Coles. The story, said Grigsby, was both entertaining and captivating.[45] Coles loved an audience and was ever able to talk of his connections to figures of history that added to his own celebrity.

Illinois journalist Hooper Warren (who dogged Coles's election in 1824 and the convention struggle that followed) had complained that Coles told stories to a point well beyond boredom. Evidently, Philadelphia was more appreciative. Randall came to regard Coles as an important source with firsthand knowledge of Jefferson. Coles received a letter dated 13 September 1856 asking his views as to the existence of a monarchical party during the first six presidents.[46] Coles also provided Randall with a detailed memoir of the meeting with John Adams in 1811 that led (indirectly) to the affectionate reconciliation of Adams with Jefferson and the celebrated friendship that remains as a beacon of republican creativity and civility in American letters.[47] Randall completed his biography in 1858 and straightaway sent a note to Coles announcing that a copy of the third volume would follow presently. Coles was among the first few contributors acknowledged in the preface.[48]

* * *

What can one make of this history-making of Edward Coles? His history of the Northwest Ordinance (such as it was)? His efforts to shape the legacy of Madison as antislavery republican? His attempt to cast Jefferson as the common-man republican president of the United States and champion of a free Northwest? Were Madison and Jefferson not the same men who had rebuffed Coles's challenges to demonstrate their republican virtue in one way or another? Had each not failed the republican cause by retaining their slaves even unto death? Yet, Coles remained ever committed to the ideals of republican virtue writ plain. He believed in the Declaration of Independence as a covenant to be taken literally, a covenant that made a higher calling than did political party. Madison and Jefferson embodied that covenant in the public's legacy of American history (mythology and all).

Coles believed, to his very core, that both founding fathers were antislavery, procolonization, and antiabolitionist. In that sense, Coles's efforts in shaping the historical record was, as Suzanne Cooper Guasco asserts, "managing memory" of the founding fathers in support of his own aspirations to end slavery in America and fulfill the promise embodied by the Declaration of Independence.[49] He joined a long queue of historians, politicians, and enthusiasts of every stripe who would cast that promise in the mold of their own vision.

Edward Coles was a consort of the Virginia dynasty. His personal commitment was to emancipation. He was otherwise one with Jefferson and Madison, loyal to them as men and to their views as republicans. He was a republican prince in the court of the founding fathers.

13

The Preacher

Robert Crawford continued overseeing the Prairieland Farm and its rental for some years, remaining Edward Coles's agent, watching over and caring for the business interests of Coles's investment at his Pin Oak farm until at least 1843.[1] Crawford appears to have flourished in freedom, and his faithfulness as an agent was well met by his reliable, if rough-hewn, personal qualities. Among those qualities was a gift for preaching.

In the early decades after Edward Coles moved to Pin Oak Township in Illinois, a track of ten miles wound through the woodlands and prairie east of Edwardsville toward the little community of Marine. In some parts, the open prairie was awash with grain. Otherwise, gently rolling hills and woodlands prevailed. At one point, this Edwardsville-Marine Road flattened out, and the view opened to a wooded glen containing the Ebenezer Camp meeting ground.

Ebenezer was, according to G. C. Lusk, who lived in Edwardsville until 1839, the great center of agricultural, political, social, and religious intercourse in the Pin Oak area. A log building stood there enfolded by a small stand of trees; a clearing opened up beyond and made way for a cemetery. Neighbors flocked to Ebenezer for song and preaching or to bury their own. Preachers came in, and neighbors gathered from all around to hear the Word. If the weather allowed, they would sit "under the drippings of the sanctuary" made by the spreading canopy of trees.[2]

Robert Crawford preached there. People in Edwardsville as well as Pin Oak came to hear the natural-born preacher. In all likelihood, the man many called "Uncle Bobby" could neither read nor write, but he knew the scripture, and he taught it powerfully and faithfully.[3] Captain A. L. Brown, editor of the *Edwardsville (Illinois) Democrat* in 1912, brought Crawford's preaching to mind in a reminiscing article. Uncle Bobby Crawford would draw scores of white people from the neighboring towns to hear the Bible brought to life in his unique fashion.[4]

A Nurturing Presence

Twenty years after becoming a free man, Robert Crawford abetted the formation of a church organization that would, in its way, ring in a new era for black influence in America. Crawford was not the central figure in this story. He was a significant, even a leading figure, a source of enduring support, and a nurturing presence. The story of Uncle Bobby Crawford is entwined with the development and expansion of reputedly the longest-lived and still-operational black Baptist organization in America. The national movement of African American Baptist Conventions owes much to the faithful efforts of men like Robert Crawford and others in western Illinois who set the church on a road of community development and social conscience. It was John Livingston and Alfred H. Richardson who provided the power and the glory; Uncle Bobby Crawford gave the Amens of support and foundation.

In 1837 and 1838, the Union Baptist Church of Alton, the Salem Baptist Church of Ogle Creek, and the Mt. Zion Baptist Church of Ridge Prairie were all formed in western Illinois under the leadership of Richardson, a free black man from Tennessee. Robert Crawford became a member of the Mt. Zion Baptist Church (sometimes called the Ridge Prairie Church).[5]

Pin Oak Township and that part of it known as Ridge Prairie had become a home place for freed black persons. The Crawfords (Robert and Kate) lived there. Michael Lee moved there sometime after 1817 and married Polly Crawford in 1822. Other free black men and women moved in (Samuel Vanderberg, Henry Daugherty, and Thomas Seton among them). In time, the community supported a milk dump at Kuhn Station, a general store, and a grain elevator. And it supported two churches, one Methodist, the other the Mt. Zion Baptist Church. Several preachers emerged among the black population.

White preachers were in the Pin Oak township also. James Lemen Sr., a white Virginian, had lived in Ridge Prairie since 1802. If preaching were magnetic, compasses pointed to Pin Oak township. It was to Lemen that Richardson wrote in contacting the Illinois Union Baptist Association, a regional organization of white churches, asking for membership on behalf of the black churches then being ministered to by Reverend Livingston.[6] Their membership was accepted in 1838. Richardson followed with a request that an association of black Baptist Churches be formed. This, too, was agreed.

On 27 April 1839, representatives of the Union Baptist Church of Alton, Salem Baptist Church of Ogle Creek, and the Mt. Zion Baptist Church of Ridge Prairie met at the home of Samuel Vincent in St. Clair County. Lemen, now moderator of the Illinois Union Baptist Association, officiated at the formation of the Colored Baptist Association and Friends to Humanity.[7]

At Mt. Zion in Ridge Prairie (Pin Oak Township), the first meeting of the new association of black churches was called to order on Friday, 13 September 1839. Elder Henry Smith (of the African Church of St. Louis) gave the introductory sermon from Ephesians 2. Mt. Zion presented three messengers to the new association; Robert Crawford was identified as elder of the church in minutes that have come down from that first meeting. On Saturday, Robert Crawford delivered the sermon "from the stand."[8] Prayers were offered, minutes of the previous day read, rules of decorum adopted, and other business completed. Resolutions accepted were to support religious and moral education of the children through Sabbath schools, to teach and support temperance, to prepare a circular letter for the next meeting. Elder J. B. Meacham was appointed to preach the introductory sermon at the association meeting to be held the following year (Elder Robert Crawford would be the alternate preacher).

The evening of the second day of the first annual meeting of the Colored Baptist Association and Friends to Humanity closed with a candle-lit service. Brother S. S. Ball addressed the congregation, drawing upon the Acts of the Apostles 2:37–38. And a Pentecostal shower anointed the congregation that evening, a fine drizzle that was more blessing than soaking.[9] Annual meetings rotated among the member churches. Robert Crawford was active in each of the first eight meetings and attended sporadically thereafter. He was regularly called upon to plan the meetings and to preach. In 1840, Crawford was identified now in minutes as the pastor of the Mt. Zion Church.[10]

From the beginning, the Colored Baptist Association was a highly organized operation. It had a constitution and rules of decorum. Elected officers included a moderator, clerk, standing secretary, corresponding secretary, and treasurer. A committee on missions was set up at the fifth session. A schedule of monthly meetings was prepared and promoted via the organization's circular letters and its annual newsletter. Minutes were always taken. A committee on public exercises managed the agenda of the annual sessions; more often than not, Uncle Bobby Crawford provided leadership here. Ad hoc committees were formed. A nominating committee recommended officers to the annual session. A committee on the next annual session recommended the location. By the fifth annual session, the organization had grown to ten churches. By 1849 (ten years after formation), the Colored Baptist Association had become a community of thirteen little churches and 243 church members.[11]

The struggle against slavery formed an increasingly important mission of the Colored Baptist Association as the years rolled on. Initially, antislavery activities were restricted to annual resolutions, prayer meetings, and vigils. There was, however, a sentiment among many (especially in the earliest years) that the association should not focus on slavery (it being an issue tied up with "things of this world"). Effort should focus instead on temperance, the saving of souls, and spreading of the Gospel. It may be, in fact, that this reluctance to address slavery in the early years helped to ensure survival of the black churches. Edward Coles may have made the American Bottom a focal point of antislavery during the convention battle, but later incidents, such as the killing of Elijah P. Lovejoy in 1837, proved that racism and opposition to radical abolitionism still existed.

* * *

During the first dozen years of its existence, the Colored Baptist Association appears to have been quiet in its opposition to slavery. Prayers, vigils, and resolutions constituted resistance. As time went on, however, and as younger preachers began to have influence, the association grew more bold in its opposition. At first, it was a trickle. Association articles denounced slavery in religious and secular publications. Later, antislavery petitions and letters flowed freely from the association. And fugitive slaves from the south were actively protected and provided with support.[12]

Sometime between August 1851 and August 1853, the name of the Colored Baptist Association was changed to the Wood River Colored

Baptist Association. The WRCBA provided much of the leadership and resources for the formation and development of the Western Colored Baptist Association, organized in St. Louis in 1853 and in operation until the Civil War. The methods and traditions of the WRCBA, dating from the very first days in 1839 (the meticulous keeping of records, the reliance on formalized rules. the assertion of mutual support) formed a model that was emulated by black Baptist organizations in much of Illinois and in surrounding states.

Following the Civil War, the WRCBA restarted the Western Colored Baptist Association (later renamed the Northwestern Colored Baptist Association).[13] Through active support of the Western Colored Baptist Association (personnel and financing) and through collaboration with other emerging Baptist Conventions, the Wood River Baptist District Association, as it became known later, earned considerable influence and a fair share of credit for the strength of the national convention movement that emerged in the Baptist church during the later half of the nineteenth century. Later, it provided financial and leadership support for the developing National Association for the Advancement of Colored People.[14]

The Wood River Baptist District Association is now the longest-lived black Baptist organization in America. It was not the first of its kind. The Providence Baptist Association in southern Ohio predates it (1834), as does the Union Baptist Association of Ohio (1836). These organizations disbanded; the Wood River Baptist District Association continues today. Other associations played critical roles in the movement that give the African American Baptist Church strength through mutual support. But the Wood River Baptist District Association should be remembered as a sturdy and reliable column of support in the nascent convention movement of the Baptist church.

What was Robert Crawford's role in all of this? He was a faithful supporter of the association in its earliest days. He was assigned to major committees. He was pastor of one of the three first churches. He preached a storm of Baptist commitment to the Gospels. Beyond that, Crawford was not the moving force of the nascent Wood River Baptist District Association. He was a faithful member, a pioneer of sorts. He was a laborer in the vineyard.

Dear Master

Robert Crawford had married Kate Crawford in December of 1826. Kate's daughter Betsy had married Jesse Price in October. Three of Kate's children by her earlier marriage to Ralph Crawford remained close. Thomas, who since birth had been weak in the right arm and leg, was now about twenty-four years of age. Mary was about eighteen, and William was all of sixteen.[15] But Kate and Robert had formed a new family. In 1831, Kate bore Ferdenand. And in 1835, she bore Richard.[16]

Robert and Kate Crawford heard from Edward Coles in February 1837 in an effusive and jubilant letter that survives. Coles's pride fairly bursts from the lines:

> I have experienced great pleasure in witnessing, & I now have much in braving this testimony to the good conduct of those to whom I restored their liberty; & the conduct of none has been so conspicuously praiseworthy as that of the two I am now addressing. You both have fulfilled your parts, and have in every respect maintained as fair a character under your brown faces, as the fairest of your fair faced neighbours. I take pleasure in speaking so highly in your praise, not only because worth is deserving of praise & should be thus encouraged, but because there is a prejudice in narrow minds ag[ains]t you, because your God and their God has seen fit to give your skin a darker hue . . .
>
> P.S. You say nothing in your letter about my Farm near you, which I left in your care. Mr. Prickett wrote me you had handed to him for me $13. Is it possible this is all the remit which has been paid for the last two years? I wish you would attend to it, & do the best you can for me.
>
> I hope you have not sold the two quarter sections of land I gave you. It is becoming daily more valuable. I sold a quarter section of mine, not far from yours, lately for $500 cash—& some land in that part of the State has been sold by a man here for $1500 the quarter section.[17]

In 1843, Kate and Robert did sell the property that Edward Coles had deeded to them in 1819.[18] Robert signed his name, and Kate signed her mark. Their 180 acres returned $2,000 in the sale to Isaac Prickett.[19]

Two letters remain in correspondence from Robert Crawford to Edward Coles; one is presented here. Dated 23 October 1840, the letter was dictated to Richardson, friend of Robert Crawford and cofounder of the WRBDA (spelling and punctuation as true as possible to the original):

Dear Master,

I received your Letter of Sept 10 which Gave Me Great Satisfaction to here of your hith [health] and prosperity—I am permitted through the Great Goodness of God to onst [once] more try to Convey a few Lines to your sight Liting [letting] you know at the Sametime that My Self and Katy are well and hearty and in a reasonable State of prosperity . . .

. . . We are truly thankfull that our old master John Caules [Coles]—and his wife Rebekah ever had a son born by the Name of Edward we believe that God have made him the means of doing us this great good—We recollet [recollect] at your fathers Death that Several of the poor oppressed—that was choosing their masters But God choosed for us—that we walk around our farm and Look at the blessings of God == that we are ready to speak in the Language of the Samist [Psalmist] and Say that Lord Great things for us wharewith we are glad.

We are almost ready to call apon our horses and Cattle to praise the god whom we all ought to adoare for his great goodness but a master strive to in at the Straight gate for straight is the gate and narrow is the rode and thare be that findith it, but Brad [broad] is the rode that Leads unto Death and thousands walk together there ==Remember that this Life is not Long—but the Life to Come has no end == now I want you to tell my friends—that the Lord have done these Great things for me— and yours allso there is a day acoming when the Servant and the Master Shall Both meet at the Bare of God—to hear them finding and proving wont it be awfull indeed =[20]

Here is the voice of Robert Crawford. Here are the epiphany and the thanksgiving of the preacher Robert Crawford, broken in language but whole in spirit. Here is the Robert Crawford of the Ebenezer camp-ground and the Mt. Zion Baptist Church. Here is Robert Crawford in flight of word, sent to his former master with affection.

Robert Crawford left Pin Oak sometime before the census of 1850. The handwritten census records of J. B. Roper, committed at the end of August in that year, show that the Crawford family had moved to East Litchfield in Montgomery County (one county north and east of Madison County). The record shows that Robert was fifty-two years of age; Thomas, who was a boy of thirteen or fourteen years when he came to Illinois with his parents in 1819, was now forty. His stepbrothers, Ferdenand and Richard, were nineteen and fifteen. And there appears there another name in the rolls taken by Roper. Cordelia was listed as a black female, age fifty-two. Presumably Kate Crawford had died, and Robert may have taken another wife.[21]

Records of the Wood River Baptist District Association show that in 1854 the annual session was held at Piasa, located due north of Alton in the County of Macoupin. The opening sermon was given by Elder Jackson. The Zoar Church of Chicago requested membership in the association that year, a testament to the influence of the WRBDA in quarters quite far afield. The Rocky Branch Church of Montgomery County was also requesting admittance. Pastor Robert Crawford represented that little church in the next county to the east.[22]

With the coming of the Civil War, the WRBDA reduced operations (judging from the much-shorter lists of attendees at the annual sessions during the war years), and Robert Crawford's name fell from the rolls of active participants.[23] Crawford's health began to give way, and in June 1870, he entered into an arrangement with Archie Pettiford. This was a lease for Crawford's house and twenty-seven acres of land. In return, Crawford was to have lodging, food, and personal care whether in sickness or in health, washing and mending of clothing at a discount. Crawford signed with a mark. Robert Crawford died before the life of the contract was finished. He passed away on 29 August 1870.[24]

On 19 September, a petition testamentary was registered in the Montgomery County Court, summarizing the real and personal estate of Robert Crawford: chiefly twenty seven acres in land, three promissory notes, household furniture, and three hogs. The estate sale that followed in October lists the contents of a comfortable farm life on the Illinois prairie: a tin pie safe, a looking glass, various bedsteads with cord, blankets, a black coat, a churn, stone jars, and a coffee pot. And two pages more, detailing the remains of a long life. He was seventy-three years old when he died. Robert Crawford epitomized the hopes Edward Coles had in developing his experiment in freedom. Crawford's life was a journey from slavery to property ownership, regional leadership in a new and important network of black churches and respected standing as an influential preacher in the prairielands of Illinois.

14

Prodigal Virginian

The three Coles children grew to adulthood in a family life bathed in affection, constantly reinforced by family associations that reached from Philadelphia to Central Virginia and beyond. Mary Coles remained in Philadelphia all of her life. She never married. She devoted her energies largely to the Episcopal Church and became well known for her Tuesday missionary Bible class in Philadelphia. She mixed with bishops and other church leaders in both the United States and in England. Hers was the life of an activist: a churchly activist, traveler, and civic volunteer.[1] Edward Coles Jr. grew to be a lawyer with a practice in Philadelphia. He married Bessie Campbell in 1868; they had three children. Summers were spent at a family retreat in Maine. His was the life of success and domestic stability.

It was Roberts, the youngest of the three children, who would introduce a dark and tragic chord into the sweet harmonies of domestic life in Philadelphia. Roberts was a Coles through and through. With maturity, Roberts developed fine features, articulated by dark eyes and hair of dark chestnut, and a sweet and handsome face that hinted at a Puckish interior. He was intelligent, to be sure, and developed a strong sense of his family and its roots in Virginia. His father had given attention to documentation of the family tree, but by the mid-1850s, neuralgia in his hands made writing painful. He proposed to pass the project along to his son Roberts, who had shown the greatest interest in family history among the three children.[2]

Roberts Coles has been characterized variously as "modest, gentle and retiring to an unusual degree," alternatively as "gay and sprightly."[3]

Perhaps, these qualities are not confounding. There is ample room in a complex young man for contradiction. He was twenty-one when he broke away from the confines of family in Philadelphia to embrace the plantation life that his father had turned his back on. Roberts had been drawn to Albemarle County for some years and could not ignore the siren call of the Green Mountain and the romance of his southern pedigree. Has it happened before that a father was unable to transmit his own passions to his offspring? Surely, Roberts had no fair conception of the journey his father's life had taken in struggling against slavery. We do not know his views on slavery, but his actions suggest that its injustices could not hold him back. Not lost on this boy were love of family and abiding belief in his very personal tie to the dynasty based at Enniscorthy. The son has learned imperfectly from the father. Perhaps he has heard only the parts that he wanted to hear.

In 1860, Roberts left home for Albemarle County. Roberts Coles's cousin Tucker Skipwith Coles gave him a start by selling him (largely on credit) a nine-hundred-acre property with a small house. The deed, registered in April 1860, was fulfillment of a romantic desire. It held the promise of an auspicious future steeped in the genteel and "respectable" culture of Virginia's aristocracy. The Plantation, as Roberts's new homestead had been known of late, was carved out of the original fifteen-hundred-acre tract Clarkson farm on the Hardware River, located in the northern portion of the family's holdings at Enniscorthy and adjoining his Uncle John Coles's property Estouteville.[4] And with the conveyance of the property complete, Tucker Coles began the construction of a new dwelling house in the southern part of the property on a hill overlooking the Beaverdam Creek. Roberts put down these roots, and they were not yet enough. He met and fell in love with Jeannie C. Fairfax. He lost his heart completely to this prominent young lady from Richmond's upper social reaches. They became engaged.

The Civil War broke out on 12 April 1861. It was just a year since Roberts Coles had become a bona-fide Virginian. Would he return to the bosom of his father in Philadelphia or spend the war in Virginia? Unreferenced sources indicate that Edward Coles pleaded with his son not to support the Confederacy.[5] Roberts opted to support it. He mustered into the Forty-sixth Albemarle Infantry (Company I, the "Green Mountain Grays") on 16 July 1861 and kept this from his parents.[6] Ninety men from Albemarle, Fluvanna, Amherst, and Nelson Counties gathered that day at the old African church close to Carter's bridge at the very foot of the Green Mountain (and scarcely a stone's throw from his own front porch at the Plantation).[7] They gathered to sign up for a one-year tour of duty. Roberts was elected captain.

The Shells Fly Thick

Henry Wise and his Confederate command of twenty-seven hundred men were, at the time, dug in behind breastworks at Tyler Mountain, not far from Charleston in western Virginia (now, of course, West Virginia). Wise had been a member of the U.S. House of Representatives as a Jacksonian Democrat from 1833 to 1844. He had been minister to Brazil for a short time and then served as governor of Virginia from 1856 to 1860. The final act of his administration had been the execution of John Brown. Wise rejoiced in the war when it came and offered his services to the Confederacy's war effort. His lack of military experience was a problem, but his political popularity and enthusiasm for the cause could spur recruitment in a politically sensitive area. He was given command of a regiment that would focus on keeping western Virginia in the Confederacy, where feelings about the war were very mixed. So the new Virginia Forty-sixth (not yet joined by the recruits from Albemarle) was in the Charleston area in July 1862, wearied from marching about the mountains in pursuit of phantom Yankees.

In August, Captain Roberts Coles and the Green Mountain Grays left their bivouac by Carter's Bridge and made their way to Charlottesville, where a train took them west as far as the Jackson River. They marched to White Sulphur Springs, where they joined up with Brigadier General Henry Wise and other newly recruited companies of the Wise Brigade. Two weeks later camp was broken and the regiment marched along the old stage line toward Charleston, stopping at Tyler Mountain. Various excursions from Tyler Mountain to targets thought to be in Union hands brought the regiment into occasional light contact with the enemy, but no major battle was joined.

The Union was as eager as the South to win western Virginia. Union victories over a second regiment in western Virginia, under Brigadier General Robert S. Garnett at Rich Mountain and Laurel Hill led to a collapse of the Confederate effort in western Virginia, so Wise retreated eastward to Gauley Bridge. Casks of whiskey were found by some of the men. Prudently, the officers broke the casks in order to prevent drunkenness, leading the men to their only reasonable course: scooping up the amber medicine out of the wagon ruts in the road and taking their whiskey with a mud chaser.[8]

By 2 August, the Forty-sixth and the other brigades of Wise's legion had retreated back to White Sulphur Springs, were reequipped, and set off to try and regain lost territory. General John B. Floyd arrived at the camp on 5 August with twelve hundred men. Floyd had the same rank as did Wise, but with an earlier commission, Floyd was entitled to seniority and general command over the entire brigade. Floyd determined to retreat all the way back to the Kanawha valley, but Wise was strongly against it. Wise proposed, instead, to go only as far as Sewell Mountain. There he went, in defiance of orders from Floyd. And there Wise made camp—named it after his own disposition, as it were. There he sat at Camp Defiance. From there, also, he was removed from his command and recalled to Richmond.

While at Sewell Mountain, Captain Roberts Coles was able to write a letter to his uncle, John Rutherfoord in Richmond; he had bought a quire of paper for seventy-five cents and made ink out of gunpowder, water, and brown sugar. By this time his parents had learned of his enlistment.

Camp Defiance, October 13th
My dear Uncle,

    I should have long ago answered your first letter, but for the peculiar state of our affairs in Sewell Mt. The letter was rec'd at the time of the expected attack on our position. . . . I do not believe father ever supposed my entering the army was in want of respect for him; he knows too well the love I bear him, & which he so well deserves at the hands of all his children. I do not believe any family was ever more perfectly devoted to each other than my parents & their children. I know not what I would give if I could but correspond with them now & even occasionally see them. . . . Although born in Phila I have always regarded myself as a Virginian. V^a is the land of my father. Out of a large family not one has ever yet been buried off its soil. My own most pleasant associations have all been connected with Albemarle. I have always looked forward to my annual visits there as a boy as the principle objective during the year. The name of Coles has always seemed to me to belong to Va. At school, the boys used frequently to joke me for calling myself a Virginian, & disclaiming myself as a Philadelphian. I cannot account for the real veneration & lure I have always felt for the old State. My father and mother know my feelings as well as do I. I claim my share of paternity in Enniscorthy, & the corresponding right to defend it. . . . I know that father, long as he has been separated from the land of his birth, and in spite of his objections to its institutions still preserves undiminished the pride of State & would shudder at the thought of its being overrun by any invader. The charge if ever brought against him of being a Black Republican, because he remains at the North, is false. . . . My every feeling of patriotism is enlisted in the present struggle, my love towards my parents draws me in an opposite direction. Give my love to Aunt Emily & your circle & believe me your aff nephew

Roberts Coles[9]

The regiment learned, on 10 December, that it was being recalled to Richmond.[10] The Forty-sixth marched to Salem, then moved by rail to Norfolk. Orders soon bade them move south to Albemarle Sound. They camped for two weeks at "Naggs Head," in the vicinity of a strategic but neglected Confederate position on the North Carolina coast.[11]

General Wise, recalled to Richmond late in the fall of 1861, grew adamant that his command should be returned to him. The War Department, perhaps with some reluctance, handed him the apparently straightforward assignment of overseeing the defenses of Roanoke Island. Captain Roberts Coles and the Green Mountain Grays, together with the other companies of the Forty-sixth, remained at Nagg's Head, located across the inland channel from the northern point of Roanoke Island: a reserve for the main defensive unit on the island.

* * *

North Carolina is shielded from the full force of the Atlantic by a wisp of sandy capes reaching four hundred miles from Virginia Beach in the north to Cape Fear in the south. Although only a mile or so in width in most places (less, even, in some) and composed entirely of fickle dunes and shifting sandy promontories that appear spindly and fragile on any map, the capes of North Carolina provide a deadly barrier of sand bars to ocean vessels.

Ships can gain access to the east coast of North Carolina only by first passing into Pamlico Sound at one of only a few inlets: places like

Hatteras, Ocracoke, Swash (smaller boats might squeak through elsewhere). Once inside the cape, overland access to Norfolk, Petersburg, and the Confederate capital at Richmond can be gained then by running north into Albemarle Sound. The entrance to Albemarle Sound from Pamlico is a narrow passage corked up by Roanoke Island.

Roanoke Island controlled the entrance to Albemarle Sound and points inland. Despite its strategic importance, little attention had been expended on Roanoke Island by the Confederacy. Three small fortifications had been erected, protected by a few small cannon and defended by five small gunboats and a minor hatchery of untrained and unpaid troops, twenty-five hundred overall.[12]

* * *

Early in February, Brigadier General Ambrose Everett Burnside, the battle-hardened commander of the newly commissioned North Carolina Expeditionary Corps (dramatically referred to in excited front-page articles in the northern papers as the "Burnside Expedition"), steamed into Pamlico Sound with his Union expedition of three brigades and twenty-seven ships (carrying a force of seventy-five hundred men). On 6 February, Burnside sat comfortably on the south side of Roanoke Island; Wise had been struck with pneumonia and fever and lay bedridden at Nagg's Head. Command of the Confederate troops passed to Colonel H. M. Shaw of the Eighth North Carolina Regiment.

At 10:00 A.M. on 7 February, Company A (under Captain Obediah J. Wise, son of the infirm brigadier general) and Company I (under Captain Roberts Coles) were towed by steam tug from Nagg's Head to Roanoke Island. As the boat splashed through the sound, Coles quickly scratched a note in pencil on a torn sheet of paper to his fiancée, Jeannie Fairfax, Clifton House, Richmond:

On board transport—Feb 7th

The battle has commenced. In five minutes we will be on Roanoke Island. The light is beautiful. Our gun boats & batteries are engaging the enemy in full view & the shot & shell are whistling around us. If I fall God grant you a happy life, as happy a one as I would have tried to have made it. Be assured my last thoughts on Earth will be of you my dearest Jeannie. Your picture will be the last sight I shall see if time is given me to look once more upon it. I have volunteered for this service. What honor I crave is only craved that you may share it. May God Almighty bless you and may we meet in the world to come if denied that blessing again here. And now I strike for Virginia. Again, Good bye.

Yours forever
Roberts Coles

I have but the moment to write. The shells fly thick.[13]

Arrival brought into view the battle for the island, already in progress. The little fleet of reinforcements was soon discovered by the Federal forces; the two companies retreated under fire, discovering later a possible landing spot at the northern point of the island.[14] They struggled through the swamps on the island's northern point to join their comrades at about 6 P.M., forming a defensive line at a clearing near the middle of the ruddy and primitive island. Company I moved to the right flank; A to the left. A steady rain fell that night; the men slept in shifts as best they could.

At 7 the next morning, Burnside began his march on the redoubts. Firing commenced as the Twenty-third and Twenty-seventh Massachusetts emerged through the woods on the southern side of the battlefield's open clearing. In short order, the musket balls from the Massachusetts regulars were joined by grape. Captain Wise was wounded in the wrist. While bandaging himself and pleading to his subordinates that the wound was but trifling, a ball caught him full in the breast.

The Federals were held off for three hours as Burnside tried repeatedly to turn the flanks. The right flank was finally breached at about noon. The Yankee line charged ahead. Captain Roberts Coles took a bullet in the chest; he was killed on the spot.

With the Federals at the quick charge and the Confederate line squeezed against the northern shore, the island was quickly lost. In all about twenty-five hundred Confederate soldiers were captured. Twenty-two were killed; sixty-two were missing. Roanoke Island was in the hands of Union forces, and prisoners were marched into the Yankee camp that evening.

* * *

The Burnside Expedition to open a landing site for a push to the Confederate capitol had been a matter of front-page interest in the Philadelphia papers since the day after the battle.[15] Descriptions of the Burnside expedition and its departure from Fort Monroe at Norfolk were all that appeared in print for a day or two. Then, on 10 February, the headlines (sent in by telegraph to Philadelphia's *Daily Evening Bulletin*): "GLORIOUS

NEWS FROM NORTH CAROLINA." The entire rebel army had been destroyed or captured, and the Rebel gunboats had been taken or burned, the story said. Coverage ran to two full columns; details were many, but a cohesive overview of the battle was not yet available.

On 15 February, a complete review of the battle appeared on page 5 of the Philadelphia *Daily Evening Bulletin* by a *New York Times* correspondent. He described the geography and the disposition of the troops; he went over the movements of the ships as they threaded their way between Roanoke Island and the mainland. He reported on the commencement of the battle on 7 February and troop movements next morning, the taking of the forts, and the resistance felt by the Federal troops. He told about the turning of the tide at noon and the final capture of the rebel army. Then he reported on the aftermath. On the third column, midway down the page:

> At the right of the battery, scattered over the field were several rebel officers and soldiers, their bodies still warm, and the life-blood oozing from ghastly wounds. Among these I came upon one officer who lay near a tree where he had fallen, pierced by a bullet in the left breast. His long, pale features, which were calm as those of a person asleep, indicated more than ordinary character, and his dark hazel eye still half open bespoke intelligence not often met with on the field. He was plainly but neatly dressed, though without anything like a uniform to indicate his rank. I thought of the parents of this rash, misguided man, and though I had no clue to his identity, could not resist the desire to remove a lock of his hair as a memento. Soon afterwards I met a prisoner in the person of Dr. Walter Coles, who was in search of Capt. Coles, of the Wise Legion. I showed him the body, which he identified as that of his cousin, and he stated that his parents resided in Philadelphia. Several others of the rebel dead lay on the field.[16]

News of the battle of Roanoke Island brought a thrill to households throughout Philadelphia, but the household of Edward Coles was deeply buried in grief. They were overwhelmed and powerless, lost, and in anguish. Perhaps the newspapers have it wrong? Maybe seriously wounded but alive?

Three days later, Edward Coles Jr. wrote an anguished note to his uncle in Richmond inquiring about the fate of his younger brother. Was there any chance that the identification of his body was faulty?[17]

Walter Coles accompanied the body to Richmond. Roberts Coles was buried in the family cemetery at Enniscorthy surrounded by graves of the family that had so captured his devotion. In about 1895, his sister, Mary, removed his remains to Philadelphia, where they were reinterred at the Woodlands Cemetery. Roberts lies beside his mother, and next to her is his father, Governor Edward Coles.[18]

* * *

On a grassy hill overlooking Beaverdam Creek in southern Albemarle County, the shell of a new home lay unfinished as of February 1862. With spring, the redbud would proclaim new growth, and white and pink dogwood flowers would brighten the view down the valley made by Eppes Creek. Tucker Coles never advanced the project he had begun before Roberts Coles went away to war. The house they were building for Roberts and his bride-to-be was abandoned. The roof was not up, and the floors were open to the spring rains. New plaster fell off in bits and chunks.

The Plantation went to Tucker's brother Peyton (a term of Roberts's will). After the end of the war, Peyton Coles conveyed the property back to his brother in payment of part of the deed of trust held by Tucker for the property. Outstanding on the deed of trust was a debt of $5,000. It was paid by Edward Coles Sr. The empty house on the little hill overlooking Beaverdam Creek decayed, and eventually the remains were hauled away.[19]

15

The Woodlands

Edward Coles left his western business interests in the hands of solicitor Isaac Prickett of Edwardsville, Illinois. Letters indicate that Prickett was, altogether, an unsatisfactory steward of Coles's holdings. Coles traveled back to Illinois and Missouri every few years in order to effect business that Prickett had failed to manage satisfactorily. Coles had, for instance, loaned money to Messrs. Wilson and Edwards of Edwardsville, secured by mortgage. Under personal financial distress, Edwards had been forced to assign the property to creditors (property that was, of course, not his to assign). Coles came up empty. Prickett took little or no action. Coles was forced to travel to settle the matter. He went to St. Louis in May 1839 and to Edwardsville in May 1842.[1] He watched carefully over his assets and traveled to supervise their management as long as his health permitted.

Edward Coles battled poor health for the final decade of his life, but ultimately he receded into privacy. Aching joints and troublesome digestion kept him housebound for much of the 1860s. Letters have not survived. His renown surely declined even as his life quieted to a certain stillness. Friends and family were all that were left.

Lincoln

Coles's lifelong efforts to weaken slavery (and to strengthen the republican ethos) together with his association with the founding fathers earned for him a share of affection in Philadelphia. Perhaps, it even reached to a modest level of esteem. He was no titan. His was, rather, a minor star in the Philadelphia firmament. Yet, there was warmth of feeling toward him.

Abraham Lincoln, the lawyer from Illinois, formed the Republican ticket with Hannibal Hamlin of Maine. On the evening of 18 May 1860, the Republicans called an impromptu meeting in celebration of the blessed event: the emergence of a ticket that had a reasonable hope of beating Stephen A. Douglas, who was leading the race for nomination by the Democrats. Lincoln had, after all, shown that he was a match for Douglas in a series of barnstorming public debates two years before. The meeting hall at the corner of Seventh and Chestnut was crowded that night. A band helped to amplify the excitement of the day with patriotic tunes. Dr. Smith, chair, called on William M. Bull, who roared out a collective congratulation on the success of the convention and outlined the life of Lincoln for the benefit of those not yet acquainted. Bull brayed "when the news spread through our city there was seen no smile on the faces of the Democracy. They had calculated upon Seward, and then they might have been successful. But now Douglas has not a shadow of a chance!"[2]

Moses A. Dropsie was next in the line of speakers, then William S. Pierce, and after him, Henry M. Brunner. No doubt the crowd was somewhat worn down by the oratory, so the stationary celebration graduated to a parade in the streets. Fireworks were already appearing in the night skies. A band was placed at the head of the procession. On they went, then, to the home of Judge John M. Read on Chestnut Street, gleefully marching and swaying to the trumpets and drum. It was both serenade and ballyhoo. Then the crowd marched to the home of Edward Coles on Spruce Street. Coles was too ill to make an appearance. He was too weak to address the crowd, so Moses Dropsie (still not at a loss for words, remarkably) lectured to the churning mass of Republicans in front of Mr. Coles's brownstone residence. Dropsie pointed out that it was Coles who had furthered the Republican cause in Illinois, and that so long as Republicanism shall survive, the likes of James Madison and Edward Coles will never be forgotten.[3]

Three cheers were tossed to the heights for the Honorable Edward Coles. Cheers followed for the newly formed Republican ticket. The band played some. After a time, the clamor died down, and the crowd dissolved into the city. The night air remained agitated with excitement until the small hours. Thirty-six years before, a small riot had gathered below the window of Edward Coles's room in Vandalia to hurl their venom at him. On that night, the crowd had despised its new governor; it had derided his resistance to slavery. He was, to them, little more than a traitor. But recollection of Coles's stand for racial fairness had traversed half a continent and survived for a generation and more. Now the Republicans gathered to celebrate what he had done. Under the window of his modest house in Philadelphia, they cheered as fireworks lit the night of Lincoln's nomination.

* * *

The election was held on 6 November 1860. The weather was bad, and Coles was unwell. Concerned that the combination of weather and infirmity would keep Coles from voting, Nicholas Trist offered his arm in support and accompanied the governor to the polling station.[4] Coles voted for Lincoln.

Douglas pocketed the electoral votes from only two northern states: Lincoln took the rest. The election was his with 180 electoral votes. A delegation of Philadelphians was successful in the coming weeks in persuading the president-elect to visit the city on his way from Illinois to the inauguration. Plans were laid, and the great city of Philadelphia mounted a public display to welcome Lincoln on the very day of Washington's birth, normally a grand occasion in its own right.

Lincoln arrived at the Kensington Depot just before four o'clock on Thursday, 21 February. Huge crowds pressed against the fence surrounding the depot; squads of police formed on display within. As Lincoln's train slowed to a graceful halt, a salute of thirty-four guns was blasted by the Minute Men of '76, under Captain Caspar M. Berry. A storm of confusion churned the throng. Noise and cheering rose in gusts. Then the procession formed to see the president-elect to his residence in the newly completed Continental Hotel (said to be not only the newest big hotel but also the biggest big hotel in the nation). Fire-company bells and cheers rose to meet the barouches and carriages carrying the president-elect and his party as it made a clangorous entrance to the downtown. The parade route was choked with bunting and flags, and streets were bursting with a ruck of citizens, all straining for a view.

The crowds were of such size and the parade of such breadth that they did not reach the Continental Hotel until darkness was falling. Ninth Street had been cleared, so the entrance of the hotel received its guests without much difficulty. The mayor and other leading figures, with the president-elect and vice president–elect, made their way to the second-story balcony overlooking the clotted boulevard. The crowds surged to take up every space below as the first speech of welcome commenced. Little could be heard below, of course: cheers and shouts drowned out the speechmaking. Following the reception ceremony, Lincoln and his party retired to their apartments and took hurried meals. Then selected dignitaries of the town (city counselors and such) were ferried briefly into one of the parlors of the hotel for the thrill of meeting the president-elect.

They were well behind schedule by the time general citizenry were invited to see Lincoln, standing at the top of the landing of the grand staircase. The band played airs and marches on the balcony to the wild scene in the streets.

Edward Coles must have improved in health since the election. He was at the Continental Hotel, fighting the crowds for a better view. He made his way through the sea of Philadelphians near the front door until he managed to get close to the front of the crowd. His pocket was picked. Someone grabbed his wallet, even with squads of policemen at hand, repeatedly shouting "Move on, Gentlemen! Move on, Gentlemen!" to the mob. Getting Lincoln's attention, Coles was able finally to make his way to the side of this man who was being honored as president-elect on Washington's birthday. The two men from Illinois shared a moment of mutual recognition. Lincoln was delighted by this brief meeting and told Coles that he was still revered throughout Illinois. Coles took Lincoln's warmth as a tribute and cherished the acknowledgment of his role in the state.[5]

On 23 September 1862, the Emancipation Proclamation was signed by the President of the United States under powers granted to him by the state of war then in effect. Edward Coles would live to see the proclamation activated on 1 January the next year and to see the ratification of the Thirteenth Amendment to the Constitution. He would live to see the end of slavery.

Photograph of Edward Coles taken shortly before his death. Courtesy Winterthur Museum.

* * *

Of his family's generation, only one sister outlived Edward. Isaac Coles had died in 1841. Enniscorthy, the family seat and Isaac's home, had burned to the ground a week before Christmas two years prior. It was mid-day when an outdoor fire northwest of the house was whipped into a blaze by local winds. It ignited the gable end of the main building. The house was destroyed. Gone with the fire were most of the towering tulip poplars that framed and shaded the house. Burnt were the shrubs and plantings that graced the family house on Green Mountain. Most of the furniture, paintings, and the library were saved.[6]

Both Sallie and John III passed away in 1848. The following year, Rebecca died. Walter died in 1854, and Mary in 1856. Tucker died five years later, followed by Elizabeth in 1865.

Edward passed away on 7 July 1868 in his home at 1303 Spruce Street. He was eighty-two years old. Emily would die three years later at the age of seventy-six. A notice of Edward Coles's death appeared in Philadelphia's *Daily Evening Bulletin* on 8 July. It was two lines in length. It gave the date of death and the age. The note was repeated the next day.[7]

Edward Coles was buried at Woodlands, a gracious parkland cemetery with curving roads and walkways surrounding the Woodlands Mansion in western Philadelphia. The family plot is a teardrop of grass enclosed by a raised curb.[8] Governor Coles was laid in the family vault at the heart of the plot. He was joined by his wife, Sallie, on 7 April 1883 and by his daughter Mary on 29 October 1920. And Roberts, his youngest, who had perished at the Battle of Roanoke Island, was moved to the vault also. Roberts was placed there beside his mother on 25 September 1895.

On Saturday, 11 July 1868, an obituary appeared in the *Daily Evening Bulletin* of Philadelphia under "City Bulletins." It was one of eight minor notices. Just a single column-inch of small type noting Edward Coles's passing, his former relationship with James Madison, his ties to a political era of the past, and his role as Governor of Illinois when political affairs in the west were primitive.

Epilogue

The cause of racial freedom in Illinois moved forward slowly and with hesitation. The convention struggle of 1824 ended talk of legalizing slavery in Illinois and set the state on an uneven road toward greater racial justice. Racial injustice remained a fact of life, however. Free black persons could be kidnapped with impunity well into the 1830s. Legislation restricting the arrival of free black people in the state was passed in 1829 and in 1848 and again in 1853. More than fifteen years after Illinois' political watershed of 1824, black people were finally relieved of the legal obligation to prove they were not slaves (the case of *Bailey v. Cromwell* in 1841, argued by Abraham Lincoln). "French slaves" were finally set loose from the ties perpetuating their bondage six years after that (*Jarrott v. Jarrott*, 1845). The Underground Railway carried large numbers of slaves through three Illinois branch lines to Canada, signifying both resistance to slavery and viable support for the sanctity of ownership of slave property. By 1848, the antislavery Liberty Party won majorities in eighteen northern counties (only eight years after its founding in the east). And the state constitution was revised in 1848—it forbade slavery once and for all. Edward Coles was not responsible in any direct sense for these changes. His contribution was in standing firmly against a tide toward slavery in Illinois. His perseverance in that stand and the victory that came of it formed a pivot point in Illinois history that is palpable. The stand he took made a difference. It is not too much to say that the path by which Illinois headed toward racial justice had the tenure and good faith of Edward Coles at its crossroad.

Accolades to Edward Coles have been modest. In 1885, when the Phillips Decorative Company of Chicago produced eight murals for the walls of the north and south corridors of what is now the first floor of the capitol in Springfield, Illinois, Edward Coles was cast as a heroic subject. The moment of freedom when on the Ohio River Coles announced his intention to his slaves is captured in one of these murals as a signal moment in Illinois history. Artistic license was taken with some of the details, but there is no error in its sentiment: the State of Illinois recognizes and officially celebrates the symbolic and moral meaning of its second governor's poignant and principled battle against slavery. In 1953, the National Urban League, under the authority of Illinois Governor William G. Stratton, laid a wreath on the grave of Edward Coles.[1] In 1967, as the sesquicentennial of Illinois approached, the well-known choral director Norman Luboff composed an oratorio about Edward Coles and the freeing of his slaves.[2] A singular biography of Coles—an affectionate and partisan trumpet to the heroic side of this story—was published in 1882. Occasional summary articles have appeared in regional history journals, pointing to fitful rediscovery of the story every decade or so. More frequent, Edward Coles has made cameo appearances in many books on the antebellum south to illustrate the high road not taken or to explore the paradoxes of Jefferson's character.

The name of Edward Coles has played among the footnotes of great and celebrated Americans. Yet, he has not surfaced as a significant historical worthy, and the reasons bear consideration. First, Edward Coles has no home. He turned his back on Virginia, renouncing it as a slaveholding blot on the republican covenant. He turned away from Illinois after scarcely ten years of tumultuous life on the frontier and lived the rest of his life, quietly, in Pennsylvania. He was tied to principle more than to place, so no place has called him son. A secondary reason why Coles's legacy resides in the footnotes rather than the main text of history is emancipation is a sure road to obscurity.

Coles's dim legacy tracks with those of other great emancipators. Robert Carter III, whose manumission of more than 450 slaves has, until very recently, won him little notice in Virginia history. The emancipation stories of John Randolph and Robert Pleasants are similarly obscure in the telling of the history of Virginia. We take delight in grand scale and in history that is big and durable with sweep, majesty, and moment. The emancipators have not made that impression on us. Their good deeds were primarily private, occurring offstage. They attracted more derision than admiration, overall, and imitators did not rush to their side. Even John Hammond Moore, who produced a unique and generally balanced review of slavery in Virginia's Albemarle County, was somewhat dismissive of Coles's emancipation. Coles was, after all, wealthy and could well afford the financial sacrifice.[3]

As a matter of historical moment, private emancipations form significant reminders that support for slavery was never entire. Slavery proponents often harbored great passion, and as men of property, they controlled the engines of government and had great influence over the means and directions of broad public opinion. Support for slavery gave the appearance of being monumental in the south, but it never lacked fissures and cracks. Some exploited those cracks and doubts, pushing back, often quietly and privately, with freedom through deeds of gift and wills. A few took on the institution more directly with courage and fierce insistence. Racism covered the entire enterprise with a pervasive shroud that helped to perpetuate both privilege and injustice. The emancipators provide a subtle but frequent reminder that it was possible to give freedom, and they point to the moral and literal meanings of the country's founding premises and the Bible's core instruction. The grand flow of history in America is surely supported and in some measure constituted by these smaller currents.

Perhaps time and history have caught up with Edward Coles. Perhaps Edward Coles and Robert Carter III and Robert Pleasants and the many hundreds of other Virginians who freed their slaves at various times are emerging, now, as historical worthies. Two songs are to be sung to this new melody in the American story. First, the histories of emancipations in America neatly confirm what historian John Hope Franklin claims: black histories and white histories, treated separately, fall short. In joining black and white stories together, American history takes on depth and meaning that better reflects the struggles that have marked our past. Second, histories of emancipation lay threadbare the tapestry of rationalizations, circumstances, and financial tangles that held back Virginians, Illinoisans, and others from living up to the national covenant with freedom. Still, durable patches of resistance to slavery persisted in the south, and they, too, are part of the story. The histories of emancipations in America show that it was difficult but possible to give freedom. These stories add weight to the costly failures by so many (founding father and common citizen alike) who were witness to and aware of the inhumanity of slavery and did not act. The life of Edward Coles demonstrates the enduring truth of one republican belief: justice is not the exclusive product of the great men of history. It is very often the product of great citizens.

NOTES
BIBLIOGRAPHY
INDEX

Notes

"Dust in the Balance": An Introduction

1. E. Coles, "Autobiography," n.p.
2. Alvord, *Governor Edward Coles*, ix.
3. E. Coles, "Autobiography," n.p.

1. River and Opportunity

1. W. B. Coles, *Coles Family of Virginia*, 35. John Coles (1705–47) was the grandfather of Edward Coles.
2. Ibid., 35.
3. Langhorne, Lay, and Rieley, *Virginia Family and Its Plantation Houses*, 6; W. B. Coles, *Coles Family of Virginia*, 35.
4. Ward, *Richmond*, 22.
5. Many families of Richmond were intermarried and thus related. Mary Ann Winston's sister married Patrick Henry Sr., so the Coles's families counted the Henrys among their in-laws and relations.
6. W. B. Coles, *Coles Family of Virginia*, 35.
7. Ibid., 40.
8. J. Coles II, Ledger of John Coles, 1780–1807, Smith-Carter Papers.
9. W. B. Coles, *Coles Family of Virginia*, 51–57.
10. J. Coles II, Ledger of John Coles, 1780–1807, Smith-Carter Papers.
11. Ibid.
12. Langhorne, Lay, and Rieley, *Virginia Family and Its Plantation Houses*, 27.
13. W. B. Coles, *Coles Family of Virginia*, 52. The children of John Coles were as follows: John "Jack" (1769–73), Walter (1772–1854), John III (1774–1848), Mary Elizabeth (1776–1856), Isaac (1778–78), Isaac (1780–1841), Tucker (1782–1861), Rebecca (1784–1849), Edward (1786–1868), Sarah (1789–1848), Elizabeth (1791–1865), William (1793–94), and Emily Anne (1795–1871). Ibid.
14. R. B. Davis, *Intellectual Life in Jefferson's Virginia 1790–1830*, 14–15.
15. "Notes on Edward Coles, 1863," E. Coles Papers, Historical Society of Pennsylvania. See also W. B. Coles, *Coles Family of Virginia*, 18; E. Woods, *Albemarle County in Virginia*, 290.

16. Monroe, *Founding of the American Public School System*, 61–62.
17. "Notes on Edward Coles, 1863," E. Coles Papers, Historical Society of Pennsylvania; Woods, *Albemarle County in Virginia*, 88.
18. Morrison, *College of Hampden-Sydney*, 131; passport certificate, 1814, E. Coles Papers, Historical Society of Pennsylvania.
19. Edward Coles to John Coles [II], 6 December 1805, E. Coles Papers, Historical Society of Pennsylvania.
20. Edward Coles to John Coles [II], 5 September 1805, E. Coles Papers, Historical Society of Pennsylvania.
21. James Madison, "Manifestations of the Beneficence of Divine Providences toward America," 4.
22. Ibid.
23. See Bailyn, *Ideological Origins of the American Revolution* and *Origins of American Politics*; Wood, *Creation of the American Republic, 1776–1787*, *Radicalism of the American Constitution*, and *Revolutionary Characters*; Buel, *Securing the Revolution*; May, *Enlightenment in America*; Shalhope, "Toward a Republican Synthesis"; Appleby, "Social Origins of American Revolutionary Ideology" and *Capitalism and a New Social Order*; Yazawa, *From Colonies to Commonwealth*; and Diggins, *Lost Soul of American Politics*.
24. Appleby, *Capitalism and a New Social Order*, 95.
25. The best discussions can be found in Bailyn, *Ideological Origins of the American Revolution*, and Wood, *Creation of the American Republic, 1776–1787*.
26. See especially Crowe, "Bishop James Madison and the Republic of Virtue."
27. Bishop J. Madison, "Address to the Members of the Protestant Episcopal Church in Virginia," 22.
28. May, *Enlightenment in America*, 138.
29. Crowe, "Bishop James Madison and the Republic of Virtue," 58.
30. Edward Coles to John Coles, 6 December 1805, E. Coles Papers, Historical Society of Pennsylvania.
31. Edward Coles to John Coles, 6 November 1806, E. Coles Papers, Historical Society of Pennsylvania.
32. E. Coles, "Autobiography," n.p.
33. Ibid.
34. Ibid. For more on the paradox of slavery and American life, see J. C. Miller, *Wolf by the Ears*, and Morgan, *American Slavery, American Freedom*. Miller shows the dilemma Coles faced: his elders agreed that slavery was evil and had to come to an end but shrugged their shoulders about how to achieve its demise.
35. John Coles [II] to Edward Coles, 7 May, 30 April, and 1 April 1807, E. Coles Papers, Historical Society of Pennsylvania.
36. John Coles [II] to Edward Coles, 10 June 1807, E. Coles Papers, Historical Society of Pennsylvania.
37. Ibid.

38. Rebecca Coles, copy of memoranda from almanac, 1803–27, Coles Family Papers, Historical Society of Pennsylvania.

39. E. Coles, "Emancipation," n.p.

2. Man of Property

1. John Coles, will, Will Book 4:289, Register of Wills, Circuit Court, Albemarle County, VA. John Coles lived from 1745 to 1808.

2. Ibid.

3. Elizabeth Langhorne to K. Edward Lay, 1983, Langhorne Papers.

4. The property is located on State Road 635, off State Road 6 at about Greenfield at the west end of the Rockfish Valley in Virginia's Nelson County.

5. Lay, "Coles Family Houses," n.p.

6. John Coles II, "Ledger of John Coles, 1780–1807," acc. no. 9533, E. Coles Papers, Small Special Collections Library.

7. The land, located at Beaverdam, was transferred in 1785 and was close to a Coles grist mill on the Hardware River. See Langhorne, Lay, and Rieley, *Virginia Family and Its Plantation Houses*, 23.

8. John Coles II, "Ledger of John Coles, 1780–1807," acc. no. 9533, E. Coles Papers, Small Special Collections Library.

9. E. Coles, "Autobiography," n.p.

10. John Coles to Edward Coles, 24 December 1812, deed book 240, Albemarle County Court house.

11. Burin, *Slavery and the Peculiar Solution*, 108.

12. E. Coles, "Autobiography," n.p.; E. Coles, "Emancipation," n.p.

13. Cappon, "Personal Property Tax List of Albemarle County, 1782."

14. Moore, *Albemarle*, 85; Cappon, "Personal Property Tax List of Albemarle County, 1782."

15. Dunn, *Dominion of Memories*, 50.

16. Levy, *First Emancipator*.

17. Wolf, *Race and Liberty in the New Nation*; Sheppard, "Question of Emancipation in Virginia from the Revolution to the Slavery Debate of 1832," 193.

18. Ibid.

19. T. S. Babcock, "Manumission in Virginia 1782–1806," 50, 52, 54.

20. Irving Brant, *James Madison*, 2:401; D. Madison, *Memoirs and Letters of Dolley Madison*, 4.

21. D. Madison, *Memoirs and Letters of Dolley Madison*, 5, 8.

22. Blair, *Negro in Virginia*, 41.

23. "Notes of Edward Coles," 1863, E. Coles Papers, Historical Society of Pennsylvania.

24. In 1816, this law was further amended, permitting newly freed slaves to petition the legislature for permission to remain in the state, based on meritorious service and good behavior. J. C. Miller, *Wolf by the Ears*, 128; Schwarz, *Slave Laws in Virginia*, 57.

25. Schwarz, *Migrants Against Slavery*, 13.

26. E. Coles, "Autobiography," n.p.

27. Lippincott, "Edward Coles, Second Governor of Illinois," 60.

28. E. Coles, "Autobiography," n.p., and "Emancipation," n.p. In the latter, he commented that his family "reminded me that I had no profession, and would not have the means of supporting myself."

29. E. Coles, "Autobiography," n.p., and "Emancipation," n.p.

30. Stagg, Cross, and Perdu, *Papers of James Madison*, 2:351; Bear and Stanton, *Jefferson's Memorandum Books*, 1147.

31. Stagg, Cross, and Perdu, *Papers of James Madison*, 2:351; W. B. Coles, *Coles Family of Virginia*, 93.

32. Stagg, Cross, and Perdu, *Papers of James Madison*, 2:151.

33. Isaac Coles to James Madison, 12 December 1809, E. Coles Papers, Chicago Historical Society. This incident was not the last time Isaac's temper and violent streak got him in trouble. He would be involved in a similar situation as an officer on the northern front during the War of 1812. That attack led to his resignation from the army, once again under a cloud of controversy. For further details about his resignation, see E. Coles Papers, Perkins Library.

34. Stagg, Cross, and Perdu, *Papers of James Madison*, 2:151.

35. W. B. Coles, *Coles Family of Virginia*, 99.

36. Edward Coles to James Madison, 8 January 1810, E. Coles Papers, Princeton University Library.

37. E. Coles, "Autobiography," n.p. See also Ketcham, "Dictates of Conscience," 51. His sister Rebecca records that his departure from Green Mountain was on 12 January 1810. Rebecca Coles, memoranda from the almanacs of Rebecca Coles, Coles Family Papers, Historical Society of Pennsylvania.

38. Young, *Washington Community*, 40–46; Wills, *James Madison*, 59–62.

39. Young, *Washington Community*, 181.

40. Wood, *Revolutionary Characters*, 169. Gordon S. Wood argues that Madison strongly supported the embargo as a strategy to avoid war but achieve its aims. Ibid.

41. Ibid., 133–34, 197, 226, 233.

42. Seale, *President's House*, 123.

43. Ibid., 128.

44. Ferling, *Adams vs. Jefferson*, 44.

45. Furman, *White House Profile*, 57.

46. Hunt-Jones, *Dolley and the "Great Little Madison,"* 42.

47. Edward Coles to Hugh Blair Grigsby, 23 December 1854, container 85, Rives Papers.

48. Young, *Washington Community*, 222–23.

49. William Pinckney to Edward Coles, n.d., E. Coles Papers, Princeton University Library.

50. Joseph Hawkins to Edward Coles, 10 February 1813, E. Coles Papers, Princeton University Library.

51. Edward Coles to James Madison, 20 April 1813, E. Coles Papers, Chicago Historical Society; Nicholas Biddle to Edward Coles, 6 November 1813, E. Coles Papers, Princeton University Library. Nicholas Biddle (1786–1844) had a varied and erudite career. He was secretary for James Monroe (while U.S. minister to England), editor of *Port Folio* magazine, state legislator (and promoter of public education), and editor of Lewis and Clark's report on their travels to the Pacific Ocean. Biddle is primarily remembered, however, for his role as president of the Bank of the United States for twenty years (1819 to 1839).

52. For instance, Joseph Story to Edward Coles, 28 November 1811; Richard Rush to Edward Coles, 25 November 1811; and Christopher Hughes to Edward Coles, 5 February 1814, all in E. Coles Papers, Princeton University Library.

53. Edward Coles to James Madison, 22 May 1813, E. Coles Papers, Chicago Historical Society.

54. White, *Jeffersonians*, 323.

55. Edward Coles to his brother [John], 30 November 1810, E. Coles Papers, Historical Society of Pennsylvania.

56. Robert Fulton to Edward Coles, 17 January 1815, E. Coles Papers, Princeton University Library.

57. Edward Coles to John Coles, 18 March 1811, E. Coles Papers, Historical Society of Pennsylvania.

58. James Monroe to Edward Coles, 19 May 1811, Princeton University Library; 25 May 1811, E. Coles Papers, Princeton University Library.

59. Edward Coles to his mother, 26 May 1813, E. Coles Papers, Historical Society of Pennsylvania.

60. Edward Coles to Dolley Payne Madison, 10 June 1811, E. Coles Papers, Princeton University Library. For a more detailed review of the Smith Pamphlet Affair and the role played by Coles in informing Dolley Madison on matters political, see Allgor, *Perfect Union*, 259–61.

61. James Monroe to Edward Coles, 19 May 1811 and 25 May 1811, E. Coles Papers, Princeton University Library.

62. James Monroe to Edward Coles, 19 May 1811, E. Coles Papers, Princeton University Library for the Gerry information. For Coles's version of the Jefferson-Adams friendship, see Edward Coles to Henry S. Randall, 11 May 1857, E. Coles Papers, Princeton University Library; also printed as appendix 25 in Randall, *Life of Thomas Jefferson*, 639.

63. Thomas Jefferson to Benjamin Rush, 5 December 1811, in Ford, *Writings of Thomas Jefferson*, 298.

64. See Kraut and Fox, *Completion of Independence 1790–1830*, 5:200–201; Perkins, *Prologue to War*, 425–26; Risjord, "1812," 201.

65. Ketcham, *James Madison*, chap. 19.

66. Edward Coles to John Coles, 6 May 1812, E. Coles Papers, Historical Society of Pennsylvania.

67. Edward Coles to Payne Todd, 3 January 1815, E. Coles Papers, Princeton University Library. John Payne Todd (1792–1852) was the son of Dolley Madison; the sole surviving child of her marriage to John Todd.

68. Ibid.

69. Edward Coles to Nicholas Biddle, 29 January 1815, Miscellaneous Autograph File.

70. Edward Coles to Payne Todd, 3 January 1815, E. Coles Papers, Princeton University Library.

71. Edward Coles to Nicholas Biddle, 29 January 1815, Miscellaneous Autograph File; Nicholas Biddle to Edward Coles, 17 January 1815, E. Coles Papers, Princeton University Library. Coles believed that the national government should be the supreme power in waging war, and the states should defer once the declaration was passed. Biddle's handwriting becomes more hurried and messy as the letter proceeds, suggesting the depth of emotion he felt on the matter of Congress's actions. See also Nicholas Biddle to Edward Coles, 19 February 1815, E. Coles Papers, Princeton University Library.

72. Edward Coles to John Coles, 25 November 1812, signed, E. Coles Papers, Princeton University Library.

73. "Naval Entertainment," *National Intelligencer*, 28 November 1812.

74. Brant, *James Madison*, 5:122, gives a full account of the events. Ketcham notes that the party was so convivial that the secretary of the navy became "totally drunk."

75. The battle occurred on 25 October 1812, and the prize arrived in New York harbor on 4 December 1812.

76. Edward Coles to John Coles, 30 November 1810, E. Coles Papers, Historical Society of Pennsylvania.

77. Edward Coles to John Coles, 28 January 1811, E. Coles Papers, Princeton University Library; Coles to family, 3 February 1810, E. Coles Papers, Historical Society of Pennsylvania.

78. Edward Coles to his mother, 30 December 1819, E. Coles Papers, Historical Society of Pennsylvania. Examples of Edward's concern about his bachelor status are in Edward Coles to Nicholas Biddle, 15 May 1816, Miscellaneous Autograph File; James Madison to Edward Coles, 13 September 1819, E. Coles Papers, Princeton University Library.

79. Edward Coles to John Coles, 27 February 1810, E. Coles Papers, Historical Society of Pennsylvania.

80. Edward Coles to John Hawkins, 1 or 7 March 1809, E. Coles Papers, Princeton University Library.

81. Tench Ringgold to Edward Coles, 12 April 1815, E. Coles Papers, Princeton University Library.

82. Edward Coles to John Coles, 6 May 1812, E. Coles Papers, Historical Society of Pennsylvania.

83. Ibid. Nothing is known about Miss A., and she is not spoken of in any of the other correspondence.

84. Ibid. Also see Dolley Madison to Edward Coles 6 March 1816, E. Coles Papers, Princeton University Library. Tench Ringgold, a college friend, teased Coles about his Miss Swann on several occasions. In one letter, he spent two pages on the subject. Tench Ringgold to Edward Coles, 12 and 23 April 1815, E. Coles Papers, Princeton University Library.

85. Quoted in Anthony, *Dolley Madison*, 204.

86. Edward Coles to John Coles, 17 December 1810 and Edward Coles to family, 3 February 1810, E. Coles Papers, Historical Society of Pennsylvania; Edward Coles to Campbell, Spring 1808, E. Coles Papers, Princeton University Library. The romantic side of the Virginia cavalier is borne out in Coles's letters.

87. Samuel Lockwood to Thomas Mather, 6 March 1822, Mather Papers. The letter indicates that Coles was still trying to marry in Illinois.

88. Edward Coles to John Coles, 27 February 1810, E. Coles Papers, Historical Society of Pennsylvania; Isaac Coles to James Madison, 29 October 1810, E. Coles Papers, Chicago Historical Society. Both letters discuss the raising of sheep in Albemarle County and the success of pippin apples.

89. E. Coles, "Autobiography," n.p.

90. Edward Coles to John Coles, 27 February 1810, E. Coles Papers, Historical Society of Pennsylvania.

91. Edward Coles to John Coles, 28 January 1811, E. Coles Papers, Princeton University Library; Edward Coles to John Coles, 26 March 1812, E. Coles Papers, Historical Society of Pennsylvania. The letters reveal Edward's frustration at not being able to sell his plantation.

92. Coles to Mother/sisters, 4 February 1810, E. Coles Papers, Historical Society of Pennsylvania.

93. Edward Coles to John Coles, 6 May 1812, E. Coles Papers, Historical Society of Pennsylvania.

94. Ibid.

95. Edward Coles to John Coles, 1 July 1814, E. Coles Papers, Historical Society of Pennsylvania.

96. Edward Coles to Isaac Coles, 18 September 1815, E. Coles Papers, Historical Society of Pennsylvania.

97. Edward Coles to John Coles, 30 November 1810, E. Coles Papers, Historical Society of Pennsylvania; E. Coles, Edward Coles to W. C. Flagg, 28 March 1861, E. Coles, "To W. C. Flagg," 61–62. See also E. Coles, "Autobiography," n.p.

98. E. Coles, "Notes," 1863, folder 23, box 3, Coles Family Papers, Historical Society of Pennsylvania.

99. Edward Coles to John Coles, 3 November 1810, E. Coles Papers, Historical Society of Pennsylvania.
100. Edward Coles to James Madison, 22 September 1812, E. Coles Papers, Chicago Historical Society.
101. Brant, *James Madison,* 5:162.
102. Edward Coles to John Coles, 25 November 1812, E. Coles Papers, Princeton University Library.
103. See Shryock, *Medicine and Society in America 1660–1860,* 59–60, for information on Dr. Physick, who was known as the father of American surgery.
104. Edward Coles to John Coles, 28 March 1813, E. Coles Papers, Historical Society of Pennsylvania.
105. Edward Coles to his mother, 3 May 1813, E. Coles Papers, Historical Society of Pennsylvania.
106. Edward Coles to James Madison, 15 May 1813, E. Coles Papers, Chicago Historical Society. A sign of his improved health was the gossipy letter he wrote to Dolley Madison. Edward Coles to Dolley Madison, 22 May 1813, E. Coles Papers, Chicago Historical Society.
107. Edward Coles to John Coles, 8 September 1813, E. Coles Papers, Historical Society of Pennsylvania.
108. Edward Coles to James Madison, 10 August 1814, E. Coles Papers, Chicago Historical Society.
109. Edward Coles to his mother, 30 December 1819, E. Coles Papers, Historical Society of Pennsylvania.

3. Release

1. Green, *Washington,* 92.
2. For a recent discussion of the slave trade in the District of Columbia and efforts to control it after Coles had left, see Gudmestad, *Troublesome Commerce,* 35–61.
3. See Blair, *Negro in Virginia,* 177.
4. Horton, "Genesis of Washington's African American Community," 26.
5. For evidence of his favors for family and friends, see Edward Coles to John Coles, 1 August 1814, E. Coles Papers, Historical Society of Pennsylvania.
6. Edward Coles, "Autobiography," n.p.
7. Ibid.
8. Thomas Jefferson to John Manners, 22 February 1814; Thomas Jefferson to L. H. Girardin, 14 March 1814 ; Thomas Jefferson to Chevalier Luis de Onis, 28 April 1814; Thomas Jefferson to Thomas Law, 13 June 1814, all in Lipscomb and Bergh, *Writings of Thomas Jefferson,* vol. 14.
9. Thomas Jefferson to Dr. Thomas Cooper, 10 September 1814, in Lipscomb and Bergh, *Writings of Thomas Jefferson,* 14:179.
10. Edward Coles to Thomas Jefferson, 31 July 1814, E. Coles Papers, Princeton University Library.

11. Ibid.

12. Coles is often used as an example of the second generation leaving Virginia, fleeing slavery to end his own involvement in the institution. A more recent example of this interpretation is Whitman, *Challenging Slavery in the Chesapeake*, 102–3.

13. See, for example, J. C. Miller, *Wolf by the Ears*, 205–6; Schwarz, *Migrants Against Slavery*, 77; Kennedy, *Mr. Jefferson's Lost Cause*, 82.

14. Thomas Jefferson to Edward Coles, 25 August 1814, E. Coles Papers, Princeton University Library.

15. He did, in fact, go a little further. In his "Autobiography," Coles reports that Jefferson showed his letter to Coles to "a number of young and talented men," encouraging them to form a "phalanx" to eradicate slavery. Coles knows this because Jefferson confirmed it, and several of the young men contacted Coles and confirmed Jefferson's actions. April 1844.

16. Ellis, *American Sphinx*.

17. Peterson, *Jefferson Image in the American Mind*, 9–11.

18. J. C. Miller, *Wolf by the Ears*, 89.

19. Jefferson to Dr. Walter Jones, 31 March 1801, in Lipscomb and Bergh, *Writings of Thomas Jefferson*, 14:256.

20. Peterson, *Jefferson Image in the American Mind*, 174.

21. Thomas Jefferson to Dr. Thomas Cooper, 10 September 1814, in Lipscomb and Bergh, *Writings of Thomas Jefferson*, 179.

22. Edward Coles to Thomas Jefferson, 26 September 1814, E. Coles Papers, Princeton University Library.

23. All three letters were published without abridgment in E. B. Washburne's 1882 biography of Coles. For a useful discussion of the letters, see Malone, *Sage of Monticello*, 320. For the two letters written by Coles to Jefferson, see also E. Coles, "Letters of Edward Coles: Edward Coles to Thomas Jefferson."

24. This summary scarcely does adequate service to Oakes's argument; for the full treatment, see Oakes, *Slavery and Freedom*.

25. The private residence of Colonel John Tayloe III, located still at Eighteenth Street and New York Avenue NW, Washington, had been in use by French minister Louis Serurier, who offered the house to the president's use as he was planning to move temporarily to Philadelphia. The building is currently home to the American Architectural Foundation.

26. Edward Coles to R.S.M., extract, 21 March 1815, E. Coles Papers, Princeton University Library. The recipient is probably the president's nephew Robert Madison who lived at the White House at various times during the Madison's tenure. Coles tells Biddle much the same thing in an extract dated 6 April 1815 to the same recipient, E. Coles Papers, Princeton University Library, but here he stresses the permanence of any move west.

27. Tench Ringgold to Edward Coles, 23 April 1815, E. Coles Papers, Princeton University Library.

28. Edward Coles to Nicholas Biddle, 6 April 1815, E. Coles Papers, Princeton University Library. The letter presented is an extract in Coles's hand. A similar letter, written to "R.S.M." (probably Robert Madison) shares much the same language as that of Biddle but focuses less on family resistance to his views on slavery and acknowledges the 24 August 1814 letter he has received from Jefferson.
29. Edward Coles to James Madison, 25 July 1815, E. Coles Papers, Chicago Historical Society. See also Edward Coles to John Coles, 28 July 1815 and 11 September 1815, E. Coles Papers, Historical Society of Pennsylvania.
30. Edward Coles to Isaac Coles, 11 September 1815, E. Coles Papers, Historical Society of Pennsylvania.
31. Ibid.
32. Ibid.
33. Billington, "Frontier in Illinois History," 93–94.
34. For instance, to Payne Todd he had written, "I must therefore in the spring, however reluctantly, retire to the woods of the west . . . [but] before I bury myself in my retirement." Edward Coles to Payne Todd, 3 January 1815, E. Coles Papers, Princeton University Library.
35. E. Coles, account book, E. Coles Papers, Historical Society of Pennsylvania, n.p.
36. Nicholas Biddle to Edward Coles, 11 April 1816, E. Coles Papers, Princeton University Library.
37. Edward Coles to Nicholas Biddle, 15 May 1816, Miscellaneous Autograph File.
38. Ibid.
39. Ibid.
40. Payne Todd to Edward Coles, December 1815, E. Coles Papers, Princeton University Library.
41. James Madison to Edward Coles, 13 September 1819, E. Coles Papers, Princeton University Library.
42. Washburne, *Sketch of Edward Coles*, 39.
43. Ammon, *James Monroe*, 350; Levett Harris to William Pinckney, 10 October 1816, Diplomatic Dispatches, Russia. A fuller account is in Levett Harris to James Monroe, 13 October 1816, Diplomatic Dispatches, Russia. Edward Coles to James Monroe, 14 December 1816, Special Agents, speaks of Daschkoff's pro-British feelings.
44. Levett Harris to William Pinckney, 10 October 1816, Diplomatic Dispatches, Russia; James Madison to Edward Coles, 9 July 1816, E. Coles Papers, Chicago Historical Society.
45. James Madison to Edward Coles, 7 July 1816 and 9 July 1816, E. Coles Papers, Chicago Historical Society. Madison offered Coles the standard rate of pay, $6.00 a day, plus transportation costs.
46. E. Coles, "Autobiography," n.p.

47. Benjamin Harris to B. W. Crowninshield, 19 July 1816, Miscellaneous Collections of the Office of Naval Records. See also Benjamin Harris to William Bainbridge, 31 July 1816, and W. B. Crowninshield to A. J. Wadsworth, 2 August 1816, both in Miscellaneous Collections.

48. Edward Coles to Levett Harris, 30 September 1816, E. Coles Papers, Princeton University Library.

49. Edward Coles to John Coles, 4 October 1816, E. Coles Papers, Historical Society of Pennsylvania.

50. Edward Coles to Levett Harris, 5 October 1816, E. Coles Papers, Princeton University Library. A copy of the same letter is in the E. Coles Papers, Chicago Historical Society. Attached to this letter of protest is a note explaining that it was never sent because Harris had argued against such an action. Typically with a firm eye on his reputation, Coles was being very careful about his responsibility.

51. Edward Coles to James Monroe, 14 December 1816, ALS (copy), folder 16, box 1, E. Coles Papers, Princeton University Library.

52. Ibid.

53. Ibid.; William Eustis to James Monroe, 4 January 1817 and 17 January 1817, Diplomatic Dispatches, Netherlands.

54. "Notes on the Life of E. C.," E. Coles Papers, Historical Society of Pennsylvania, n.p.

55. George Mann to Edward Coles, n.d., and A. H. Rowan to Edward Coles, n.d., both in E. Coles Papers, Princeton University Library.

56. Adams, *Memoirs of John Q. Adams*, 477, 507.

57. See Birkbeck, *Notes on a Journey in America*, 8–9; Flower, *History of the English Settlement in Edward County Illinois*, 24–25.

58. Edward Coles to William Barry, 25 June 1858, E. Coles Papers, Chicago Historical Society.

59. E. Coles, "Autobiography," n.p.

60. Ibid.

61. Payne Todd to Edward Coles, December 1815, E. Coles Papers, Princeton University Library.

62. "History of Edward Coles," *Edwardsville Spectator*, 27 November 1821.

63. Edward Coles to William Barry, 25 June 1858, E. Coles Papers, Chicago Historical Society.

64. E. Coles, "Autobiography," n.p. The traditional sources that attribute the letter to Coles generally refer to Buck, *Illinois in 1818*.

65. George Churchill, "Diary," Churchill Papers.

66. E. Coles, "Autobiography," n.p.

67. Ibid.

68. Edward Coles to James Monroe, 11 October 1818, Coles Family Papers, Historical Society of Pennsylvania.

69. E. Coles, "Emancipation," n.p.

70. The scene is alluded to in ibid.

71. Lay, "Coles Family Houses."

72. E. Coles, "Autobiography," n.p.

73. Robert "Preacher" Crawford to Edward Coles, 23 October 1841, E. Coles Papers, Princeton University Library.

74. E. Coles, "Emancipation," n.p.; Edward Coles, letter to the editor, *Edwardsville Spectator*, 24 June 1822.

75. Ages and general descriptions of the slaves are taken from "Charges of County Commissioners of Madison County against Edward Coles, March 1824," in Alvord, *Governor Edward Coles*, 205. It is possible that the elderly slaves were named Molley, Frankey, or Grace. These slaves were transferred to Edward Coles in 1812 but did not travel with him to Illinois. Richardson in "Virginian Who Made Illinois a Free State" names the two women, Aunt Amanda and Aunt Sophie, but no source is given, and no direct evidence has been uncovered to confirm.

76. E. Coles, "Emancipation," n.p.

77. Ibid.

78. E. Coles, ledger of Edward Coles, 1819 to 1836, E. Coles Papers, Historical Society of Pennsylvania.

79. Coles sets the date of departure as 30 March 1819 in "Emancipation," but other sources indicate that the date was 1 April 1819. E. Coles, "Emancipation," n.p.

80. The route taken by the Coles slaves to Brownsville, Pennsylvania, is nowhere recorded. The route described in this narrative is conjectural. It is based on roads known to exist at the time and constitutes the most-direct means of traveling from Rockfish to Edwardsville, Illinois.

81. E. Coles, "Emancipation," n.p.; Edward Coles to John Coles, Brownsville, [PA], 11 April 1819, acc. no. 1729, E. Coles Papers, Small Special Collections.

82. Milton no longer exists, its buildings long gone and its foundations grown over entirely. Milton was a vibrant center for some generations during the golden years of tobacco but has left scarcely a mark on the Albemarle countryside.

83. Edward Coles to John Coles, Brownsville, [PA] 11 April 1819, acc. no. 1729, E. Coles Papers, Small Special Collections.

84. Pollard, *Under the Blue Ledge*, 39.

85. Edward Coles to John Coles, Brownsville, [PA], 11 April 1819, acc. no. 1729, E. Coles Papers, Small Special Collections Library.

86. Cramer, *Navigator*, 41.

87. Brownsville lived and died by the National Road. When the railroad from Philadelphia to Pittsburgh was completed, Brownsville began a decline, and it never recuperated. Many buildings of 1819 still stand in Brownsville. They are empty, darkened by time and all but forgotten, wondrous testaments to the noble role played by Brownsville, Pennsylvania, in America's expansion westward.

88. Edward Coles to John Coles, Brownsville, [PA], 11 April 1819, acc. no. 1729, E. Coles Papers, Small Special Collection.

89. Edward Coles to his mother, 24 April 1819, E. Coles Papers, Historical Society of Pennsylvania.

90. E. Coles, "Autobiography," n.p.

91. E. Coles, ledger of Edward Coles, 1819 to 1836, E. Coles Papers, Historical Society of Pennsylvania.

92. The story of Green is a detail for which there is no adequate context. According to Coles's later letter to James Madison, Green was the son of a General Green from Culpeper, Virginia. This letter implies that Green joined the party in Brownsville, but Green very soon dropped from notice in any correspondence from Coles. Explanation as to who the man is, his relationship to Coles, and his subsequent history are not available. Edward Coles to James Madison, 20 July 1819, in Daly, "Some Letters of Edward Coles," 5.

93. E. Coles, "Autobiography," n.p.

4. Beginning

1. E. Coles, "Autobiography," n.p.

2. Edward Coles to his mother, 24 April 1819, E. Coles Papers, Historical Society of Pennsylvania. The letter was "written 10 miles above Louisville."

3. Cramer, *Navigator*, 68.

4. Edward Coles to James Madison, 20 July 1819, in Daly, "Some Letters of Edward Coles," 5.

5. General James Taylor (1769–1848) was quartermaster general of the northwestern army during the War of 1812.

6. Edward Coles to his mother, 24 April 1819, E. Coles Papers, Historical Society of Pennsylvania.

7. E. Coles, "Autobiography," n.p.; E. Coles, "Emancipation," n.p.

8. E. Coles. "Emancipation," n.p.

9. E. Coles, "Autobiography," n.p.

10. Edward Coles to his mother, 24 April 1819, E. Coles Papers, Historical Society of Pennsylvania.

11. Ibid.

12. Quoted in Marie George Windell, ed., "The Road West in 1818, the Diary of Henry Vest Bingham," *Missouri Historical Review* 40, no. 1 (1945), 21–54, quoted in McCord, *Travel Accounts of Indiana 1679–1961*, 89.

13. E. Coles, "Emancipation," n.p.

14. Pyne, "Battling the 'National Sin,'" 72.

15. Harris, *History of Negro Servitude in Illinois*, 2.

16. Gillespie, *Recollections of Early Illinois and Her Noted Men*, 8.

17. Pyne, "Battling the 'National Sin,'" 72; J. E. Davis, *Frontier Illinois*, 54.

18. J. E. Davis, *Frontier Illinois*, 91.

19. Sutton, "Edward Coles and the Constitutional Crisis in Illinois, 1822–1824," 38.

20. Hand, "Negro Slavery in Illinois," 42–43.

21. William Morrison to Eliza Morrison, 27 August 1815, William Morrison Papers.

22. John Graham quoted by Judge Gillespie in E. B. Washburne, *Sketch of Edward Coles*, 62. Vincennes (or Post Vinsan, as it was often referred to) was the territorial capital of Indiana Territory from 1800 until 1809 when Illinois was formed as a separate territory.

23. Buck, *Illinois in 1818*, 184; J. E. Davis, *Frontier Illinois*, 116.

24. Pyne, "Battling the 'National Sin,'" 72.

25. Buck, *Illinois in 1818*, 187.

26. Boggess, *Settlement of Illinois, 1778–1830*, 179.

27. Buck, *Illinois in 1818*, 216.

28. Dillon, "Antislavery Movement in Illinois, 1809–1844," 38–42; Buck, *Illinois in 1818*, 218; Sweet, *Religion on the American Frontier, 1783–1840*, 1:94; T. Ford, *History of Illinois from Its Commencement as a State in 1818 to 1847*, 1:15.

29. Buck, *Illinois in 1818*, 255; T. Ford, *History of Illinois from its Commencement as a State in 1818 to 1847*, 72; W. R. Thompson, "Illinois Constitutions," 65. Edward Coles, who attended as an observer, believed that many (but not a majority) of the delegates favored making Illinois a slave state.

30. Dillon, "Antislavery Movement in Illinois, 1809–1844," 48; Buck, *Illinois in 1818*, 266.

31. U.S. Census for 1820.

32. For a description of the salt production in Illinois saline country, see Ben Gelman, "Industry in Southern Illinois Has Quite a Salty Past," *Southern Illinoisan*, March 6, 2002; George Washington Smith, "Salines of Southern Illinois."

33. E. Coles, "Undated Notes on the Making of Salt in the Saline District," E. Coles Papers, Princeton University Library.

34. Ben Gelman, "Industry in Southern Illinois Has Quite a Salty Past," *Southern Illinoisan*, March 6, 2002.

35. E. Coles, "Undated Notes on the Making of Salt in the Saline District," E. Coles Papers, Princeton University Library.

36. Ibid.

37. Rohrbough, *Land Office Business*, chap. 6.

38. Rothbard, *The Panic of 1819*, ii.

39. See, for instance, Gillespie, *Recollections of Early Illinois and Her Noted Men*, 10.

40. H. H. Hall to Postmaster of Vermillion County, 13 January 1832, Williams-Woodberry Collection.

41. Peter Cartwright, quoted in Barnhardt, "Sources of Southern Migration into the Old Northwest," 56. See also Patton, "Letters from North Carolina Emigrants in the Old Northwest, 1830–1834," 263–65.

42. Dillon, "Antislavery Movement in Illinois, 1809–1844," 9–11; Brown, *Historical Sketch of the Early Movement in Illinois for the Legalization of Slavery*, 12.

43. Sweet, *Religion on the American Frontier, 1783–1840*, 44.

44. Ibid., 91, 93, 526–27, 88n50.

45. Ibid., 93.

46. Lenton, *History of Methodism in Illinois from 1793–1832*, 213. For a recent discussion of Cartwright, see Bray, *Peter Cartwright*, 103–9.

47. Lenton, *History of Methodism in Illinois from 1793–1832*, 222; Agnew, "Methodism," 540, 504–5. Cartwright was a prodigy from Kentucky who became bishop in Illinois at the very young age of twenty-four. He was typical of frontier ministers in that he made his living by farming rather than preaching.

48. *Edwardsville (Illinois) Spectator*, 18 July 1820, has several letters on the issue; the paper of 25 July 1820 contains both Kane's and Edwards' letters; the results are in 8 August 1820. See also T. C. Pease, *Frontier State 1818–1848*, 72–73; Harris, *History of Negro Servitude*, 27–29.

49. T. Ford, *History of Illinois*, 51, and *Edwardsville (Illinois) Spectator*, 16 January 1821 and 6 February 1821. See also M. Mason, *Slavery and Politics in the Early Republic*, chap. 8.

5. A Rough Land of Great Promise

1. Travous, "Illinois Years of Edwards Coles," n.p.
2. Beck, *Gazetteer of the States of Illinois and Missouri*, 105.
3. Edward Coles to James Madison, 20 July 1819, in Daly, "Some Letters of Edward Coles," 5.
4. *(Shawneetown) Illinois Gazette*, 5 May 1821; Edward Coles to Henry S. Dodge, 22 February 1821, in Alvord, *Governor Edward Coles*, 255. The common view that clearing prairie required more than two horses appears to be contradicted by Coles's experience.
5. E. Coles, "Ledger of Edward Coles," n.p.
6. Ibid.
7. Nore and Norrish, *Edwardsville*, 33; Washburne, *Sketch of Edward Coles*, 53.
8. Washburne, "Sketch of Edward Coles," 46–47.
9. E. Coles, "Emancipation," n.p.
10. Nore and Norrish, *Edwardsville*, 33.
11. Sapp, *Madison County Court Records*.
12. Washburne, *Sketch of Edward Coles*, 202. See also Travous, "Illinois Years of Edwards Coles," n.p.
13. Wright, *Views of Society and Manners in America*, 520.
14. Hempstead. "Diary of a Yankee Farmer in Missouri 1819," 272, 286.
15. Ibid., 287.
16. Springer, "Edward Coles' Letter Regarding His Slaves," *Edwardsville (Illinois) Spectator*, 6 July 1822.
17. E. Coles, "Autobiography," n.p. The apparent discrepancy between the transfer of Manuel's debt from Coles to Dr. Walker and the repayment of the same debt to Coles directly is not resolved in any known documentation. Coles reports that papers of freedom were recorded in St. Louis. See Edward Coles to J. M. Peck, 30 April 1855 in Alvord, *Governor Edward Coles*, 353.
18. E. Coles, "Autobiography," n.p.

19. Springer, "Edward Coles' Letter Regarding His Slaves," *Edwardsville (Illinois) Spectator*, 6 July 1822. Springer, Jessie E. "Edward Coles Letter regarding His Slaves." Transcription of Coles's letter to *Edwardsville Spectator*. Madison County Historical Society, Edwardsville, Illinois, June 22, 1822.

20. Edward Coles to his mother, 24 April 1819, E. Coles Papers, Historical Society of Pennsylvania.

21. Evidence of Nancy Gaines's death is given in the letter of transmission written by Edward Coles in payment of a bond. Edward Coles to Madison County Commissioners, 31 January 1825, in Alvord, *Governor Edward Coles*, 210.

22. "History of Edward Coles," *Edwardsville(Illinois) Spectator*, 27 November 1821.

23. Rohrbaugh, *Land Office Business*, 23, 25.

24. Buck, *Illinois in 1818*, 55.

25. Travous, "Illinois Years of Edwards Coles."

26. Alvord, *Governor Edward Coles*, 221.

27. J. E. Davis, *Frontier Illinois*, 205.

28. Rohrbaugh, *Land Office Business*, 173–76.

29. Edward Coles to William Crawford, 10 November 1820, in Alvord, *Governor Edward Coles*, 224.

30. Ibid.

31. Edward Coles to William Crawford, 10 November 1820, in Alvord, *Governor Edward Coles*, 225.

32. Coles's frustrations are evident in his letter to D. P. Cook: "You [Cook] who are acquainted with the illiterate [cha]racter of *French settlers* can form some idea of the time required, and the trouble attending the taking of depositions for *seventy claims*." Edward Coles to D. P. Cook, 15 November 1820, in Alvord, *Governor Edward Coles*, 254.

33. See Edward Coles to James Madison, 20 July 1819, E. Coles Papers, Chicago Historical Society; "Edward Coles Account Book," 1818 to 1839, vol. 4, E. Coles Papers, Historical Society of Pennsylvania.

34. Norton, *Edward Coles*, 29.

35. E. Coles, "Emancipation," n.p.

36. Ibid.

37. Ibid.

38. The story is retold from E. Coles, "Emancipation," n.p.

39. Edward Coles to J. M. Peck, 30 April 1855, in Alvord, *Governor Edward Coles*, 353.

40. Edward Coles to Isaac Prickett, 24 June 1843, in ibid., 308.

41. Woods, *Albemarle County in Virginia*, 102.

42. Edward Coles to William Berry, 25 June, 1858, in Alvord, *Governor Edward Coles*, 364.

43. *(Shawneetown) Illinois Gazette*, 20 November 1819.

44. Simeone, *Democracy and Slavery in Frontier Illinois*, 63.

45. Faux, "Faux's Memorable Days in America," 289.

46. T. C. Pease, *Frontier State 1818–1848*, 16; Edward Coles to William Berry, 25 August 1858, E. Coles Papers, Chicago Historical Society, Chicago; *Illinois Intelligencer*, 13 December 1823; *(Shawneetown) Illinois Gazette*, 5 May 1821; Edward Coles to Henry S. Dodge, 22 February 1821, in Alvord, *Governor Edward Coles*, 255.

47. *(Shawneetown) Illinois Gazette*, 5 May 1821; Edward Coles to Henry S. Dodge, 22 February 1821, in Alvord, *Governor Edward Coles*, 255.

48. Edward Coles to William Berry, 25 August 1858, E. Coles Papers, Chicago Historical Society.

49. Beck, *Gazetteer of the States of Illinois and Missouri*, 105.

50. Buck, *Illinois in 1818*, 264, 319. The population figure of 34,610 for 1818 assumes that the true Illinois population does not include persons enumerated during the supplemental census called for by the Territorial Government (believed to include people who were passing through to other destinations).

6. Contest and Convention

1. *(Vandalia) Illinois Intelligencer*, 30 October 1821.

2. Edward Coles to Mary Carter, 18 April 1821, acc. no. 1729, Smith-Carter Papers.

3. *Edwardsville (Illinois) Spectator*, 20 February 1821.

4. One man underscored Coles's obscurity by claiming that Coles was not running for governor. He had asked Coles about his candidacy, and Coles had denied being a candidate! He had probably talked to one Edward Cowles who lived in this man's county. "An Inquirer from Kaskaskia," *Illinois Intelligencer*, 27 November 1821.

5. Sutton, "Edward Coles and the Constitutional Crisis in Illinois, 1822–1824," 37.

6. *Edwardsville (Illinois) Spectator*, 26 March 1822; *Shawneetown (Illinois) Gazette*, 13 April 1822.

7. *Edwardsville (Illinois) Spectator*, 18 May 1822.

8. "Justice," *(Vandalia) Illinois Intelligencer*, 4 December 1821.

9. "Answer to Justice," *(Vandalia) Illinois Intelligencer*, 4 December 1821.

10. *Edwardsville (Illinois) Spectator*, 27 November 1821.

11. *(Vandalia) Illinois Intelligencer*, 4 December 1821.

12. *Edwardsville (Illinois) Spectator*, 19 February 1822.

13. "Warren's Reply to Peck," *Free West*, 3 May 1855, in Alvord, *Governor Edward Coles*, 339.

14. For a discussion of the preference for more traditional elites over upland Southerners (like Warren) in the politics of this era, see Etcheson, *Emerging Midwest*.

15. Typical of many first gubernatorial races, Bond had been a compromise candidate for governor, while Edwards was given one of the senate seats. Bond had run unopposed.

16. Horatio Newhall to J. & J. Newhall, 11 May 1822, Newhall Collection. The *Edwardsville (Illinois) Spectator*, 19 March 1822, contained several letters urging voters to question candidates closely. See also Horatio Newhall to J. & J. Newhall, 10 August 1822, Newhall Collection.

17. E. Coles, "Emancipation," n.p.

18. Indenture Records, Madison County, 178.

19. Michael Lee is listed as living in Madison County in the U.S. Census of 1850. His age was given as fifty-three and his occupation as farmer. Listed with him are Mary, sixteen, Martha, eleven, and Susan, nine. Polly is listed as age fifty.

20. *Edwardsville (Illinois) Spectator*, 13 July 1822.

21. 9 February 1822; "Peter Newman," 5 March 1822; "Neptune," 19 February 1822, all in *Edwardsville (Illinois) Spectator*; Horatio Newhall to J. & J. Newhall, 11 May 1822, Newhall Papers.

22. Other than Warren, few said much about slavery per se in the 1822 campaign. We suspect that as the abolitionist fever arose in later decades, the participants of 1822 tended to look upon slavery in hindsight as more important than it was at the time of the election. For additional comments on the candidates' views of slavery, see W. R. Thompson, "Illinois Constitutions," 109; Brown, *Historical Sketch of the Early Movement in Illinois for the Legalization of Slavery*, 17–19; T. Ford, *History of Illinois*, 20–21, 51; and Alvord, *Governor Edward Coles*, 50.

23. Ress, *Governor Edward Coles and the Vote to Forbid Slavery in Illinois, 1823–1824*, 128.

24. Alvord, *Governor Edward Coles*, 52; T. C. Pease, *Frontier State, 1818–1848*, 77.

25. *Edwardsville (Illinois) Spectator*, 24 August 1822; *(Shawneetown) Illinois Gazette*, 21 September 1822; *Kaskaskia (Illinois) Republican Advocate*, 4 January 1823.

26. *Kaskaskia (Illinois) Republican Advocate*, 4 January 1823.

27. Hooper Warren, "Replication by Warren," 10 May 1855, in Alvord, *Governor Edward Coles*, 347.

28. Norton, *Edward Coles*, 16; Alvord, *Governor Edward Coles*, 52; Cassidy, "Issue of Freedom in Illinois under Governor Edward Coles," 286; Richardson, "Virginian Who Made Illinois a Free State," 13.

29. For further discussion of the nature and balance of debate in the election of 1822, see Leichtle, "Rise of Jacksonian Politics in Illinois." See also Sutton, "Edward Coles and the Constitutional Crisis in Illinois," 39.

30. *(Vandalia) Illinois Intelligencer*, 28 December 1822. Coles's inaugural address gives further evidence that issues other than slavery were involved in the election. See Leichtle, "Rise of Jacksonian Politics in Illinois."

31. James Madison to Edward Coles, 19 October 1822, E. Coles Papers, Princeton University Library.

32. Edward Coles to James Madison, 30 October 1822, E. Coles Papers, Chicago Historical Society.

33. Stroble, *High on the Okaw's Western Bank*, 14.

34. Ibid., 18. Tunstall was not, apparently, a chimney man. The legislature was forced to charge the town trustees with hiring a suitable repairman to replace the flue as the one chimney was found to supply as much smoke as heat. See Baringer, *Lincoln's Vandalia*, 18.

35. "Thomas Lippincott's Recollections," *Alton (Illinois) Telegraph*, 17 March 1868.
36. Ibid.

7. A Prairie Firestorm

1. Edward Coles to James Madison, 25 April 1823, E. Coles Papers, Princeton University Library.
2. *(Vandalia) Illinois Intelligencer*, 10 December 1822.
3. *(Richmond, Virginia) Enquirer*, rept. in *(Vandalia) Illinois Intelligencer*, 29 March 1823. Hezekiah Niles parodied Coles's ire in a column printed in the *(Shawneetown) Illinois Gazette*, 23 February 1822.
4. J. M. Thompson, *Pike County History*; Simeone, *Democracy and Slavery in Frontier Illinois*; Stevens, "Shaw-Hansen Election Contest," 393.
5. The text of the inaugural address appeared in several state papers. See, for example, *(Vandalia) Illinois Intelligencer*, 7 December 1822.
6. *(Vandalia) Illinois Intelligencer*, 7 December 1822.
7. Stevens, "Shaw-Hansen Election Contest," 393. See also Dillon, "Antislavery Movement in Illinois, 1809–1844," 79–81.
8. Coles reflected on this point in an 1824 letter to Roberts Vaux. He had made his slavery proposals to smoke the slavery advocates out and reveal that slavery was the planned goal of constitutional revision. Edward Coles to Roberts Vaux, 21 January 1824, Vaux Family Papers. See also Alvord, *Governor Edward Coles*, 57; Edward Coles to Nicholas Biddle, 22 April 1823, E. Coles Papers, Princeton University Library.
9. Hopper Warren, ed., *(Chicago) Free West*, 21 December 1854, in Alvord, *Governor Edward Coles*, 313.
10. J. E. Davis, *Frontier Illinois*, 168.
11. Richard Flower to John Quincy Adams, 13 July 1823, Letter File, Illinois State Historical Library.
12. Brown, *Historical Sketch of the Early Movement in Illinois for the Legalization of Slavery*, 21.
13. See Pyne, "Battling the 'National Sin,'" 79; Sutton, "Edward Coles and the Constitutional Crisis in Illinois, 1822–1824," 40.
14. *(Vandalia) Illinois Intelligencer*, 7 December 1822; Alvord, *Governor Edward Coles*, 60.
15. *(Vandalia) Illinois Intelligencer*, 7 December 1822; Alvord, *Governor Edward Coles*, 87–89.
16. *(Kaskaskia, Illinois) Republican Advocate*, 4 January 1823; *(Vandalia) Illinois Intelligencer*, 14 December 1822.
17. *(Vandalia) Illinois Intelligencer*, 21 December 1822; *(Kaskaskia, Illinois) Republican Advocate*, 4 January 1823.
18. *(Vandalia) Illinois Intelligencer*, 21 December 1822.
19. Alvord, *Governor Edward Coles*, 71, 72.
20. Ibid., 72.

21. Churchill, "Early Days in Madison County," 31–32; Harris, *History of Negro Servitude*, 36.
22. Brown, *Historical Sketch*, 25.
23. Simeone, *Democracy and Slavery in Frontier Illinois*, 122–23.
24. Brown, *Historical Sketch*, 23–26.
25. Ibid., 48–50.
26. Simeone, *Democracy and Slavery in Frontier Illinois*, 127.
27. *Edwardsville (Illinois) Spectator*, 15 February 1823.
28. T. C. Pease, *Frontier State 1818–1848*, 78–79.
29. Washburne, *Sketch of Edward Coles*, 88.
30. Simeone, *Democracy and Slavery in Frontier Illinois*, 130; *Edwardsville (Illinois) Spectator*, 22 February 1823.
31. *(Vandalia) Illinois Intelligencer*, 30 January 1824; *(Kaskaskia, Illinois) Republican Advocate*, 27 February 1823.
32. Washburne, *Sketch of Edward Coles*, 89.
33. Brown, *Historical Sketch*, 27.
34. Harris, *History of Negro Servitude in Illinois*, 37; Simeone, *Democracy and Slavery in Frontier Illinois*, 130; T. C. Pease, *Frontier State 1818–1848*, 78; Alvord, *Governor Edward Coles*, 83. Harris asserts that there were two mob scenes, one each on the nights of 11 and 12 February. Simeone agrees. Others (Pease, also Washburne citing Ford) have reported only one mob scene of 12 February. Harris stipulates that Hansen was burned in effigy on 11 February, while both Pease and Washburne/Ford report that it was 12 February.
35. Brown, *Historical Sketch of the Early Movement in Illinois*, 29.
36. H. Newhall to J. & J. Newhall, 22 March 1823, Newhall Collection. For additional comments, see Brown, *Historical Sketch of the Early Movement in Illinois*, 29–30; T. Ford, *History of Illinois*, 60–61; George Churchill to Editor, *(Princeton, Illinois) Bureau Advocate*, 2 May 1851; and Alvord, *Governor Edward Coles*, 319.
37. Washburne, *Sketch of Edward Coles*, 98.
38. "Message to Senate," 14 February 1823, in Alvord, *Governor Edward Coles*, 113–14; L. D. Ewing to Joseph Gillespie, 30 January 1840, Gillespie Papers.
39. Edward Coles to John G. Lofton, 16 February 1823, rept. in Washburne, *Sketch of Edward Coles*, 140.

8. The Chasm
1. Washburne, *Sketch of Edward Coles*, 86, 89.
2. Stevens, "Shaw-Hansen Election Contest," 398.
3. Birkbeck, *To the People of Illinois on the Question of a Convention*, 4.
4. Brown, *Historical Sketch*, 27.
5. *Edwardsville Spectator*, 1 March 1823.
6. Harris, *History of Negro Servitude in Illinois*, 39; Brown, *Historical Sketch*, 1823.
7. *(Vandalia) Illinois Intelligencer*, 4 January 1823.
8. T. C. Pease, *Frontier State 1818–1848*, 195–96.

9. *Kaskaskia Republican Advocate,* 25 January and 1 February 1823.

10. *(Vandalia) Illinois Intelligencer,* 15 February 1823.

11. T. C. Pease, *Frontier State 1818–1848,* 56.

12. *(Vandalia) Illinois Intelligencer,* 28 December 1822.

13. Ibid., 4 January 1823.

14. *Kaskaskia Republican Advocate,* 17 January 1823.

15. T. C. Pease, *Frontier State 1818–1848,* 100–101; Gillespie, *Recollections of Early Illinois and Her Noted Men,* 14.

16. T. C. Pease, *Frontier State 1818–1848,* 97–99.

17. Edward Coles to William Crawford, 1 July 1824, E. Coles Papers, Chicago Historical Society.

18. Horatio Newhall to J. & J. Newhall, 24 November 1824, Newhall Collection.

19. Alvord and Greene, *Executive Letterbook 1818–1835,* 4:47–50; and Edward Coles to James S. Johnson, 1 November 1825, ibid., 92–94.

20. Harris, *History of Negro Servitude in Illinois,* 41.

21. *(Vandalia) Illinois Intelligencer,* 8 March 1823.

22. Alvord, *Governor Edward Coles,* 86.

23. Ibid., 85; Dillon, "Antislavery Movement in Illinois, 1809–1844," 85–86.

24. Simeone, *Democracy and Slavery in Frontier Illinois,* 138, 138, 139.

25. "Edward Coles, Second Governor of Illinois," 61.

26. Ibid., 62.

27. *(Vandalia) Illinois Intelligencer,* 31 May 1823.

28. Ibid., 24 May 1823.

29. Edward Coles to William Barry, 25 June 1858, E. Coles Papers, Chicago Historical Society. Also see "Jonathan Freeman," and "John Rifle," both in (Shawneetown) *Illinois Gazette,* 21 June 1823.

30. Edward Coles to Robert Vaux, 27 June 1823, in Alvord, *Governor Edward Coles,* 127. Vaux was an active leader in the Pennsylvania Colonization Society and had worked diligently against slavery in general.

31. *(Vandalia) Illinois Intelligencer,* 24 May 1823.

32. Harris, *History of Negro Servitude in Illinois,* 43.

33. Reynolds, "Friendship's Offering," 10.

34. Dillon, "John Mason Peck," 389. Also Washburne, *Sketch of Edward Coles,* 169; Harris, *History of Negro Servitude in Illinois,* 42, 43. See also John Mason Peck to Hooper Warren, 27 March 1855 in Alvord, *Governor Edward Coles,* 332.

35. Dillon, "John Mason Peck," 389. Dillon argues that the history was significantly colored by Peck's letter to Warren, cited in note 34, and by John Reynolds's history, which acknowledges the great assistance of Peck in a letter.

36. Ibid., 390.

37. Bray, *Peter Cartwright,* 107.

38. Simeone, *Democracy and Slavery in Frontier Illinois,* 183.

39. Birkbeck, *To the People of Illinois on the Question of a Convention,* 39.

40. Edward Coles to William Berry, 25 June 1858; in Alvord, *Governor Edward Coles*, 364.

41. Edward Coles to James Madison, 25 April 1823, and Edward Coles to Nicholas Biddle, 22 April 1823, E. Coles Papers, Princeton University Library.

42. Edward Coles to Editor, *Genius of Emancipation*, 18 April 1823, E. Coles Papers, Princeton University Library. See also E. Coles, "Notes on Slavery" and "Scrapbook," E. Coles Papers, Princeton University Library.

43. Edward Coles to Nicholas Biddle, 22 April 1823, E. Coles Papers, Princeton University Library.

44. Nicholas Biddle to Edward Coles, 26 May 1823, and Nicholas Biddle to Edward Coles, 20 May 1823, both in Alvord, *Governor Edward Coles*, 123.

45. Ryan, "Moral Reform and Democratic Politics," contains a general discussion of Vaux' background.

46. Nicholas Biddle to Edward Coles, 26 May 1823, E. Coles Papers, Princeton University Library.

47. Roberts Vaux to Edward Coles, 27 May 1823, in Alvord, *Governor Edward Coles*, 126.

48. Roberts Vaux to Edward Coles, 24 June 1823, in ibid., 129–30.

49. T. C. Pease, *Frontier State 1818–1848*, 83; *(Vandalia) Illinois Intelligencer*, 9 July 1824.

50. Edward Coles to Nicholas Biddle, 18 September 1823, E. Coles Papers, Princeton University Library.

51. *(Vandalia) Illinois Intelligencer*, 2 July 1824.

52. Edward Coles to Nicholas Biddle, 18 September 1823, E. Coles Papers, Princeton University Library.

53. Edward Coles to Rebecca Coles, 6 September 1823, E. Coles Papers, Historical Society of Pennsylvania.

54. Edward Coles to Andrew Stevenson, 7 April 1824, E. Coles Papers, Princeton University Library.

55. Edward Coles to James Madison, 25 April 1823, in Daly, "Letters of Edward Coles," 34. See also Samuel Lockwood to Thomas Mather, 6 March 1822, Mather Papers.

56. Edward Coles to James Madison, 25 April 1823, in Daly, "Letters of Edward Coles," 34.

57. Simeone, *Democracy and Slavery in Frontier Illinois*, 140.

58. See Edward Coles to Roberts Vaux, 11 December, 1823, and Edward Coles to Morris Birkbeck, 29 January 1824, in Washburne, *Sketch of Edward Coles*, 162, 182.

59. Simeone, *Democracy and Slavery in Frontier Illinois*, 133, 245.

60. *(Vandalia) Illinois Intelligencer*, 5 July 1823.

61. Reynolds, *My Own Times*, quoted in Alvord, *Governor Edward Coles*, 111.

62. T. Ford, *History of Illinois*, 53–54.

63. Brown, *Historical Sketch of the Early Movement in Illinois*, quoted in Alvord, *Governor Edward Coles*, 112.

64. Simeone, *Democracy and Slavery in Frontier Illinois*, 135.

65. Edward Coles to Roberts Vaux, 11 December 1823, in Washburne, *Sketch of Edward Coles*, 164.

66. Edward Coles to Morris Birkbeck, 29 January 1824, in ibid., 148.

67. Simeone, *Democracy and Slavery in Frontier Illinois*, 140; original in *Edwardsville (Illinois) Spectator*, 13 December 1823.

68. Alvord, *Governor Edward Coles*, 206–7.

69. E. Coles, "Emancipation," n.p.

70. Affidavit signed by Andrew Banks, 26 January 1826, E. Coles Papers, Princeton Collection.

71. E. Coles, "Emancipation," n.p.

72. Ibid.

73. Summons, 7 January 1824, E. Coles, Miscellaneous Papers.

74. Richardson, "Virginian Who Made Illinois a Free State," 16.

75. E. Coles, "Autobiography," n.p. Hail Mason was well aware of the certificates of Emancipation that had been registered by Coles with the county court on 4 July 1819. Mason had been a witness to the registration of the documents. See Nore and Norrish, *Edwardsville*; Sapp, *Lathrop*.

76. Coles to Morris Birkbeck, 29 January 1824, in Alvord, *Governor Edward Coles*, 148–51.

77. Washburne, *Sketch of Edward Coles*, 201.

78. Harris, *History of Negro Servitude in Illinois*, 46.

79. John Mason Peck to Hooper Warren, 27 March 1855, in Alvord, *Governor Edward Coles*, 335.

80. For a listing of the newspaper alliances with the convention factions, see Harris, *History of Negro Servitude in Illinois*, 42n3.

81. John Mason Peck to Hooper Warren, 27 March 1855, in Alvord, *Governor Edward Coles*, 335.

82. *(Vandalia) Illinois Intelligencer*, 14 May 1824.

83. "Yankee," *(Vandalia) Illinois Intelligencer*, 30 March 1823.

84. *(Vandalia) Illinois Intelligencer*, 28 May 1824.

85. *(Vandalia) Illinois Intelligencer*, 4 June 1824.

86. Edward Coles to Thomas Jefferson, 26 September 1814, E. Coles Papers, Princeton University Library.

87. *(Vandalia) Illinois Intelligencer*, 13 June 1824.

88. E. Coles, "Emancipation," n.p.; E. Coles, "Autobiography," n.p.

89. Fox, *American Colonization Society*, 46; Burin, *Slavery and the Peculiar Solution*, 19.

90. Stebbins, *Facts and Opinions Touching the Real Origin*, iv.

91. Mayer, *All On Fire*, 134–41.

92. Ketcham, *James Madison*, 628.

93. Burin, *Slavery and the Peculiar Solution*, 11–12, 19.

94. *(Vandalia) Illinois Intelligencer*, 28 July 1827.

95. Ibid., 3 March 1827.
96. Henry Eddy to A. J. Grant, 9 and 10 December 1820, Eddy Collection.
97. Edward Coles to Thomas Jefferson Randolph, 29 December 1831, abridged, by E. Coles in E. Coles Papers, Princeton Collection.
98. H. Newhall to J. & J. Newhall, 29 May 1824, Newhall Collection.
99. T. C. Pease, *Frontier State 1818–1848*, 80–81.
100. *Illinois Gazette,* 10 April 1824.
101. Ibid., 10 July 1824.
102. "Edward Coles, Second Governor of Illinois," 61.
103. Brown, *Historical Sketch,* 44. They agree with the county-by-county results reported in Washburne, *Sketch of Edward Coles,* 191, although the statewide totals therein are incorrect. Harris reports the election results as 6,640 against the convention; 4,972 for the convention (giving a 14 percent margin). He cites official returns as given in records at Springfield. Harris, *History of Negro Servitude in Illinois,* 48. The results are also given in Simeone, *Democracy and Slavery in Frontier Illinois,* but the map key is reversed, giving inverted results.
104. See Shankman, "Partisan Conflicts, 1838–1841 and the Illinois Constitution."
105. Harris, *History of Negro Servitude in Illinois,* 48.
106. Sam Butler to Jacob Harlan, 5 October 1824, Harlan Papers.
107. Kingston, "Early Western Days," 315–16.
108. Sutton, "Edward Coles and the Constitutional Crisis in Illinois, 1822–1824," 45.
109. Edward Coles to Richard Flower, 12 April 1823, and Edward Coles to Nicholas Biddle, 18 September 1823, in Alvord, *Governor Edward Coles,* 120.

9. The Complaint

1. H. Newhall to J. & J. Newhall, 17 August 1824, Newhall Collection.
2. E. Coles, "Autobiography," n.p.; E. Coles, "Edward Coles to W. C. Flagg, 28 March 1861," 63; "Edward Coles to Joel R. Poinsett, 15 March 1851," "Letters of Edward Coles," *William and Mary Quarterly,* 2nd series, 7, 113; E. Coles, *History of the Ordinance of 1787,* 27.
3. E. Coles, "Autobiography." n.p.
4. "Affidavit of Andrew Banks," 26 January 1826, E. Coles Papers, Princeton University Library.
5. E. Coles, "Emancipation," n.p.
6. Ibid.
7. Washburne, *Sketch of Edward Coles,* 201.
8. E. Coles, "Emancipation,"n.p.
9. Ibid.
10. "Verdict Against Edward Coles," Alvord, *Governor Edward Coles,* 208.
11. Buck, *Illinois in 1818,* 304.
12. T. C. Pease, *Frontier State 1818–1848,* 130.
13. "Reasons for a New Trial Advanced by Edward Coles, September 22, 1824," in Alvord, *Governor Edward Coles,* 209.

14. Edward Coles to Morris Birkbeck, 22 September 1824, in Washburne, *Sketch of Edward Coles*, 194.

15. "Governor's Message," 16 November 1824, in Alvord, *Governor Edward Coles*, 267.

16. Washburne, *Sketch of Edward Coles*, 197.

17. Edward Coles to William Barry, 25 June, 1858, in Alvord, *Governor Edward Coles*, 375.

18. In his "Emancipation," Coles asserts that this law was introduced without his knowledge and passed almost unanimously. 7.

19. "Plea of Edward Coles for Discontinuance of Action of County Commissioners, March 1825," in Alvord, *Governor Edward Coles*, 210.

20. E. Coles, "Emancipation," n.p.

21. Washburne, *Sketch of Edward Coles*, 166.

22. Ibid., 222.

23. "Bill of Exceptions Advanced by Edward Coles, March 1825," in Alvord, *Governor Edward Coles*, 213.

24. E. Coles, "Emancipation," n.p.

25. "Opinion of Supreme Court of Illinois in Suit of Edward Coles versus County of Madison, June 1826," in Alvord, *Governor Edward Coles*, 213.

26. E. Coles, "Emancipation," n.p..

27. Idzerda, Loveland, and Miller, *Lafayette*, 54.

28. Ibid.

29. Ketcham, *James Madison*, 664.

30. Lafayette to Edward Coles, 12 April 1825, in Alvord, *Governor Edward Coles*, 188.

31. Swain, "Lafayette on the Centenary of His Visit to Illinois, 1825," 2.

32. Horatio Newhall to J. & J. Newhall, 28 April 1825, Newhall Collection.

33. Edward Coles to Lafayette, 28 April 1825, in Alvord, *Governor Edward Coles*, 189.

34. Swain, "Lafayette on the Centenary of His Visit to Illinois, 1825," 3; Klamkin, *Return of Lafayette*, 150.

35. Dodge is believed to be Henry Dodge, 1782 to 1867, who was governor of the Territory of Wisconsin 1836 to 1841 and 1846 to 1848.

36. Klamkin, *Return of Lafayette*, 151.

37. Henrotin, "Visit of Lafayette to Illinois in 1825," 84.

38. Edward Coles to Adolphus Hubbard, 22 June 1825, in Alvord and Greene, *Executive Letterbook 1818–1835*, 4:89.

39. Edward Coles to Roberts Vaux, 8 February 1826, in Washburne, *Sketch of Edward Coles*, 219.

40. Ibid.

41. T. C. Pease, *Frontier State 1818–1848*, 111.

42. T. Ford, *History of Illinois*, 38.

43. Edward Coles to Andrew Stevenson, 7 April 1824, in Washburne, *Sketch of Edward Coles*, 219.

44. Ibid.

45. E. Coles, "Emancipation,"

46. Springer, "Notes of Jessie Springer on the Crawford Family."

47. It is believed that both families ultimately moved to Decatur, but the dates of these moves are not known and may not have happened until the 1830s.

48. E. E. Williams, "A Bit of Unwritten History," 1.

49. E. Coles, "Emancipation," n.p.

50. Montgomery County, Illinois, U.S. Census for 1850, dwelling entry 299.

51. Edward Coles to Isaac Prickett, 24 June 1843, in Alvord, *Governor Edward Coles*, 308.

52. "Governor's Message," December 5, 1826, in Alvord, *Governor Edward Coles*, 277.

53. "Governor's Message," *(Vandalia) Illinois Intelligencer*, 9 December 1826.

54. Rothman, *Discovery of the Asylum*, xxix.

55. McCoy, *Elusive Republic*, 237.

56. W. Archer to Jacob Harlan, 8 December 1826, Sargent Papers.

57. Nicholas Hansen to Edward Coles, 23 December 1826, in Alvord, *Governor Edward Coles*, 82.

58. Ibid. See also "Doctor Fell," *(Vandalia) Illinois Intelligencer*, 2 December 1826. Edwards, on the other hand, believed that his plans were best for the people. Ninian Edwards to Henry I. Mills, 26 December 1826, Edwards Collection.

59. *(Vandalia) Illinois Intelligencer*, 28 July 1827.

60. *(Vandalia) Illinois Intelligencer*, 9 December 1826 and 30 June 1827.

61. W. B. Archer to Jacob Harlan, 13 December 1823, Sargent Papers.

62. Snyder, *Adam W. Snyder and His Period in Illinois History*, 52.

63. W. B. Archer to Jacob Harlan, 13 December 1828, Sargent Papers.

64. John Reynolds to Ninian Edwards, 4 September 1829, Edwards Collection.

65. Leonard, "Ironies of Partyism and Antipartyism," 22.

66. *Kaskaskia (Illinois) Advocate*, 23 February 1831.

67. Ibid., 20 May 1831 and *(Vandalia) Illinois Intelligencer*, 16 April 1831.

68. *Kaskaskia Advocate*, 20 May 1831.

69. *Kaskaskia Advocate*, 10 June 1831 and 15 July 1831.

70. Ibid., 20 May 1831.

71. For the returns, see *Kaskaskia Advocate*, 12, 19, 26 August and 2, 9 September 1831.

72. Leonard, "Ironies of Partyism and Antipartyism," 30, 34.

73. Edward Coles to James Madison, 16 January 1831, and 13 July 1825, E. Coles Papers, Chicago Historical Society.

10. The Emancipator

1. A. G. Freehling, *Drift toward Dissolution*, 2.

2. For a discussion of the eclipse, see Masur, *1831*, chap. 2, "Slavery and Abolition," 9.

3. *Richmond (Virginia) Constitution Whig*, August 29, 1831, n.p.

4. Perdue, Barden, and Phillips, *Weevils in the Wheat*, 35.

5. Edward Coles to Thomas Jefferson Randolph, 29 December 1831, abridged in E. Coles, "Letters of Edward Coles: Edward Coles to Thomas Jefferson," 105.
6. A. G. Freehling, *Drift toward Dissolution*, 132.
7. Edward Coles to Thomas Jefferson Randolph, 29 December 1831, abridged in E. Coles, "Letters of Edward Coles: Edward Coles to Thomas Jefferson," 105.
8. Ibid., 106.
9. The term *post-nati* refers to a law that is to affect only those born after a date certain. Those born prior to this given date would not be affected.
10. A. G. Freehling, *Drift toward Dissolution*, 122, 124.
11. Ibid., 129.
12. Shade, *Democratizing the Old Dominion*, 224.

11. The Devastating Truth of Madison's Will

1. James Madison to Edward Coles, 8 November 1830; Edward Coles to James Madison, 4 November 1830; James Madison to Edward Coles, 23 Jan. 1831; James Madison to Edward Coles, 28 June 1831, all in E. Coles Papers, Princeton University Library.
2. Edward Coles to Hugh Blair Grigsby, 23 December 1854, container 85, Rives Papers.
3. See Genovese, "World the Slaveholders Made," for an extensive discussion of the role of noblesse oblige in southern society.
4. Berlin, "Slaves without Masters," 92.
5. Edward Coles to Hugh Blair Grigsby, 23 December 1854, container 85, Rives Papers.
6. Edward Coles to James Madison, 8 January 1832, folder 30, box 1, E. Coles Papers, Princeton University Library.
7. James Madison, will, copy made by Peter Carr for Edward Coles, folder 27, box 2, E. Coles Papers, Princeton University Library.
8. Extract of Letter to S. C. Stevenson, dated Newport, 28 July 1836, in E. Coles, "Letters of Edward Coles: Edward Coles to Thomas Jefferson," 107.
9. Boykin, *Victoria, Albert, and Mrs. Stevenson*, 5–9.
10. Edward Coles to Daniel Webster, 12 July 1834; Daniel Webster to Edward Coles, 23 July 1834; Edward Coles to Andrew Stevenson, 16 January 1835; Edward Coles to John Tyier, 26 January 1835; John Tyier to Edward Coles, 31 January 1835; Edward Coles to Andrew Stevenson, 7 January 1835; Edward Coles to Andrew Stevenson, 31 January 1835, all in E. Coles Papers, Princeton Collection.
11. Edward Coles to Sarah Coles Stevenson, 28 July 1836, in "Letters of Edward Coles: Edward Coles to Thomas Jefferson," 107.
12. Edward Coles to Hugh Blair Grigsby, 23 December 1854, container 85, Rives Papers.
13. Edward Coles to Sarah Coles Stevenson, 28 July 1836, in "Letters of Edward Coles: Edward Coles to Thomas Jefferson," 107.

14. Ibid., 108.
15. Note in the hand of Edward Coles, Warm Springs, VA September 1849, E. Coles Papers, Princeton Collection.
16. Edward Coles to Nellie Willis, 10 December 1855, E. Coles Papers, Princeton Collection, Princeton University.
17. John Willis to Edward Coles, 19 December 1855, E. Coles Papers, Princeton Collection.
18. Ibid. Evidence that Dolley Madison knew her husband's wish is strengthened by the appearance in the *Albany (Georgia) Patriot*, in 1848 of a short review of Dolley's relations with her slaves. Included is an assertion that she well knew her husband's wishes that slaves be freed. Hampden Washington, letter to editor, "Mrs. Madison's Slaves Again," *Albany (Georgia) Patriot*, 9 March 1848.
19. Jennings, *Colored Man's Reminiscences of James Madison*, 17.
20. Katharine Anthony cites a note in the handwriting of Daniel Webster indicating that Webster had paid $120 for the freedom of Paul Jennings. Anthony, *Dolly Madison*, 386. The bill of sale for the purchase of Jennings from Dolley Madison and the associated receipt are in a private collection. Beth Taylor, former Director of Education, Montpelier.
21. Anthony, *Dolly Madison*, 16.
22. A list of the five slaves owned by Dolley Madison in 1846 (three years before her death) is provided in an indenture contract she entered into with Richard D. Cutts. MS 2988, box 3, Madison Family Papers.
23. James H. Causten Jr. to John C. Payne, 16 February 1852, Dolley Madison Papers, Greensboro Historical Museum, quoted in Arnett, *Mrs. James Madison*, 400.
24. See Dolley Madison to Eliza Lee, April 1836, in Arnett, *Mrs. James Madison*, 32; Dolley Madison to Andrew Jackson, 20 August 1836, Dolley Madison Papers, Library of Congress.
25. Catherine Allgor struggles to understand Dolley's actions as well. Though the final judgment is less harsh, she concludes, "Dolley's failure to act on her slaves' behalf, either on her own or in accordance with James's wishes, sullied her reputation." *Perfect Union*, 405.

12. The Aging Historian

1. Trollope, *Domestic Manners of the Americans*, chap. 26.
2. Royall, *Sketches of History, Life, and Manners, in the United States*, 207.
3. Edward Coles to James Madison, 25 November 1833, E. Coles Papers, Chicago Historical Society.
4. W. B. Coles, *Coles Family of Virginia*, 113.
5. E. Coles, "Edward Coles to W. C. Flagg, 28 March 1861," 59–60. See also Isaac Coles to James Madison, 2 February 1835; Edward Coles to James Madison, 5 October 1834; Edward Coles to James Madison, 31 October 1834' and Edward Coles to James Madison, 2 February 1836, all in E. Coles Papers, Chicago Historical Society.

6. W. B. Coles, *Coles Family of Virginia*, 223.

7. Edward Coles to Matt R. Singleton, Philadelphia, 13 March 1846, MS, 1845–65, acc. no. 1626, Singleton Papers.

8. Edward Coles to John Rutherfoord, 6 November 1847, Rutherfoord Papers.

9. His business dealings are contained in a series of letters to his lawyer. See Edward Coles to Wash, E. Coles Papers, Princeton University Library. Also see the account books in E. Coles Papers, Historical Society of Pennsylvania.

10. Later analysts, however, tend to accept Peter Temin's exoneration of Jackson. Britain's new opium trade in China, Temin contends in his classic review *The Jacksonian Economy*, had the indirect effect of seriously restricting the availability of Mexican silver in America. Temin, *Jacksonian Economy*, 173. See also Wallis, "What Caused the Crisis of 1839?" 2.

11. Wallis, "What Caused the Crisis of 1839?" 1–2.

12. Washburne, *Sketch of Edward Coles*, 177; Edward Coles to James Tyler, 10 April 1841, E. Coles Papers, Princeton University Library.

13. Edward Coles to James Tyler, 20 July 1841, 6 July 1841, and 7 July 1841, and James Tyler to Edward Coles, 31 January 1835, all in E. Coles Papers, Princeton University Library.

14. Edward Coles to Winfield Scott, 29 April 1842, E. Coles Papers, Princeton University Library. Coles may also have been relying upon his association with Scott's wife (née Maria Mayo), who was a regular member of the White House family of President Madison while Coles was secretary.

15. Winfield Scott to Edward Coles, 30 April 1842, E. Coles Papers, Princeton University Library. Scott, as requested, passed the letters on to Tyler. Winfield Scott to James Tyler, n.d., E. Coles Papers, Princeton University Library.

16. Edward Coles to Winfield Scott, 3 May 1842, and Edward Coles to James Tyler, 5 April 1843, both in E. Coles Papers, Princeton University Library.

17. "Population Schedule," *U.S. Manuscript Census*, 1850.

18. Edward Coles to William Berry, 25 June 1858, in Alvord, *Governor Edward Coles*, 365.

19. R. Babcock, *Memoir of John Mason Peck*, 349.

20. The authors recognize the work of Suzanne Cooper Guasco in identifying and exploring the significance of the Randall-Grigsby-Coles association. Her presentation at the SHEAR conference of 2000 identified important correspondence and proposed major themes for further study regarding Edward Coles's senior years. Her proposition that Coles's efforts to burnish the antislavery reputations of Jefferson and Madison were efforts to dispel north-south tensions and avert a civil war is innovative but probably overreaching. Guasco, "Managing Memory," 3–5.

21. *Rives* is pronounced like the surname *Reeves*.

22. McCoy, *Last of the Fathers*, 327; William Cabell Rives to Edward Coles, 9 January 1856, E. Coles Papers, Princeton University Library.

23. McCoy, *Last of the Fathers*, 329–34.

24. William Cabell Rives to Edward Coles, 9 January 1856, E. Coles Papers, Princeton University Library.

25. Edward Coles to William C. Rives, 21 January 1856, E. Coles Papers, Princeton University Library.

26. Edward Coles to William C. Rives, 19 June 1857 and 26 March 1858, both in E. Coles Papers, Princeton University Library.

27. James Madison to Robert Walsh 2 November 1819, quoted in Edward Coles to William C. Rives, 19 June 1857, E. Coles Papers, Princeton University Library.

28. A brief but penetrating review of the Madison-Walsh letters in the context of the Missouri Compromise is given in McCoy, *Last of the Fathers*, 107–11.

29. *(Washington, DC) National Intelligencer*, August 10, 1852, 1.

30. Ibid.

31. Edward Coles to Charles Sumner, August 1852, E. Coles Papers, Princeton University Library.

32. Charles Sumner to Edward Coles. 23 August 1852, E. Coles Papers, Princeton University Library.

33. Ibid.

34. Edward Coles, "Who Was the Author of the Ordinance of 1787?" *(Washington, DC) National Intelligencer*, 4 January 1853.

35. E. Coles, *History of the Ordinance of 1787*.

36. Ibid., 15.

37. Ibid., 28.

38. Berkhofer, "Jefferson, the Ordinance of 1784, and the Origins of the American Territorial System," 241; Kennedy, *Mr. Jefferson's Lost Cause*, 249–51.

39. Stephen A. Douglas, "Debate in Senate: Nebraska and the Missouri Compromise," *(Washington, DC) National Intelligencer,* 2 February 1854.

40. Edward Coles, "To Senator Douglas," *(Washington, DC) National Intelligencer*, 18 February 1854.

41. Ibid.

42. Stephen A. Douglas to Edward Coles, Washington, DC, 18 February 1824, in Johannsen, *Letters of Stephen A. Douglas*, 290.

43. H. Grigsby to H. Randall, 18 February 1856 in Klingberg and Klingberg, *Correspondence between Henry Stephens Randall and Hugh Blair Grigsby 1856–1861*, 34.

44. Some details of the friendly society to which Coles became attached are discernable in the letters of Henry Stephens Randall and Hugh Blair Grigsby. See ibid.

45. H. Grigsby to H. Randall, 29 February 1856, in ibid., 38.

46. Henry S. Randall to Edward Coles, 13 September 1856. E. Coles Papers, Princeton University Library.

47. Edward Coles to Henry S. Randall, 11 May 1857, E. Coles Papers, Princeton University Library.

48. Randall, *Life of Thomas Jefferson*, frontispiece.

49. Guasco, "Managing Memory," 5.

13. The Preacher

1. Edward Coles to Isaac Prickett, 24 June 1843, in Alvord, *Governor Edward Coles*, 308.

2. G. C. Lusk, in Nore and Norrish, *Edwardsville* 34.

3. The letters from Crawford to Coles were dictated to Alfred Richardson, the local preacher and regional leader in the formation of Baptist Churches.

4. Norton, *History of Madison County, Illinois*, 596; *Edwardsville (Illinois) Democrat*, August 1, 1912.

5. Mabry, *History of Wood River Baptist District Association*, 15.

6. Ibid., 32.

7. "Minutes of the First Colored Baptist Association and Friends to Humanity," 7.

8. Ibid., 4.

9. Ibid., 5.

10. Mabry, *History of Wood River Baptist District Association*, 17.

11. Ibid., 50.

12. Ibid., 79.

13. Ibid., 75; Fitts, *History of Black Baptists*, 68.

14. Mabry, *History of Wood River Baptist District Association*, introduction.

15. "Charges of County Commissioners of Madison County against Edward Coles," in Alvord, *Governor Edward Coles*, 205.

16. Montgomery County, Illinois, *U.S. Census*, 1850, entry 299.

17. Edward Coles to one of his former slaves [Robert Crawford], 7 February 1841, folder 3, box 2, E. Coles Papers, Princeton University Library.

18. *Grantee Record Book 23*, Madison County, Illinois, 508, Madison County Historical Society.

19. There is no evidence that any of the properties Edward Coles gave to his former slaves was ever improved or farmed by them.

20. Robert and Kate Crawford (former slaves) by Alfred H. Richardson to Edward Coles, 23 October 1840, C0037, folder 5, box 2, E. Coles Papers, Princeton University Library. Three additional letters of correspondence between Coles and the Crawfords are known: Edward Coles to one of his former slaves, 8 February 1837, folder 3, box 2, E. Coles Papers, Princeton University Library; Robert and Calle Croford [Kate Crawford] to Mr. Coles, 1841, folder 3, box 3, E. Coles Papers, Princeton University Library; Robert "Preacher" Crawford to Edward Coles, 23 October 1846, E. Coles Papers, Illinois State Historical Library.

21. Montgomery County, Illinois, *U.S. Census*, 1850, entry 299.

22. Mabry, *History of Wood River Baptist District Association*, 55.

23. Ibid., 81–108.

24. Last Will of Robert Crawford, filed 19 September 1870, Record Book B, Montgomery County (Illinois) Court House, 3.

14. Prodigal Virginian

1. W. B. Coles, *Coles Family of Virginia*, 224.
2. Edward Coles to his nephew, 21 December 1856, Rutherfoord Papers.
3. W. B. Coles, *Coles Family of Virginia*, 700; Langhorne, Lay, and Rieley, *Virginia Family and Its Plantation Houses*, 141.
4. Langhorne, Lay, and Rieley, *Virginia Family and Its Plantation Houses*, 141.
5. W. B. Coles, *Coles Family of Virginia*, 701; Collins, *46th Virginia Infantry*, 12.
6. Britton, "So Many Dangers Seen and Unseen," 13. The company was originally called H, but in August 1862 a reshuffling of company rosters led to the renaming of the Green Mountain Grays as Company I. Coles expected that the war would be short-lived and that he would have an opportunity to explain his decision to join the Confederate Army to his mother in short order. Roberts Coles to John Rutherfoord, 13 October 1862, MSS1 R9337b3, Rutherfoord Family Papers, Virginia Historical Society.
7. Britton, "So Many Dangers Seen and Unseen," 71.
8. Collins, *46th Virginia Infantry*, 9.
9. Roberts Coles to John Rutherfoord, 13 October 1861, MSS1 R9337b3, Rutherfoord Family Papers, Virginia Historical Society.
10. Collins, *46th Virginia Infantry*, 24.
11. Britton, "So Many Dangers Seen and Unseen," 74.
12. Collins, *46th Virginia Infantry*, 28.
13. Roberts Coles to Jeannie Fairfax, 7 February 1862, MSS2 C6799a1, Roberts Coles Papers.
14. Collins, *46th Virginia Infantry*, 29.
15. "News from the South," *(Philadelphia) Daily Evening Bulletin*, 10 February 1862, 1.
16. Ibid., 15 February 1862, 5. The Walter Coles in question here is the grandson of Edward Coles's brother Walter. Walter Coles, 25 February 1839 to 9 August 1892, was a physician who, after the war, practiced in St. Louis. See W. B. Coles, *Coles Family of Virginia*, 311.
17. Edward Coles Jr. to John Rutherfoord, 18 February 1862, Rutherfoord Papers.
18. W. B. Coles, *Coles Family of Virginia*, 225.
19. Ibid., 704.

15. The Woodlands

1. Edward Coles to Isaac Prickett, 10 May 1838, 5 November 1838, 4 September 1848, 12 June 1840, all in E. Coles Papers, Chicago Historical Society; Edward Coles to William Gillespie, 15 November 1842, Gillespie Papers; and Edward Coles to Prickett, 24 June 1843, 11 May 1843, 20 December 1842, and 2 September 1842, E. Coles Papers, Chicago Historical Society.
2. "Reception of the News of the Nomination in Philadelphia," *Philadelphia Daily Evening Bulletin*, 19 May 1860, 1.

3. Ibid. Coles was not, of course, the first governor of Illinois. That honor went to Shadrach Bond (1773–1832). The error was a slip excusable by the impromptu nature of the gathering.
4. Preface (by Nicholas Trist in his hand), Edward Coles to Abraham Lincoln, 15 July 1862, container 7, Trist Papers.
5. Ibid.
6. W. B. Coles, *Coles Family of Virginia*, 99.
7. "Died," *(Philadelphia) Daily Evening Bulletin*, 8 and 9 July 1868.
8. Woodlands is located at 4000 Woodland Avenue, Philadelphia. The Coles family plot is located in section E, lot 218. Burial records of Woodlands Cemetery Company of Philadelphia.

Epilogue

1. Sutton, "Edward Coles and the Constitutional Crisis in Illinois, 1822–1824," 44.
2. Luboff and Stracke, *Freedom Country*.
3. Moore, *Albemarle*, 121.

Bibliography

Academic Records. Hampden-Sydney College, Farmville, Virginia.

Adams, John Q. *Memoirs of John Q. Adams.* Edited by Charles Francis Adams. Vol. 5. Philadelphia: Lippincott, 1874–77. Reprint, New York: AMS, 1970.

Agnew, Thomas L. "Methodism on the Frontier." In *The History of American Methodism.* Edited by Emory Stevens Bucke. 3 vols. Nashville, TN: Abingdon, 1964.

Allgor, Catherine. *Parlor Politics: In Which the Ladies of Washington Help Build a City and a Government.* Charlottesville: University Press of Virginia, 2002.

———. *A Perfect Union: Dolley Madison and the Creation of the American Nation.* New York: Owl, Holt, 2006.

Alvord, Clarence W. *Governor Edward Coles.* Springfield: Illinois State Historical Library, 1920.

Alvord, Clarence, and Evarts B. Greene, eds. *Executive Letterbook 1818–1835.* Vol. 4. Springfield: Illinois State Historical Society, 1909. 47–50.

Ammon, Harry. *James Monroe: The Quest for National Identity.* New York: McGraw-Hill, 1971.

Angle, Paul. "Nathaniel Pope, 1784–1850: A Memoir." In *Illinois State Historical Society Transactions for the Year 1936.* Springfield: Illinois State Historical Society, 1937. 111–81.

Anthony, Katharine. *Dolly Madison: Her Life and Times.* Doubleday, 1949.

Appleby, Joyce. *Capitalism and a New Social Order.* New York: New York University Press, 1984.

———. "The Social Origins of American Revolutionary Ideology." *Journal of American History* 64 (March 1978): 935–58.

Arnett, Ethel Stephens. *Mrs. James Madison: Incomparable Dolley.* Greensboro, NC: Piedmont, 1972.

Ayres, S. Edward. "Albemarle County, 1744–1770: An Economic, Political and Social Analysis." *Magazine of Albemarle County History* (1966–67): 36–71.

Babcock, Rufus. *Memoir of John Mason Peck.* Carbondale: Southern Illinois University Press, 1965.

Babcock, Theodore Stoddard. "Manumission in Virginia 1782–1806." Master's thesis, University of Virginia, 1974.

Bailyn, Bernard. *Ideological Origins of the American Revolution*. Boston: Belknap Press, 1992.

――――. *The Origins of American Politics*. New York: Knopf, 1968.

Barbour, James. *Eulogium upon the Life and Character of James Madison*. Washington, DC: Gales & Seaton, 1836.

Baringer, William E. *Lincoln's Vandalia: A Pioneer Portrait*. New Brunswick, NJ: Rutgers University Press, 1949.

Barnhardt, John D. "Sources of Southern Migration into the Old Northwest." *Mississippi Valley Historical Review* 22 (June 1935): 49–62.

Bear, James A., Jr., and Lucia C. Stanton, eds. *Jefferson's Memorandum Books*. Princeton, NJ: Princeton University Press, 1997.

Beck, Lewis C. *A Gazetteer of the States of Illinois and Missouri*. Albany, NY: Webster, 1823. Reprint, New York: Arno, 1975.

Berkhofer, Robert F. "Jefferson, the Ordinance of 1784, and the Origins of the American Territorial System," *William and Mary Quarterly*, 3rd. ser., 29, no. 2 (1972): 231–62.

Berlin, Ira. *Many Thousands Gone: The First Two Centuries of Slavery in North America*. Cambridge, MA: Harvard University Press, 1998.

――――. *Slaves without Masters—the Free Negro in the Antebellum South*. New York: Pantheon, 1974.

Betterly, Richard. "Seize Mr. Lincoln: The 1861 Baltimore Plot." *Civil War Times Illustrated*, February 1987, 14–21.

Biddle Family. Papers. Historical Society of Pennsylvania, Philadelphia.

Billington, Ray A. "The Frontier in Illinois History." In *An Illinois Reader*, edited by Clyde C. Walton. DeKalb: Northern Illinois University Press, 1970. 28–45.

Birkbeck, Morris. *Notes on a Journey in America*. Philadelphia: Lippincott, 1818.

――――. *To the People of Illinois on the Question of a Convention*. Shawneetown, IL: Jones, July 1823.

Blair, John F. *The Negro in Virginia*. Winston-Salem, NC: Writer's Program of the Work Projects Administration, State of Virginia, 1994.

Boggess, Arthur C. *Settlement of Illinois, 1778–1830*. Madison: Wisconsin State Historical Society, 1908. Reprint, Ann Arbor, MI: University Microfilms, 1968. Citations are to the 1968 edition.

Boyer Lewis, Charlene M. *Ladies and Gentlemen on Display: Planter Society at the Virginia Springs, 1790–1860*. Charlottesville: University Press of Virginia, 2001.

Boykin, Edward. *Victoria, Albert, and Mrs. Stevenson*. New York: Rinehart, 1957.

Brant, Irving. *James Madison*. 6 vols. Indianapolis: Bobbs-Merrill, 1941–61.

Bray, Robert. *Peter Cartwright: Legendary Frontier Preacher*. Urbana: University of Illinois Press, 2005.

Britton, Rick. "Edward Coles and the 'Peculiar Institution.'" *Albemarle Magazine*, February–March 1998, 60–66.

———, ed. "So Many Dangers Seen and Unseen: A Civil War Memoir by James Addison Leathers." *Magazine of Albemarle County History* 59 (2001): 69–83.

Brodie, Fawn M. *Thomas Jefferson: An Intimate History*. New York: Norton, 1974.

Brown, William H. *An Historical Sketch of the Early Movement in Illinois for the Legalization of Slavery*. Chicago: Church, Goodman, & Donnelly, 1865.

Brydon, George Maclaren. *Virginia's Mother Church*. Vol. 2. Philadelphia: Church Historical Society, 1952.

Buck, Solon J. *Illinois in 1818*. 2nd rev. ed. Urbana: University of Illinois Press, 1967. Originally published in 1917 by the Illinois Centennial Commission.

Buel, Richard, Jr. *Securing the Revolution: Ideology in American Politics*. Ithaca, NY: Cornell University Press, 1972.

Bulfinch, Thomas. "Prometheus and Pandora." In *Bulfinch's Mythology: The Age of Fable*. Garden City, NY: Doubleday, 1948. 30–38.

Burin, Eric. *Slavery and the Peculiar Solution: A History of the American Colonization Society*. Gainesville: University Press of Florida, 2005.

Cappon, Lester J. "Personal Property Tax List of Albemarle County, 1782." *Magazine of Albemarle County History* 5 (1945): 47–73.

Cassidy, John Thomas. "The Issue of Freedom in Illinois: Under Governor Edward Coles." *Illinois State Historical Society Journal* 57 (1964): 284–88.

Chambers, Douglas B. *Murder at Montpelier: Igbo Africans in Virginia*. Jackson: University Press of Mississippi, 2005.

"Charges of County Commissioners of Madison County against Edward Coles, March 1824." In Alvord, *Governor Edward Coles*. 205–6.

Christian, Charles M. *Black Saga: The African American Experience*. Boston: Houghton Mifflin, 1995.

Churchill, George. "Early Days in Madison County—Annotations of Reverend Thomas Lippincott." Churchill Papers, Illinois Historical Survey, Urbana.

———. Papers. Illinois State Historical Library, Springfield.

Coke, Ben H. *Early Landowners Near Greenfield, Virginia, and the Bell Family Who Once Lived There*. Utica, KY: McDowell. 1993.

Coles, Edward. "Autobiography." April 1844, Coles Collection, Historical Society of Pennsylvania.

———. "Edward Coles to W. C. Flagg, 28 March 1861." *Journal of the Illinois State Historical Society* 3 (Fall 1910): 59–64.

———. "The Emancipation of the Slaves of Edward Coles." October 1827. Folder 21, box 3, Coles Family Papers, Historical Society of Pennsylvania, Philadelphia.

———. *History of the Ordinance of 1787*. Philadelphia: Historical Society of Pennsylvania, 1856.

———. "Letters of Edward Coles." *William and Mary Quarterly*, 2nd series, 7, no. 1 (January 1927): 32–41.

———. "Letters of Edward Coles." *William and Mary Quarterly*, 2nd series, 7, no. 3 (July 1927): 158–73.

———. "Letters of Edward Coles: Edward Coles to Thomas Jefferson." *William and Mary Quarterly*, 2nd series, 7, no. 2 (April 1927): 97–113.

———. Papers. Albert and Shirley Small Special Collections Library, University of Virginia, Charlottesville.

———. Papers. Chicago Historical Society, Chicago.

———. Papers. Illinois State Historical Library, Springfield.

———. Papers. Manuscript Department, William R. Perkins Library, Duke University, Durham, NC.

———. Papers. Princeton University Library, Princeton, NJ.

Coles Family Papers. Collection 1458. Historical Society of Pennsylvania, Philadelphia.

———. Earl Gregg Swem Library, College of William and Mary, Williamsburg, VA.

———. Virginia Historical Society, Richmond, VA.

Coles, Roberts. Papers. Virginia Historical Society, Richmond, VA.

Coles, William B. *The Coles Family of Virginia*. Baltimore: Gateway, 1989.

Collections of the Illinois State Historical Library. Vol. 4. Springfield: Illinois State Historical Library, 1909.

Collins, Darrell L. *46th Virginia Infantry*. Appomattox, VA: Howard, 1992.

Côté, Richard N. *Strength and Honor: The Life of Dolley Madison*. Mount Pleasant, SC: Corinthian, 2005.

Cox, Isaac J. "Thomas Sloo Jr.: A Typical Politician of Illinois." In *Transactions of the Illinois State Historical Society for the Year 1911*, 29–30. Springfield: Illinois State Historical Society, 1912.

Cramer, Zadok. *Navigator: Containing Directions for Navigating the Monongahela, Allegheny, Ohio, and Mississippi Rivers*. Pittsburgh: Cramer & Spear, 1818.

Crowe, Charles. "Bishop James Madison and the Republic of Virtue." *Journal of Southern History* 30, no. 1 (1964): 58–70.

———. "The Reverend James Madison in Williamsburg and London, 1768–1771." *West Virginia History* 25, no. 4 (1964): 270–78.

———. "The War of 'Pure Republicanism' against Federalism, 1794–1801: Bishop James Madison on the American Political Scene." *West Virginia History* 24, no. 4 (1963): 355–62.

Cunningham, Noble E., Jr. *In Pursuit of Reason: The Life of Thomas Jefferson*. Baton Rouge: Louisiana State University Press, 1926.

Dabney, Virginius. *Richmond: The Story of a City*. Charlottesville: University Press of Virginia, 1990.

Daly, Ann, ed. "Some Letters of Edward Coles, Second Governor of Illinois to James Madison." *Bulletin of the Chicago Historical Society*, series 2, 1, no. 1 (1934): 1–8.

Davis, David Brion. *The Problem of Slavery in the Age of Revolution*. Ithaca, NY: Cornell University Press, 1999.

Davis, James E. *Frontier Illinois*. Bloomington: Indiana University Press, 1999.

Davis, Bailey Fulton. *The Deeds of Amherst County, Virginia, 1761–1807 and Albemarle County, Virginia 1748–1763*. Easley, SC: Southern Historical, 1979.

Davis, Richard Beale. *Intellectual Life in Jefferson's Virginia 1790–1830*. Knoxville: University of Tennessee Press, 1972.

De Alba, Susan. *Country Roads: Albemarle County, Virginia*. Berryville, VA: Rockbridge, 1993.

Diggins, John P. *The Lost Soul of American Politics: Virtue, Self-interest, and the Foundations of Liberalism*. New York: Basic Books, 1984.

Dillon, Merton L. "The Antislavery Movement in Illinois, 1809–1844." PhD diss., University of Michigan, 1950.

———. "John Mason Peck: A Study of Historical Rationalization." *Journal of the Illinois Historical Society* 50, no. 4 (Winter 1957): 383–90.

Diplomatic Dispatches. Netherlands. Vol. 1.5. National Archives and Records Administration, Washington, DC.

———. Russia. Vol. 5. National Archives and Records Administration, Washington, DC.

Dunn, Susan. *Dominion of Memories—Jefferson, Madison, and the Decline of Virginia*. New York: Basic Books, 2007.

Eddy, Henry. Papers. Illinois Historical Survey, University of Illinois, Urbana.

"Edward Coles, Second Governor of Illinois—Correspondence with the Reverend Thomas Lippincott." *Journal of the Illinois State Historical Society* 3 (January 1911): 59–63.

Edwards, Ninian. Collection. Chicago Historical Society, Chicago, IL

Ellis, Joseph J. *American Sphinx: The Character of Thomas Jefferson*. New York: Knopf, 1996.

———. *Founding Fathers: The Revolutionary Generation*. New York: Knopf, 2000.

Etcheson, Nicole. *The Emerging Midwest: Upland Southerners and the Political Culture of the Old Northwest, 1787–1861*. Bloomington: Indiana University Press, 1996.

Faux, William. *Faux's Memorable Days in America—November 27, 1818–July 21, 1820*. 1823. Reprint, Carlisle, MA: Applewood, 2007.

Ferguson, Eugene S. *Truxtun of the Constellation*. Baltimore: Johns Hopkins Press, 1956.

Ferling, John. *Adams vs. Jefferson: The Tumultuous Election of 1800*. New York: Oxford University Press, 2004.

Finkelman, Paul. *Jefferson and Slavery*. Charlottesville: University Press of Virginia, 1993.

———. "Thomas Jefferson And Antislavery." *Virginia Magazine of History and Biography* 102, no. 2 (April 1994): 193–228.

Fischer, David Hackett, and James C. Kelly. *Bound Away: Virginia and the Western Movement*. Charlottesville: University Press of Virginia, 2000.

Fitts, Leroy. *A History of Black Baptists*. Nashville: Broadman, 1985.

Flanagan, John T. "The Destruction of an Early Illinois Library." *Illinois State Historical Society Journal* 49 (Winter 1956): 387–93.

Flower, George. *History of the English Settlement in Edward County Illinois*. 2nd ed. Chicago: Fergus, 1902.

Ford, Paul L., ed. *The Writings of Thomas Jefferson*. New York: Putnam, 1898.

Ford, Thomas. *A History of Illinois*. Chicago: University of Illinois Press, 1995.

———. *A History of Illinois from Its Commencement as a State in 1818 to 1847*. Edited by Milo M. Quaife. Vol 1. Chicago: Lakeside, 1945.

Fox, Earl Lee. *The American Colonization Society: 1817–1840*. Baltimore: Johns Hopkins University Press, 1919.

Freehling, Alison Goodyear. *Drift toward Dissolution: The Virginia Slavery Debate of 1831–1832*. Baton Rouge: Louisiana State University Press, 1982.

Freehling, William. "The Founding Fathers and Slavery." *American Historical Review* 77, no. 1 (1972): 81–93.

Furman, Bess. *White House Profile*. Indianapolis: Bobbs-Merrill, 1951.

Genovese, Eugene. *The World the Slaveholders Made*. Middletown, CT: Wesleyan University Press, 1988.

Gillespie, Joseph. Papers. Chicago Historical Society.

———. *Recollections of Early Illinois and Her Noted Men*. Chicago: Fergus, 1880.

Goodwin, Edward Lewis. *The Colonial Church in Virginia*. Milwaukee, WI: Morehouse, 1927.

Gordon-Reed, Annette. "Logic and Experience: Thomas Jefferson's Life in the Law." In *Slavery and the American South*, ed. Winthrop D. Jordan. Jackson: University Press of Mississippi, 2003. 3–28.

Gore, Mary Jane. *Slavery in Albemarle: To Buy, To Sell, To Own a Human Being*. Charlottesville, VA: Jennings, 1997.

"Governor Coles' Autobiography: Letter From Governor Edward Coles to the Late Senator W. C. Flagg." *Journal of Illinois State Historical Society* 3 (October 1910): 59–64.

Green, Constance M. *Washington: Village and Capital 1800–1878*. Princeton: Princeton University Press, 1962.

Guasco, Suzanne Cooper. "Confronting Democracy: Edward Coles and the Cultivation of Authority in the Young Nation." PhD diss., College of William and Mary, 2004.

———. "The Deadly Influence of Negro Capitalists: Southern Yeomen and Resistance to the Expansion of Slavery in Illinois." *Civil War History* 47, no. 1 (March 2001). 7–29.

———. "Managing Memory: The Cultivation of Elite Authority in Jacksonian America." Paper presentation, annual conference, Society for Historians of the Early American Republic (SHEAR) Conference, Buffalo, NY, 20–23 July 2000.

Gudmestad, Robert H. *A Troublesome Commerce: The Transformation of the Interstate Salve Trade.* Baton Rouge: Louisiana State University Press, 2003.

Gwaltney, Mary S. "Bishop James Madison's Letters on Politics, 1787–1809." Master's thesis, College of William and Mary, 1983.

Gwathmey, John H. *Historical Register of Virginians in the Revolution: Soldiers, Sailors, Marines, 1775–1783.* Baltimore, MD: Genealogical, 1938.

Hand, John P. "Negro Slavery in Illinois." *Transactions of the Illinois State Historical Society* 15 (1910): 42–50.

Harlan Family. Papers. Illinois State Historical Library, Springfield.

Harris, Norman Dwight. *History of Negro Servitude in Illinois and of the Slavery Agitation in That State, 1719–1864.* Ann Arbor: University Microfilms, 1968. First published 1904 by McClurg, Chicago.

Hawks, Francis L. *Contributions to the Ecclesiastical History of the United States of America.* New York: Harper, 1836.

Hempstead, Stephen, Sr. "The Diary of a Yankee Farmer in Missouri 1819: I at Home: Part IV." *Missouri Historical Society Bulletin*, series 2, 2, no. 3 (April 1958): 272–88.

Henrotin, Ellen M. "The Visit of Lafayette to Illinois in 1825." *Transactions of the Illinois State Historical Society* 12 (1907): 79–84.

Hofstadter, Richard. *The Idea of a Party System.* Berkeley: University of California Press, 1969.

Holmes, David L. *A Brief History of the Episcopal Church.* Philadelphia: Trinity Press International, 1993.

——, ed. *A Nation Mourns: Bishop James Madison's Memorial Eulogy on the Death of George Washington.* Mount Vernon, VA: Mount Vernon Ladies Association, 1999.

Horton, James Oliver. "The Genesis of Washington's African American Community." In *Urban Odyssey: A Multicultural History of Washington, D.C.,* edited by Francine Curro Cary. Washington, DC: Smithsonian Institution Press, 1996.

Hunt, Gaillard, ed. *The Writings of James Madison.* New York: Putnam's, 1900.

Hunt-Jones, Conover. *Dolley and the 'Great Little Madison.'* Washington, DC: American Institute of Architects Foundation, 1977.

Hurley, Daniel I. "Deism at the College of William & Mary, 1722–1836." Master's thesis, College of William and Mary, 1974.

Idzerda, Stanley J., Anne C. Loveland, and Marc H. Miller. *Lafayette, Hero of Two Worlds.* Lebanon, NH: University Press of New England, 1989.

Ingersoll, Charles J. *History of the Second War between the United States of America and Great Britain.* Philadelphia: Lippincott, Grambo, 1853.

Isaacs, Rhys. *The Transformation of Virginia: 1740 to 1790.* Chapel Hill: University of North Carolina Press, 1982.

Jennings, Paul. *A Colored Man's Reminiscences of James Madison.* Brooklyn: Beadle, 1865.

Johannsen, Robert W., ed. *The Letters of Stephen A. Douglas*. Champaign: University of Illinois Press, 1961.

Kemper, Charles E. "The Birth-Place of Bishop Madison." *William and Mary Quarterly*, 2nd series, 2, no 3 (July 1922): 185–86.

Kennedy, Robert G. *Mr. Jefferson's Lost Cause: Land, Farmers, Slavery and the Louisiana Purchase*. New York: Oxford University Press, 2003.

Ketcham, Ralph L. "The Dictates of Conscience: Edward Coles and Slavery." *Virginia Quarterly Review* 36 (Winter 1960): 47–62.

———. *James Madison: A Biography*. Charlottesville: University Press of Virginia, 1996.

Kingston, John T. "Early Western Days." In *Report and Collections of the State Historical Society of Wisconsin*, edited by Lyman Draper. Vol. 7. Madison: State Historical Society of Wisconsin, 1876. 297–344.

Klamkin, Marian. *The Return of Lafayette, 1824–1825*. New York: Scribner, 1975.

Klingberg, Frank J., and Frank W. Klingberg. *The Correspondence between Henry Stephens Randall and Hugh Blair Grigsby 1856–1861*. Berkeley: University of California Press, 1952.

Koch, Adrienne. *Madison's 'Advice to My Country.'* Princeton: Princeton University Press, 1966.

Kraut, John A., and Dixon R. Fox. *The Completion of Independence 1790–1830*. Vol. 5 in *A History of American Life*. New York: Macmillan, 1944. Reprint, Chicago: Quadrangle, 1971. Citations are to the 1971 volume.

Langhorne, Elizabeth. "Edward Coles, Thomas Jefferson, and the Rights of Man." *Virginia Cavalcade* 23, Summer 1973, 30–37.

Langhorne, Elizabeth, K. E. Lay, and W. D. Rieley. *A Virginia Family and Its Plantation Houses*. Charlottesville: University Press of Virginia, 1987.

Langhorne, Elizabeth Coles. Papers. Albert and Shirley Small Special Collections Library, University of Virginia.

Lay, K. Edward, et al. "Coles Family Houses: Edward Coles House, Enniscorthy, Estouteville, Old Woodville, Redlands, Tallwood." Photocopied booklet. Charlottesville: School of Architecture, University of Virginia, 1987.

Leichtle, Kurt E. "Edward Coles: An Agrarian on the Frontier." PhD diss., University of Illinois at Chicago Circle, 1982.

———. "Rise of Jacksonian Politics in Illinois." *Illinois Historical Journal* 82, no. 2 (Summer 1989): 93–107.

Lenton, James. *History of Methodism in Illinois from 1793–1832*. Cincinnati, OH: Walsen & Stowe, 1883.

Leonard, Gerald. "The Ironies of Partyism and Antipartyism: Origins of Partisan Political Culture in Jacksonian Illinois." *Illinois Historical Journal* 87 (Spring 1994): 21–40.

Letter File. Illinois State Historical Library, Springfield.

Levy, Andrew. *The First Emancipator: The Forgotten Story of Robert Carter, the Founder Who Freed His Slaves*. New York: Random, 2005.

Lewis, Charlene M. Boyer. *Ladies and Gentlemen on Display: Planter Society at the Virginia Springs, 1790–1860*. Charlottesville: University Press of Virginia, 1965.

Lippincott, Thomas. "Edward Coles, Second Governor of Illinois—Correspondence with Rev. Thomas Lippincott." *Journal of the Illinois State Historical Society* 3 (January 1911): 59–63.Lipscomb, Andrew A., and Albert E. Bergh. *The Writings of Thomas Jefferson*. Vol. 14. Washington, DC: Thomas Jefferson Memorial Association, 1903–4.

Luboff, Norman, and Winfred Stracke. *Freedom Country*. Folder 1, box 105, Norman Luboff Collection, Music Division, Library of Congress, Washington, DC.

Mabry, Eddie. *The History of Wood River Baptist District Association*. St. Louis: Swift, 1996.

Madison, (Bishop) James. "An Address to the Members of the Protestant Episcopal Church in Virginia." Richmond, VA: Nicholson, 1799. Reprint, Worchester, MA: American Antiquarian Society, 1964.

———. "Manifestations of the Beneficence of Divine Providence towards America. 1795." Early American Imprints, 1st series, no. 29016. New York: Readex Microprint, 1985.

Madison County Historical Society, Edwardsville, Illinois.

Madison, Dolley. *Memoirs and Letters of Dolley Madison, ed. by Her Grandniece*. Boston: Houghton Mifflin, 1886.

———. Papers. Greensboro Historical Museum, Greensboro, NC.

———. Papers. Library of Congress, Washington, DC.

Madison Family Papers. Albert and Shirley Small Special Collections Library, University of Virginia, Charlottesville.

Madison v. Madison. Orange County (Virginia) Circuit Court. Hollinger file no. 628. Orange, VA, 1846.

Malone, Dumas. *Jefferson the Virginian*. Vol. 1. *Jefferson and His Time*. Boston: Little, Brown, 1948.

———. *The Sage of Monticello*. Vol. 6. *Jefferson and His Time*. Boston: Little, Brown, 1981.

Mason, Matthew. *Slavery and Politics in the Early Republic*. Chapel Hill: University of North Carolina Press, 2006.

Mason, Richard Lee. *Narrative of Richard Lee Mason in the Pioneer West, 1819*. New York: Hartmann, 1915.

Masur, Louis P. *1831: Year of the Eclipse*. New York: Hill & Wang, 2001.

Mather, Thomas. Papers. Chicago Historical Society.

Mattern, David B., and Holly C. Shulman, eds. *The Selected Letters of Dolley Payne Madison*. Charlottesville: University of Virginia Press, 2003.

May, Henry F. *The Enlightenment in America*. New York: Oxford University Press, 1976.

Mayer, Henry. *All on Fire: William Lloyd Garrison and the Abolition of Slavery*. New York: St. Martin's, 1998.

McCartney, Martha W. *James City County: Keystone of the Commonwealth.* Virginia Beach, VA: Donning, 1997.

McColley, Robert. *Slavery and Jeffersonian Virginia.* Urbana: University of Illinois Press, 1964.

McCord, Shirley S. *Travel Accounts of Indiana 1679–1961.* Indianapolis: Indiana Historical Bureau, 1970.

McCoy, Drew R. *The Elusive Republic: Political Economy in Jeffersonian America.* Chapel Hill: University of North Carolina Press, 1980.

———. *The Last of the Fathers: James Madison and the Republican Legacy.* New York: Cambridge University Press, 1989.

McCue, George. *Octagon: Being an Account of a Famous Washington Residence.* Washington, DC: American Institute of Architects Foundation, 1976.

McCullough, David. *John Adams.* New York: Simon & Schuster, 2001.

Meade, Bishop William. *Old Churches, Ministers and Families of Virginia.* Vol. 1. Philadelphia: Lippincott, 1878.

Meyer, Douglas K. *Making the Heartland Quilt.* Carbondale: Southern Illinois University Press, 2000.

Miller, Ann L. *Historic Structure Report: Montpelier, Orange County, Virginia.* Montpelier, July 1990.

Miller, John Chester. *The Wolf by the Ears: Thomas Jefferson and Slavery.* Charlottesville: University of Virginia/Thomas Jefferson Memorial Foundation, 1991.

"Minutes of the First Colored Baptist Association and Friends to Humanity." Wood River Baptist District Association, Alton, Illinois, 1839.

Miscellaneous Autograph File. Illinois State Historical Library, Springfield.

Miscellaneous Collections. Office of Naval Records. Library of Congress, Washington, DC.

Monroe, Paul. *Founding of the American Public School System: A History of Education in the U.S. from the Early Settlements to the Civil War Period.* New York: Macmillan, 1940.

Moore, John Hammond. *Albemarle: Jefferson's Country, 1727–1976.* Charlottesville: University Press of Virginia, 1976.

Morgan, Edmund. *American Slavery, American Freedom.* New York: Norton, 1975.

Morrison, Alfred J. *College of Hampden-Sydney.* Hampden Sydney, Farmville, VA: Hampden-Sydney College, 1921.

Morrison, William. Papers. Illinois State Historical Library, Springfield.

Nash, Gary B. *The Failure of Gradual Emancipation in the South.* San Diego, CA: Greenhaven, 2000.

Newhall, Horatio. Papers. Illinois State Historical Library, Springfield.

Nore, Ellen, and Dick Norrish. *Edwardsville: An Illustrated History.* Edwardsville, IL: Edwardsville Historic Preservation Commission, 1996.

Norton, W. T. *Edward Coles, Second Governor of Illinois.* Philadelphia: Lippincott, 1911.

———. *History of Madison County, Illinois*. Marceline, MO: Walsworth, 1980.

Oakes, James. *Slavery and Freedom: An Interpretation of the Old South*. New York: Vintage, 1990.

Patton, James, ed. "Letters from North Carolina Emigrants in the Old Northwest, 1830–1834." *Mississippi Valley Historical Review* 47 (1960): 263–77.

Pawlett, Nathaniel Mason. *Albemarle County Roads, 1725–1816*. Richmond: Virginia Highway & Transport Research Council, 1978.

Pearce, Lydia Burger. "Recollections of Pin Oak Blacks." Handwritten notes. 1952. Madison County (Illinois) Historical Society, Edwardsville.

Pease, Theodore C. *The Frontier State 1818–1848*. Springfield: Illinois Centennial Commission, 1918.

———. *The Story of Illinois*. Chicago: University of Chicago Press, 1975.

Pease, William H., and Jane H. Pease. *Black Utopia: Negro Communal Experiments in America*. Madison: State Historical Society of Wisconsin, 1963.

Perdue, Charles L., Jr., Thomas E. Barden, and Robert K. Phillips, eds. *Weevils in the Wheat: Interviews with Virginia Ex-slaves*. Charlottesville: University Press of Virginia, 1976.

Perkins, Bradford. *Prologue to War: England and the United States, 1805–1812*. Berkeley: University of California Press, 1961.

Peterson, Merrill D. *The Jefferson Image in the American Mind*. Charlottesville: Thomas Jefferson Memorial Foundation/University Press of Virginia, 1998.

Peterson, Merrill D., and Norma S. Frankel, eds. *Thomas Jefferson: A Reference Biography*. New York: Scribner, 1986.

Politte, Violet. "Governor Edward Coles." No date. Vertical file. Madison County Historical Society, Edwardsville, Illinois.

Pollard, Oliver A., Jr. *Under the Blue Ledge: Nelson County Virginia*. Richmond, VA: Dietz, 1997.

Pyne, James. "Battling the 'National Sin.'" *Chicago History* 19 (Spring/Summer 1990): 70–83.

Randall, Henry S. *The Life of Thomas Jefferson*. New York: Derby & Jackson, 1858.

Randle, Julia E. "The Economic Benefits of Slavery to the Episcopal Church in Virginia." *Center Aisle* 2, 14 June 2006, 4.

Rawlings, Mary. *The Albemarle of Other Days*. Charlottesville, VA: Michie, 1925.

———. *Ante-bellum Albemarle*. Charlottesville, VA: Peoples National Bank of Charlottesville, 1935.

Ress, David. *Governor Edward Coles and the Vote to Forbid Slavery in Illinois, 1823–1824*. Jefferson, NC: McFarland, 2006.

Reynolds, John. "Friendship's Offering: A Sketch of the Life of Dr. John M. Peck." Belleville, IL: Advocate, 1858.

———. *My Own Times, Embracing Also, the History of My Life*. Belleville, IL: N.p., 1855.

Richardson, Eudora Ramsay. "The Virginian Who Made Illinois a Free State." *Journal of the Illinois State Historical Society* 45 (1952): 5–22.

Risjord, Norman J. "1812: Conservatives, War Hawks, and the Nation's Honor." *William and Mary Quarterly*, 3rd series, 18, no. 2 (April 1961): 196–210.

Rives, William C. Papers. Library of Congress, Washington, DC.

Rives, William C., and Philip R Fendall, eds. *Letters and Other Writings of James Madison*. Philadelphia: Lippincott, 1865.

Rohrbough, Malcolm. *The Land Office Business: The Settlement and Adminis-tration of American Public Lands, 1789–1837*. New York: Oxford University Press, 1968.

Rothbard, Murray. *The Panic of 1819: Reactions and Policies*. New York: Colum-bia University Press, 1962.

Rothman, David. *Discovery of the Asylum*. Philadelphia: Little, Brown, 1971.

Royall, Ann Newport. *Sketches of History, Life, and Manners, in the United States*. New Haven, CT: 1826. Reprint, New York: Johnson Reprint, 1970.

Russell, John H. *The Free Negro in Virginia—1619 to 1865*. New York: Dover, 1969.

Rutherfoord Family Papers. Virginia Historical Society, Richmond, VA.

Rutherfoord, John. Papers. Manuscript Department, William R. Perkins Li-brary, Duke University, Durham, NC.

Ryan, Roderick. "Moral Reform and Democratic Politics: The Dilemma of Roberts Vaux." *Quaker History* 59 (Spring 1970): 3–14.

Sapp, Peggy Lathrop. *Madison County Court Records, 1813–1818 and Indenture Records 1805–1826*. Springfield, IL: FolkWorks, 1993.

Sargent, Samuel Stephen. Papers. Abraham Lincoln Presidential Library (for-merly the Illinois State Historical Library), Springfield, IL.

Schlesinger, Catherine Savedge. *The Wren Building at the College of William and Mary: Summary Architectural Report*. Williamsburg, VA: Colonial Williams-burg Foundation, 1979.

Schwarz, Philip J. *Migrants Against Slavery: Virginians and the Nation*. Charlot-tesville: University Press of Virginia, 2001.

———. *Slave Laws in Virginia*. Athens: University of Georgia Press, 1996.

Seale, William. *The President's House*. Washington, DC: White House Associa-tion and National Geographic Society, 1986.

Seaman, C. C. *A History of Southern Rockfish Families and Old Houses*. Lovings-ton, VA: Nelson County (Virginia) Historical Society, 1999.

———. *Tuckahoes and Cohees: The Settlers and Cultures of Amherst and Nelson Counties 1607–1807*. Sweet Briar, VA: Sweet Briar College Printing Press, 1992.

Seaman, C. C., and M. G. Small. *A History of Northern Rockfish Valley*. Lov-ingston, VA: Nelson County (Virginia) Historical Society, 1998.

Shade, William G. *Democratizing the Old Dominion: Virginia and the Second Party System 1824–1861*. Charlottesville: University Press of Virginia, 1996.

Shalhope, Robert E. "Toward a Republican Synthesis: The Emergence of an Understanding of Republicanism in American Historiography." *William and Mary Quarterly*, 3rd series, no. 29 (January 1972): 49–80.

Shankman, Arnold. "Partisan Conflicts, 1838–1841, and the Illinois Constitution." *Journal of the Illinois State Historical Society* 63 (Winter 1970): 337–66.

Sheppard, Eva. "The Question of Emancipation in Virginia from the Revolution to the Slavery Debate of 1832." PhD diss., Harvard University, 2000.

Shryock, Richard. *Medicine and Society in America 1660–1860*. New York: New York University Press, 1960.

Simeone, James. *Democracy and Slavery in Frontier Illinois: The Bottomland Republic*. DeKalb: Northern Illinois University Press, 2000.

Simon, Paul. *Freedom's Champion: Elijah Lovejoy*. Carbondale: Southern Illinois University Press, 1994.

Singleton, Esther. *The Story of the White House*. Vol. 1. New York: McClure, 1907.

Singleton, Richard. Papers. Albert and Shirley Small Special Collections Library, University of Virginia, Charlottesville.

Smith, George Washington. "Salines of Southern Illinois." *Transactions of the Illinois State Historical Society* 9 (1904): 246–58.

Smith-Carter. Papers. Albert and Shirley Small Special Collections Library, University of Virginia, Charlottesville.

Snyder, John F. *Adam W. Snyder and His Period in Illinois History, 1817–1842*. Virginia, IL: Needham, 1906.

Spencer, Donald S. "Edward Coles: Virginia Gentleman in Frontier Politics." *Journal of the Illinois State Historical Society* 61, no. 2 (1968): 150–63.

Sprague, William B. *Annals of the American Pulpit*. New York: Carter, 1861.

Springer, Jessie E. "Edward Coles Letter regarding His Slaves." Transcription of Coles's 22 June 1822, letter to *Edwardsville(Illinois) Spectator*. Madison County Historical Society, Edwardsville, Illinois,.

———. "Notes of Jessie Springer on the Crawford Family." N.d. Vertical file. Madison County Historical Society, Edwardsville, IL.

Stagg, J. C. A., J. K. Cross, and S. H. Perdu, eds. *The Papers of James Madison: Presidential Series*. Vol. 2. Charlottesville: University Press of Virginia, 1992.

Stanton, Lucia. *Slavery at Monticello*. Charlottesville, VA: Thomas Jefferson Memorial Foundation, 1996.

Stebbins, G. B. *Facts and Opinions Touching the Real Origin, Character, and Influence of the American Colonization Society*. Cleveland, OH: Jewett, 1853.

Stevens, Wayne E. "The Shaw-Hansen Election Contest: An Episode of the Slavery Contest in Illinois." *Journal of the Illinois State Historical Society* 7 (January 1915): 389–401.

Stroble, Paul E. *High on the Okaw's Western Bank*. Urbana: University of Illinois Press, 1992.

Sutton, Robert M, "Edward Coles and the Constitutional Crisis in Illinois, 1822–1824." *Illinois Historical Journal* 82 (Spring 1989): 33–46.

Swain, Joseph Ward. "Lafayette on the Centenary of His Visit to Illinois, 1825." N.p.: State of Illinois, 1926(?). Reprint *Transactions of the Illinois State Historical Society* (1925).

Sweet, William Warren. *Religion on the American Frontier, 1783–1830, the Baptists.* Vol 1. Chicago: University of Chicago Press, 1931.

Temin, Peter. *The Jacksonian Economy.* New York: Norton, 1969.

Terry, Gail S. "Sustaining the Bonds of Kinship in a Trans-Appalachian Migration, 1790–1811." *Virginia Magazine of History and Biography* 102, no. 4 (1994): 455–76.

Thompson, Jess M. *The Jess M. Thompson Pike County History as Printed in Installments in the* Pike County Republican, *Pittsfield, Illinois, 1935–1939.* Reprint, Windmill, 1999.

Thompson, William R. "Illinois Constitutions." PhD diss., University of Illinois, 1960.

Travous, Louise R. "The Illinois Years of Edwards Coles." Speech delivered by Bob Lange. 1 June 1974. Vertical file. Land of Goshen Historical Society, Madison County [Illinois] Historical Society.

Trist, Nicholas. Papers. Library of Congress, Washington, DC.

Trollope, Fanny. *Domestic Manners of the Americans.* Edited by Donald Smalley. New York: Knopf, 1949.

Tyler, Lyon G. "Early Presidents of William and Mary." *William and Mary Quarterly Historical Papers* 1, no. 2 (1892): 63–75.

U.S. Bureau of the Census. *Census for 1820.* Washington, DC: Gales & Seaton, 1821.

———. *First Census of the U.S. 1790.* Washington, DC.

———. *U.S. Census for 1850.* U.S. Census Office. Washington, DC: Gales & Seaton, 1851.

U.S. Congress. Committee of the Whole House. "Report of the Committee Appointed on Eighth Instant on the Letter of I. A. Coles." Washington, DC: Weightman, 1809.

U.S. Manuscript Census for 1850. Historical Society of Pennsylvania, Philadelphia.

Vance, Joseph Carroll. "Thomas Jefferson Randolph." PhD diss., University of Virginia, 1957.

Vaux Family. Papers. Historical Society of Pennsylvania, Philadelphia.

Viles, Jonas. "Population and Extent of Settlement in Missouri before 1804." *Missouri Historical Review* 5 (July 1911): 189–213.

Wallis, John Joseph. "What Caused the Crisis of 1839?" NBER Historical Working Paper 133. Cambridge, MA: National Bureau of Economic Research, 2001.

Walsh, Lorena S. *From Calabar to Carter's Grove: The History of a Virginia Slave Community.* Charlottesville: University Press of Virginia, 1997.

Ward, Harry M. *Richmond: An Illustrated History.* Northridge: Windsor, 1985.

Washburne, E. B. *Sketch of Edward Coles, Second Governor of Illinois, and the Slavery Struggle of 1823–4.* Chicago: Jansen, McClurg, 1882. Reprint, New York: Negro Universities Press, 1969. Citations are to the 1969 edition.

Washington, James Melvin. *Frustrated Fellowship: The Black Baptist Quest for Social Power*. Macon, GA: Mercer University Press, 1986.

Weincek, Henry. *An Imperfect God: George Washington, His Slaves, and the Creation of America*. New York: Farrar, Straus, and Giroux, 2003.

Wertenbaker, Thomas J. *The Planters of Colonial Virginia*. New York: Russell & Russell, 1959.

White, Leonard. *The Jeffersonians: A Study in Administrative History*. New York: Macmillan, 1951.

Whitman, T. Stephen. *Challenging Slavery in the Chesapeake: Black and White Resistance to Human Bondage, 1775–1865*. Baltimore: Maryland Historical Society, 2007.

Wilkins, Roger. *Jefferson's Pillow: The Founding Fathers and the Dilemma of Black Patriotism*. Boston: Beacon, 2001.

Williams, Edward E. "A Bit of Unwritten History: The Negro in Madison County, Illinois." N.d. Vertical file, Madison County Historical Society, Edwardsville, IL.

Williams, John Sharp. *Thomas Jefferson: His Permanent Influence on American Institutions*. New York: Columbia University Press, 1913.

Williams-Woodberry Collection. Illinois Historical Survey, University of Illinois, Urbana.

Wills, Garry. *James Madison*. New York: Times Books, 2002.

———. *Negro President: Jefferson and Slave Power*. New York: Houghton Mifflin, 2003.

Wolf, Eva Sheppard. *Race and Liberty in the New Nation: Emancipation in Virginia from the Revolution to Nat Turner's Rebellion*. Baton Rouge: Louisiana State University Press, 2006.

Wood, Gordon S. *The Creation of the American Republic, 1776–1787*. Chapel Hill: University of North Carolina Press, 1998.

———. *The Radicalism of the American Constitution*. London: Vintage, 1993.

———. *Revolutionary Characters: What Made the Founders Different*. New York: Penguin, 2006.

Woods, Edgar. *Albemarle County in Virginia*. Charlottesville, VA: Michie, 1901.

Wright, Frances. *Views of Society and Manners in America*. London: Longman, 1821.

Yazawa, Melvin. *From Colonies to Commonwealth: Familial Ideology and the Beginnings of the American Republic*. Baltimore: Johns Hopkins University Press, 1985.

Young, James Sterling. *The Washington Community*. New York: Harcourt, 1966.

Index

AB Affair (1825), 112, 113

Adams, Abigail, 33

Adams, John, 2, 33, 144, 181

Adams, John Quincy, 47, 55, 94

Adams-Jefferson reconciliation, 34, 181

Agricultural Society of Illinois, 88–90

Albemarle Academy, 44

Albemarle Agricultural Society, 88

Albemarle County (Virginia), 7, 9, 10, 22, 61, 152, 154, 155, 173, 192, 199, 209

Alfred (Sukey's child), 59, 185, 188

American Bottom (Illinois), 51, 80, 92, 186

American Colonization Society, 127, 126–28

antislavery societies, Illinois, 115, 116, 124

Ashe Lawn (home of James Monroe), 8

Bailey v. Cromwell (1841), 207

Bank of Edwardsville, 86, 111, 112

Bank of Illinois, 111

Bank of the United States, 31, 111, 118, 170

Bank War, 170

banking in Illinois, 77, 111

Baptists, 78, 116, 117, 184–87, 189, 190

Biddle, Nicholas (1786–1844), 31, 32, 35, 36, 50, 52, 118

Birkbeck, Morris (1764–1825), 55, 56, 89, 90, 102, 109, 117, 123, 126, 130, 135–36

Black Code of 1819, Illinois, 122, 132, 136, 144

Blackwell, David, 124, 135

Blue Ridge Mountains (Virginia), 8

Bond, Shadrach, 74, 89, 92, 129

Brown, William H., 102, 105, 108, 109, 120, 124

Browne, Thomas, 93, 97

Brownsville (Pennsylvania), 60, 61, 62–63, 69, 71

Buffalo Trace (Louisville–Vincennes road, Indiana), 71

Burnside, Ambrose Everett (Brig. Gen.), 196–97

Burwell, William A., 27

Byrd, William, II, 7

Carter, Robert, III, 23, 208

Cartwright, Peter, 77, 78, 116

Charlottesville (Virginia), 8, 44, 58, 61, 193

Churchill, George, 57, 106, 107

Clay, Henry, 160, 162

Cobb, Thomas, 59, 63, 71, 80, 81, 82, 84, 87, 88, 96, 134

Coles, Edward

administration as governor, 108, 110, 112, 113, 135, 144

Agricultural Society of Illinois, formation of, 88

anticonvention activities, 113, 114, 115, 117, 119, 125–26

birth, 10

constitutional convention of 1818, Illinois, 57

convention referendum, 113

Coles, Edward (*continued*)
  death, 204
  departure from Brownsville, Pennsylvania, 63
  description, 10, 38, 94, 147
  distribution of lands to his freedmen, 84, 144
  early education, 10
  emancipation of his slaves, 1, 26, 41, 49, 64, 69, 70, 72, 82–83, 123, 143
  family orientation, 43
  Illinois Intelligencer, purchase, 124–25, 130
  illnesses, 40, 81
  inheritance, 17
  inauguration, 101
  James Madison, views on, 173
  Jefferson correspondence on slavery, 44
  land purchases, 51, 81
  migration to Illinois, 50, 60
  Peoria (Illinois) land claims, 86–87
  Philadelphia years, 149, 150, 169
  politician, 92, 96, 97, 99, 100, 131, 146–48
  Register of Lands, 57, 85, 87, 93, 94
  republican views, 100, 130, 145, 146
  sale of Rockfish property, 57, 58
  secretary to James Madison, 28, 30, 31, 34, 50
  slave owner, 38, 40, 43
  slavery debates of 1831, Virginia, 154–56
  slaves/freedmen of, 20, 58
  suit against, 121–23, 132–37, 150
  views on emancipation, 126
  views on race, 128
  views on slavery, 14, 16, 43, 55, 115, 126, 128
  western travel, 50, 56
Coles, Elizabeth (1791–1865), 10, 204
Coles, Emily Ann (1795–1871), 10, 204
Coles, Isaac (A.) (1780–1841), 10, 27, 28, 204
Coles, Edward, Jr. (1837–1907), 169, 191, 199
Coles, John (1705–47), 7
Coles, John, II (1745–1808), 8–10, 15, 17, 18, 19, 20, 25, 58, 59

Coles, John, III (1774–1848), 10, 32, 38, 39, 40, 51, 61, 63, 64, 204
Coles, Mary Eliza (1776–1856), 10, 204
Coles, Mary (1835–1920), 25, 169, 170, 191, 199, 205
Coles, Rebecca Elizabeth Tucker (1750–1826), 9, 17, 199, 204
Coles, Roberts (1838–62), 169, 191–92, 193–97, 199
Coles, Sallie Logan Robers (1809–83), 167, 169, 205
Coles, Sarah (Sallie; 1789–1848), 10, 160, 204
Coles, Tucker (1782–1861), 10, 15, 19, 192, 204
Coles, Walter (1772–1854), 7, 9, 10, 39, 56, 58, 198, 199, 204
Compromise of 1850, 178
Congress, U.S., 27, 29, 31, 32, 35, 36, 37, 44, 72, 73, 78, 79, 123, 132, 134, 138, 147, 148, 160, 173, 174, 176, 177, 179
Constellation, USS (frigate), 36
Constitutional Convention (controversy of 1822–24), 96, 103, 104, 108, 113, 115, 121, 180
  conventionist activities, 106, 114, 120, 121, 128
  social impacts, 120, 129
Constitutional Convention (Illinois, 1818), 57, 73, 74, 130
Cook, Daniel P., 74, 78, 79, 82, 97, 110, 129, 133, 135, 137
Cooper, Thomas (Dr.), 47
Corbin, George, 23
Crawford, Betsy, 58, 143, 188
Crawford, Ferdenand, 188
Crawford, Kate, 58, 80, 85, 87, 95, 143, 144, 184
Crawford, Mary, 58, 188
Crawford, Polly, 58, 80, 82, 95, 184
Crawford, Ralph, 50, 52, 58, 60, 61, 63, 70, 80, 81, 85, 87, 95, 134, 188
Crawford, Richard, 188
Crawford, Robert, 58, 80, 81, 82, 84, 87, 88, 95, 128, 143, 144, 150, 183–90

Crawford, Thomas, 58
Crawford, William (1772–1834), 87, 94, 112
Crawford, William (son of Kate Crawford), 58, 188

DaLancey, William H. (Bishop), 168
Dane, Nathan, 175–76
Decatur, Stephen (Capt.), 37
Deists, 13
Dissenters, 12
Dodge, Henry S., 89
Douglas, Stephen A., 178–80, 201
    Lincoln–Douglas debates, 3
Dunglison, Robley, 180

Edwards, Ninian, 56, 74, 78, 79, 93, 98, 112, 142, 143, 144, 145
Edwardsville, Illinois, 58, 60, 72, 78, 80, 81, 82, 83, 85, 86, 87, 88, 89, 90, 92, 93, 95, 100, 111, 114, 121, 133, 169, 183, 200
Elizabeth (Sukey's child), 59
    emancipation, 21, 23, 24, 25, 26, 27, 45, 46, 47, 59, 69, 85, 124, 126, 127, 154–56, 157–59, 162, 163, 165, 182, 208, 209
    post nati, 153, 155
Emancipation Proclamation, 203
English Settlement, Albion (Illinois), 57, 89, 102
Enniscorthy (plantation), 8, 9, 10, 14, 17, 18, 22, 50, 52, 59, 60, 170, 192, 195, 199, 204
Enniscorthy (Ireland), 7
Eppes, Francis, 7
Eustis, William, 54

Fairfax, Jeannie C., 192, 196–97
Field, Colonel Alexander, 107
Finley, Rev. Robert, 127
Flower, Richard, 57, 102, 126
Floyd, General John B., 194
Floyd, Jogn (Virginia governor, 1830–34), 154
Ford, Thomas (Illinois governor, 1842–46), 120

Frankey (Sukey's child), 59
Franklin, John Hope, 209
free blacks (Virginia), 23, 26, 153, 154
Friends of Humanity, 78, 117, 185
Fry, Colonel John, 9
Fulton, Robert, 32

Gaines, Nancy, 59, 80, 82, 85, 96, 134
Gallatin, James, 40
Gallatin County (Illinois), 75, 129
Garnett, Robert S. (Brig. Gen.), 193
Gerry, Elbridge (1744–1814), 33
Grand Prairie, 98
Granger, Gideon, 32
Great Wagon Road, 60, 61
Green Mountain Grays (46th Albemarle Infantry), 192, 193, 195
Grigsby, Hugh Blair, 172, 180

Hamlin, Hannibal, 201
Hampden-Sydney College (Farmville, Virginia.), 10, 11, 13
Hansen, Nicholas, 83, 101, 105, 106, 107, 145
Harris, Levett, 53, 54
Harrison, William Henry (Pres.), 171
Hempstead, Stephen, Sr., 83–84
Henry, Patrick, 25, 173
honor, 22, 23, 25, 43, 158
Howell, David, 175, 177
Hubbard, Adolphus, 97, 142, 143

Illinois
    Constitution of 1818, 75, 104, 114
    election of 1822, 92, 97
    free blacks, 90
    politics, 146
    population growth, 90, 130
involuntary servitude, 73, 74, 176. *See also* slavery

Jackson, Andrew (Pres.), 139, 157, 170
Jackson, Francis James, 27
Jarrott v. Jarrott (1845), 207

Jefferson, Thomas, 2, 4, 8, 9, 10, 13, 15, 27, 29, 31, 33, 34, 36, 44, 46, 49, 62, 126, 127, 139, 144, 152, 154, 155, 172, 173, 175, 176, 177, 178, 179, 180, 181, 182, 208
Adams-Jefferson reconciliation, 34, 181
Northwest Ordinance of 1784, 174–78
Jeffersonville (Indiana), 71
Jennings, Paul, 163

Kane, Elias Kent, 74, 78, 112
Kaskaskia (Illinois), 52, 74, 88, 89, 97, 98, 134, 140
Kinney, William, 103, 106

Lafayette, Marquis de, 55, 138, 139, 138–41
land business (Illinois), 76, 86
Lee, Michael, 90, 95, 144, 184
Leib, Michael, 32
Lemen, James, 78, 117, 184, 185
Liberia, 127, 128
Liberty Party, 207
Lincoln, Abraham, 3, 201, 202–3, 207
Lincoln–Douglas debates, 3
Livingston, John (Rev.), 184, 185
Louisville (Indiana), 71
Lowden, Frank O., 2
Luboff, Norman, 208
Lucinda (Sukey's child), 59

Macedonian, HMS/USS (frigate), 37, 53
Madison, Dolley Paine (1768–1849), 25, 29, 30, 33, 40, 150, 157, 158, 159, 160, 162, 163–66, 173
slavery, 165
Madison, James (Col.; 1723–1801), 164
Madison, James (Pres.), 2, 4, 8, 27, 28, 30, 31, 35, 36, 43, 49, 50, 53, 56, 89, 98, 101, 127, 139, 149, 157, 160, 162, 163, 164, 165, 172, 173, 174, 201, 205
administration of, 27, 29
slaves, 159, 161
will, 159, 160, 162, 165
Madison, James (Rev.; 1749–1812), 11–16, 44

Madison, William, 164
Madison County (Illinois), 57, 80, 88, 90, 92, 96, 106, 121, 122, 123, 132, 136, 137, 189
Manuel (Sukey's husband), 59, 64, 70, 71, 80, 83, 84, 91, 143
manumission
Charles Stockly, 23
Daniel Mifflin, 23
Elizabeth Russell, 25
George Corbin, 23
John Treackle, 23
Robert Carter III, 23, 208
Robert Pleasants, 23, 208, 209
William Parramore, 23
Mason, Hail, 82, 123, 132
Mason, James, 87, 124, 172
McGuire, James C., 173
McRoberts, Samuel, 136, 137, 147
Melton, John, 20, 38, 39
Meriwether, Frances, 18
Methodists, 78, 184
Middle Period (historiography), 172, 180
Mifflin, Daniel, 23
Milton (Virginia), 61, 103
Missouri Compromise, 78, 96, 174, 178
Moncure, Henry, 164
money, Illinois, 111
Monroe, James (1758–1831), 8, 28, 32, 54, 56, 57, 85, 138
Monticello (home of Thomas Jefferson), 8, 9, 34, 45, 46, 61, 139, 152, 160, 173
Montpelier (home of James Madison), 8, 32, 61, 157, 158, 159, 160, 161, 164
Moore, James B., 93
Moore, John Hammond, 209

National Road, 51, 62
Nelson, Roger, 27
New Albany (Indiana), 71
Nicholas, Wilson Cary, 10
Northwest Ordinance of 1784, 174–78
Northwest Ordinance of 1787, 72, 73, 96, 101, 103, 113, 174, 176, 179, 181

Octagon House, Washington, D.C., 50
Ohio, Falls of the, 71
Ohio River, 69–72, 140

Panic of 1819, 77, 79, 90
Parramore, William, 23
Payne, John (1740–92), 25
Peck, John Mason, 116, 124, 130, 172
Peoria (Illinois), 86
Pettiford, Archie, 190
Philadelphia, 25, 30, 32, 33, 35, 40, 50, 53, 64,
    118, 138, 141, 150, 152, 162, 167, 169, 170,
    171, 180, 181, 191, 192, 197, 198, 199, 200,
    202, 204, 205
Phillips, Joseph, 92, 94, 96
Phillips Decorative Company of Chicago, 207
Physick, Dr. (Philip Syng), 40
Pickering, Timothy, 177
Pinckney, William, 31
Pin Oak (Illinois), 85, 90, 95, 183, 184, 185, 189
Plantation, The (Virginia plantation of Rob-
    erts Coles), 192, 199
Pleasants, Robert, 23, 208, 209
Poydras, Julien, 32
Prairieland Farm, 81, 83, 87, 88, 95, 143, 144,
    150, 183
Price, Jesse, 143, 188
Prickett, Isaac, 188, 200
Prometheus, USS, 53, 54, 56

Quebec, Treaty of (1774), 72

Randall, Henry S., 33, 180
Randolph, Thomas Jefferson, 128, 152, 154
Rantoul, Jr., Robert, 174
Renault, Phillipe Francois, 72
Republican (ideology/political theory),
    12–16, 28, 36, 44, 55, 118, 145, 161, 172,
    174, 180, 181–82, 195, 201, 208, 210
Reynolds, John, 116, 120, 123, 132, 134, 136
Richardson, Alfred H., 184, 185, 188
Richmond (Virginia), 7, 154
Ridge Prairie (Illinois), 85, 90, 95, 184

Rives, William Cabell, 172, 173
Roanoke Island, battle of, 196–98
Roberts, Hugh, 169, 170
Rockfish Plantation, 10, 17–20, 26, 38, 39,
    52, 56, 57, 58, 60, 94, 95
Rush, Benjamin, 33, 34, 169
Rush, William, 169
Russell, Elizabeth, 25
Rutherfoord, John, 52, 170, 194

saline district, 75, 76, 102
Scott, Winfield, 171
Seward, William H., 201
Shaw, H. M. (Col.), 196
Shaw, John, 101, 105, 107
Shaw-Hansen affair, 100, 101, 107, 109
Shawneetown (Illinois), 52, 60, 71, 75, 139,
    140, 141
slavery, 15, 22, 55, 57, 74, 75, 77, 98, 115, 153,
    209
    Illinois, 113, 130, 135
    Illinois curches and, 78
    Illinois land values and, 77
    law of 1782 (Virginia), 23
    law of 1806 (Virginia), 23, 25
    law (Illinois), 74, 207
    salt industry in Illinois, 75
    Virginia, 22, 23, 151, 152
    Virginia debate of 1831, 4, 154–56
Smith, Samuel, 33
Smith, Theophilis W., 88
St. Clair, Arthur, 73, 98
St. Louis (Missouri), 80, 83, 84, 143
Stephenson, Benjamin, 86, 111, 112
Stevenson, Andrew, 160, 161
Stockly, Charles, 23
Stratton, Governor William G., 208
Sukey (Manuel's wife), 59, 70, 71, 80, 83,
    84, 91, 143
Sumner, Charles, 174

Taylor, Robert, 162, 163
Thomas, Jesse B., 74, 79, 100, 123, 132

Todd, John Payne (1792–1852), 35, 36, 40, 50, 52, 56, 164
Treackle, John, 23
Trist, Nicholas P., 180, 202
Trollope, Fanny, 167
Tunstall , Edmund, 98
Turner, Nat, 151–52
Tyler, John (Pres.), 171

Vandalia (Illinois), 94, 98, 99, 100, 101, 105, 106, 107, 108, 110, 119, 120, 121, 128, 130, 135, 141, 144, 146, 202
Vaux, Roberts, 115, 118, 141, 167, 169
Vincennes (Indiana), 71, 72, 82
Virginia, University of, 44

Walker, David V. (Dr.), 84
War of 1812, 29, 35, 37, 43, 49, 77, 93
    destruction of Washington, D.C., 49
    Treaty of Ghent, 49
Warren, Hooper, 93, 94, 96, 97, 102, 181
Washburne, Elihu B., 108, 109, 137
Washington, D.C., 29, 35, 37
    slavery, 42

Washington, George
    slaves, 157, 166
Washington, Martha, 158
Webb, Pollard, 163
Webster, Daniel, 163, 175
Whigs, 12, 36
White House, 25, 27, 28, 29–30, 35, 43, 92, 96, 161
    weekly receptions at, 30, 50
White Sulphur Springs (Virginia), 35, 50, 170, 193, 194
William and Mary, College of (Williamsburg, Virginia), 11, 12, 14, 15, 27, 49, 171
Williamsburg (Virginia), 11, 13
Willis, Nellie, 162, 163
Wilson (Sukey's child), 59
Winston, Mary Ann (wife of John Coles I), 8
Wise, Obediah J. (Capt.), 196, 197
Wise, Henry, 193, 195
Wistar, Caspar, 33
Woodlands Cemetery (Pennsylvania), 205
Wood River Baptist District Association, 187, 184–87, 190
Wright, Frances, 83

Kurt E. Leichtle is a professor of history in the history and philosophy department at the University of Wisconsin–River Falls. His work focuses on nineteenth-century American history, slavery, women in the pioneer west, and the teaching of history.

Bruce G. Carveth is a writer and editor living in Charlottesville, Virginia.